Additional Praise for *Technical Analysis and Chart Interpretations*

Ed's thorough analysis will leave you with a deeper understanding and appreciation of a vast array of technical tools and concepts. An essential guide for beginners and seasoned traders alike.

—*Jon Boorman, CMT, Broadsword Capital*

Technical Analysis And Chart Interpretations is a worthy addition to any technical analysis library. Ed Ponsi does a masterful job of taking a difficult, often confusing subject, and making it incredibly easy to digest. Whether you are a beginner or veteran student of technical analysis, this book is a must read.

—*Bob Byrne, Private Investor and Trading Coach*

Ed has written a great book not only on technical patterns and indicators, but on the pitfalls that traders will face as they embark on a trading career. This information can be applied to both longer and shorter time frames. It has value for both the investor and trader alike. I even learned some new things myself!

—*Carolyn Boroden, Founder, FibonacciQueen.com*

Ed Ponsi has taught me the value of using some of the more useful indicators on charts such as MACD. While our styles are quite different I have learned a lot from his work and I believe you can as well.

—*Helene Meisler, Contributor to Realmoney.com*

TECHNICAL ANALYSIS AND CHART INTERPRETATIONS

TECHNICAL ANALYSIS AND CHART INTERPRETATIONS

A Comprehensive Guide to Understanding
Established Trading Tactics for Ultimate Profit

Ed Ponsi

WILEY

Published by John Wiley & Sons, Inc., Hoboken, New Jersey.
Published simultaneously in Canada.

For general information on our other products and services or for technical support, please contact our
Customer Care Department within the United States at (800) 762–2974, outside the United States at (317)
572–3993 or fax (317) 572–4002.

Wiley publishes in a variety of print and electronic formats and by print-on-demand. Some material included
with standard print versions of this book may not be included in e-books or in print-on-demand. If this book
refers to media such as a CD or DVD that is not included in the version you purchased, you may download
this material at http://booksupport.wiley.com. For more information about Wiley products, visit
www.wiley.com.

Library of Congress Cataloging-in-Publication Data is available:

ISBN 978-1-119-04833-6 (Paperback)
ISBN 978-1-119-04822-0 (ePub)
ISBN 978-1-119-04823-7 (ePDF)

Cover Design: Wiley
Cover Images: Communication collage © iStock.com/archerix; Medical Abstract © kentoh/Shutterstock

Printed in the United States of America

10 9 8 7 6 5 4 3 2 1

Ride with me to the edge of the land
Ever we play in waves and sand
Night full of stars, no clouds above
Ever be strong, and know you are loved
Ever be strong, and know you are loved

CONTENTS

Every trader must follow their own path. Maybe technical analysis will be part of your path, but even if your journey takes you in another direction, it's still important to understand the concepts in this book. As you read on, the reasons why will become clear.

How did technical analysis become a part of my journey? It started with my first job interview in the financial services field, which was for a position as a stockbroker.

I was led by two senior brokers into a tiny, glass-encased room. Two more brokers were already waiting there. They began asking questions—slowly at first, then more rapidly. They bombarded me with questions to see if I could handle the pressure. My heart raced: Was I up to the challenge?

"Name your five favorite stocks," they asked.

"Ascend Communications, 3Com, Cascade, Cisco Systems," I replied.

At the time, all four companies were in the rapidly expanding computer networking sector. That sector was on fire, making headlines on a daily basis with its huge gains and wild swings.

"That's four ... keep going ... "

"Four ... Fore ... "

"Ford? Ford Motor Company?"

"No, Fore Systems."

I'd named another computer networking stock. I was five minutes into my first interview, and I'd already broken every rule of diversification. Had I blown my opportunity to break into finance?

Surprisingly, my interview caught the attention of a senior broker who specialized in technical analysis. He knew that all the stocks I'd named were in the strongly trending computer networking sector. I was hired at his recommendation and became a member of his team, which placed a heavy emphasis on technology and momentum stocks.

Our reading assignments included books such as *The Gorilla Game: Picking Winners in High Technology* by Geoffrey Moore. We were also instructed to read a number of books on technical analysis, including *Secrets for Profiting in Bull and Bear Markets* by Stan Weinstein as well as titles by John Murphy and the team of Edwards and Magee.

On our team, technical analysis was the key to every decision. While others paid close attention to fundamental research reports, our team cared only about price action. Every company's chart was to be thoroughly analyzed. I dove into the reading materials with gusto.

Total Immersion

What happened next could only be described as total immersion. We were like cult members. Our team of four would work from 8 a.m. until the closing bell. After the close, we'd look at every single chart in the S&P 500.

Then we'd go to dinner, or to the bar, or just hang around the office while the cleaning crew worked around us, and the technical analysis conversation would continue. Any remaining time was spent reading additional books on technical analysis and growth stocks as assigned by our mentor.

While I loved learning about technical analysis, I wasn't fond of being a broker. At one time I'd believed that brokers traded and managed money for their clients. This is only somewhat true; eventually, I learned that being a broker has more to do with selling than with trading.

The final straw occurred when my employer asked me to obtain a license to sell life insurance. There is nothing wrong with selling insurance to people who need it; I just didn't want to be the person who sold it to them. Instead, I wanted to use everything I'd learned about technical analysis to become a full-time professional trader. So, I quit.

The Next Step

For a long time, I'd been sending my trading track record to anyone I could find who hired traders. I'd scour the Sunday *New York Times* and collect e-mail addresses, and then bombard them with my trading record. I had a solid record, mainly thanks to the very forgiving bull market environment of the 1990s.

After months of this, with no indication that anyone noticed or cared, the phone finally rang—would I like to interview for a trading job on Wall Street?

This time, I was interviewed by just one person—and he seemed like a maniac. He stomped around his spacious Wall Street office, alternately mumbling and shouting.

His expensive suit was wrinkled and uneven, and he needed a shave. He looked as if he'd been out all night.

Suddenly, I wanted my old job back, a good paying job from which I'd walked away. What had I gotten myself into?

I didn't know it at the time, but this man was a well-known character on Wall Street. He ran several investment firms, one of which employed over 400 traders. When I told him I was willing to travel 100 miles by train to get to work every morning and another 100 miles to get home every night, he hired me on the spot.

Once again, it was a case of total immersion. I'd catch a train before dawn, always clutching a book and a copy of *Investor's Business Daily*. Eventually, one of those books would be *Confessions of a Street Addict* by legendary hedge fund manager Jim Cramer. Years later, I'd work with Jim and even merit a brief mention in one of his books.

I saw the same faces every morning on the train. Every day, a young man and an older man would board the train together, and I'd overhear them discussing technical analysis. The older gent was an experienced arbitrage trader, and the kid was a college athlete who was just getting started in the business. Every day, we'd discuss indicators and other technical concepts. Years later, we would all work together at a midtown Manhattan trading firm.

Hiding from the Boss

My first trading job could only be described as Darwinian—it was the survival of the fittest. The firm's philosophy of cutting losses quickly apparently translated to the company's attitude toward its traders. Nearly every day, another desk would be vacant, its former occupant never to return.

The company had a lengthy set of rules, particularly regarding risk management. I had trouble making money at first, as I struggled to adjust my somewhat wild trading style to fit within the company's parameters. Every day brought with it a new defeat followed by the long train ride home.

Meanwhile, the new hires I'd started with were disappearing one by one. Why had I left my secure job and gotten involved in this mess? I lost money, lost sleep, and lost my appetite. I thought I'd lose my mind.

I really thought I'd be fired, but I kept showing up. In the hallways at work, I avoided at all costs the man who hired me. I figured he'd simply forgotten to fire me, and I didn't want to jog his memory.

A few months later, after I'd gotten my act together and become profitable, I finally gathered enough nerve to march into the wild man's office. I needed to ask why he hadn't fired me while he was letting the other new hires go.

What he said startled me: "We didn't fire you because *we like the way you lose*."

He explained that while losing, I'd demonstrated "good defense." I wasn't profitable, but I hadn't lost much money, preferring to take a quick loss rather than a "hang on and hope for the best" approach. This meant that having me around wasn't a big expense to the company. My boss reasoned that since I'd already learned the proper way to lose, he might as well let me stick around for a while to see if I could learn how to win.

It All Comes Back to Technical Analysis

Of course, the entire "good defense" concept was a result of my immersion in technical analysis. All of those hours spent looking at charts had created an internal mechanism that kept me out of trouble. How could I hold on to a stock if I knew its chart was breaking down? The charts had helped me to act objectively on what was actually happening in the market.

Technical analysis had taken the emotion out of my trading. It helped me to avoid being drawn into a subjective narrative. The reality of the price trumped the inner voice that whispers, "It's a good stock, don't sell it yet, it'll come back." Once I understood that reality, it was impossible to ignore.

The game of trading is constantly changing. The recent advent of high-frequency trading has closed certain loopholes that a clever individual trader could use to his or her advantage. However, as one door closes, another one opens. There are always ways to win at this game, and if you want to win badly enough, you will find them.

This book is designed to give you an advantage. If you can read a chart, you'll know when to get into a trade; even more important, you'll know when it's time to get out. Charts provide a visual history of the price and reveal the strengths and weaknesses of the market participants. Understanding those strengths and weaknesses helps us to anticipate future turning points.

Maybe the best thing about technical analysis is this: It forces us to confront the realities of the market. Technical analysis allows us to deal with what is *actually* happening instead of what we believe *should* be happening. Belief can be a dangerous thing in trading—specifically, the belief that we know what should or will happen in any given situation. It's better to see things as they really are than as we wish to see them, and technical analysis allows us to do just that.

Ed Ponsi is the managing director of Barchetta Capital Management LLC. An experienced professional trader and money manager, Mr. Ponsi has advised hedge funds, institutional traders, and individuals of all levels of skill and experience. He has made hundreds of appearances on national and international networks such as CNN, CNBC, the BBC, and Bloomberg. A dynamic public speaker, Mr. Ponsi has lectured audiences around the world, in locations such as London, Singapore, and New York City.

PART I

THE FOUNDATION OF TECHNICAL ANALYSIS

CHAPTER 1

Why Technical Analysis?

Why would anyone want to learn about technical analysis? If we want to understand how to analyze stocks, shouldn't we concern ourselves with valuation metrics like EBITDA (earnings before interest, taxes, depreciation, and amortization) and price-to-sales ratios? Wouldn't our time be better spent listening to conference calls and digging through balance sheets instead of poring over charts in search of various patterns and formations?

In truth, there is nothing wrong with doing any of the above. Terms such as price-to-sales ratio and EBITDA fall under the auspices of "fundamental analysis." Fundamental analysis can be a useful tool for analyzing investment opportunities. Think of technical and fundamental analysis as two different sides of the same coin.

However, fundamental analysis isn't foolproof. You can learn every nuance of fundamental analysis and include every major and minor fundamental metric in your analysis, but you'll still face this problem: *You'll never know what you don't know*. You can analyze all of the information that is available to you, but you'll *never* know if you possess all of the necessary information.

Meanwhile, somebody out there usually *does* know something that you or I don't know. An investment bank that hires an army of MBAs to crunch numbers and pours millions into research *should* know more than the average individual. The market is not a level playing field, and this is particularly true when it comes to fundamental analysis.

Meanwhile, technical analysts believe that all of the necessary information, including data that may be unknown to the public, is reflected in the chart. The price of a trading instrument should reflect all that is known or knowable about that stock, commodity, or currency.

All of the information is included in the price, even inside information. We don't have to know or understand the information to observe its effect on the price.

How can this be possible?

Let's say that a mutual fund or an investment bank has discovered through its research that stock ABC is wildly undervalued and is a screaming buy. The bank starts buying the stock aggressively.

You might never know what it is they know, or who is buying the stock, but if you look at ABC's chart, you should see the effect of that buying in the form of a rising price. That rising price is trying to tell you something, even if you don't know the reason behind the move. It's not necessary to know who or what is behind every move in the market.

■ Technical and Fundamental Divergence

Fundamentally, a stock or a currency may appear to be pristine, but if the chart tells a different story, believe the chart. There have been many instances where technical analysis and fundamental analysis told very different stories. On several occasions, this divergence has led to a dramatic conclusion.

For example, back in 2001 a major energy stock began to break down for no apparent reason. Most analysts gave this $60 billion company a "strong buy" or "buy" rating. For six consecutive years, *Fortune* magazine declared it to be "America's Most Innovative Company." The stock had been one of the best performers in the energy sector, quadrupling in price in just three years.

When the stock's price began to slip, and technical support levels began to break, fundamental analysts showed little concern. As the price continued to fall, many fundamental analysts referred to the stock's depressed price as "a buying opportunity," and initiated or reiterated buy ratings on the stock.

The name of that company was Enron. That infamous name is now synonymous with fraud and deceit.

The fundamental analysts who upgraded the stock as it fell believed they possessed all of the information needed to make an informed recommendation. What they didn't know is that the company had fed them false information. The information was worthless, and so was the stock!

During the year 2000, Enron climbed above $84 per share; one year later, the stock had fallen below $1. As a result, lives were ruined, pensions became worthless, and future plans evaporated into thin air.

The fundamental analyst works under the assumption that he or she is receiving complete and accurate information, but there is no way to know for certain that this

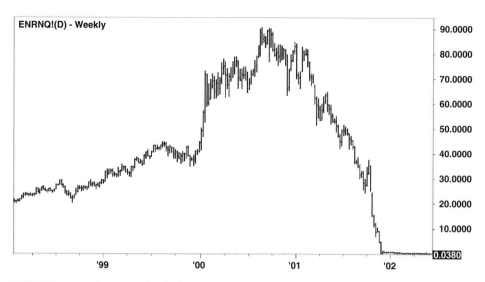

FIGURE 1.1 The Rise and Fall of Enron

is true. However, one look at Enron's chart, shown in Figure 1.1, should have made it clear that something was horribly wrong with the stock. Yet during its decline, Enron executives repeatedly insisted that there were no irregularities. They even encouraged their employees to buy more shares, just before the stock completely collapsed!

As the stock fell, it formed several bearish technical patterns. By the time you've completed this book, you'll know how to understand and apply those patterns should a similar situation arise in the future.

Enron is an extreme example, but it raises an important point: While the executives of the company were lying about the business, and while analysts were basing their assumptions about the company on those lies, the stock's price was telling the truth.

Those who knew the truth about Enron were selling their shares heavily. This is what caused the price to decline so dramatically—the truth was reflected in the stock's price. Any individual trader could have known that there was a problem by looking at the chart—and by ignoring the chorus of fundamental analysts and company officials who insisted Enron was a bargain as it fell.

■ The Collapse of Lehman Brothers

Another company that confounded analysts under a very different set of circumstances was an investment bank named Lehman Brothers Holdings. Unlike Enron, Lehman Brothers was a legitimate company with a rich history and real profits.

The investment banking company got its start in the 1850s, and by 1887 it was a member of the New York Stock Exchange. By the twenty-first century, it had grown into one of the most successful enterprises of its kind.

During 2007, shares of Lehman Brothers performed extremely well. That year, the stock reached an all-time peak, trading as high as $86.18. The company's shareholders were thrilled with the stock's performance.

Then a severe financial crisis swept the world in 2008, and the company was caught in the storm. The stock began a steep descent. There were persistent rumors that Lehman Brothers was on the verge of insolvency, which the company routinely denied.

During the summer of 2008, those rumors became more persistent, yet company officials never gave any indication to the public that the company was in trouble. The stock's decline accelerated. On September 9, 2008, the Standard & Poor's rating agency put Lehman Brothers on watch for a downgrade, citing its plunging stock price, but at the same time maintained an "A" rating on the stock.

Less than one week later, on September 15, 2008, Lehman Brothers declared bankruptcy. The stock was now virtually worthless. Later that day, Standard & Poor's removed its "A" rating from the stock.

Figure 1.2 depicts the stock's rapid decline. Technical analysts will note that Lehman's chart formed an extremely ominous technical pattern just after the stock reached its all-time peak. This pattern warned technical traders to avoid the stock, even as investors who believed the company's management were buying additional shares.

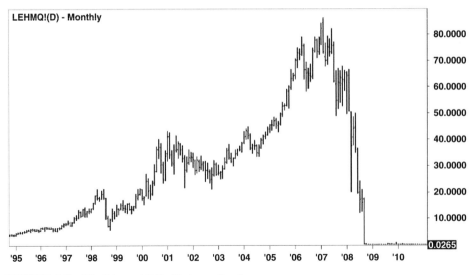

FIGURE 1.2 The Rise and Fall of Lehman Brothers

■ Price Is Truth

If fundamental analysts like those at Standard & Poor's had simply focused on the stock's price, they would have noticed a distressed chart that was breaking at all of its major support levels. One glance at that chart proved to be worth much more than countless hours of so-called expert analysis and number crunching.

Think of all the misery that could have been avoided by simply paying attention to that chart. Just as with Enron, Lehman Brothers' employees were heavily invested in the company's stock, particularly in their retirement accounts. Perhaps fundamental analysts should obtain at least a cursory knowledge of technical analysis to use as a filter or warning system in the event of situations such as these.

Years later, shares of Lehman Brothers Holdings are available on the over-the-counter market for less than three cents per share. Both the Lehman Brothers and Enron charts contained numerous clues as to what was about to transpire, thereby warning investors of the danger well before it happened. Fortunately for some investors, technical analysis allowed them to ignore the denials of management and focus on the truth of price.

Similar issues can arise at any time, with any investment, in less dramatic ways. At any given moment, your fundamental analysis of a company may be missing an important piece of information, either positive or negative. How will you know? The sad fact is, you'll only know in hindsight what you didn't know when it mattered most.

On the other hand, if you can read a chart, there's no need to understand the reason behind every move in the market. The price is already telling you everything you need to know.

■ Which Technical Analysis Method Will Work Best for You?

What is the best way to trade? Which technical analysis method should you use? How can you know which techniques will work best for you?

Everyone wants to know if there is one particular technical analysis method that works better than the others. It's a great question, because a simple answer could save a lot of time and effort.

Unfortunately, there is no simple answer. Nobody can tell you which technical analysis method will work best for you. Only you can make that determination. Here's why:

In *The Little Book of Market Wizards*, author Jack Schwager wrote the following:

> Traders must find a methodology that fits their own beliefs and talents. A sound methodology that is very successful for one trader can be a poor fit and a losing strategy for another trader.

How can that be? How is it possible that a trading strategy can work for one person and not another?

In that same book, Schwager interviewed a hedge fund manager named Colm O'Shea, who elaborated on this concept:

> If I try to teach you what I do, you will fail because you are not me. If you hang around me, you will observe what I do, and you may pick up some good habits. But there are a lot of things you will want to do differently. A good friend of mine, who sat next to me for several years, is now managing lots of money at another hedge fund and doing very well. But he is not the same as me. What he learned was not to become me. He became something else. He became him.

As a trader, you need to become you. How can you accomplish this? Study the various techniques in this book with an open mind. Consider that any of them may or may not work for you. Most likely, one or more of these concepts will resonate with you. Begin your search there.

Once you have found something that makes sense to you, apply it to your personal trading style, which will continue to evolve over time. Gain as much experience as you can, while taking as little risk as possible. After the initial excitement wears off, traders normally become less frantic and more patient. Circumstances change, people mature, and you'll find that your trading style will evolve with experience. The initial thrill of trading is gradually replaced with a calm focus.

This is important, because if you're highly excited while placing trades, you're much more likely to make a serious mistake. How would you feel about being the passenger in a vehicle whose driver is extremely emotional and excited? Or, would you want to glance up from an operating table and notice that the doctor who is about to perform surgery on you is very animated or agitated?

My trading styles have been documented in the books *Forex Patterns and Probabilities* and *The Ed Ponsi Forex Playbook*. Those styles are geared toward currency trading, but many traders have adapted them to stocks and commodities as well. However, as Mr. Schwager and Mr. O'Shea point out, there is no promise that a technique that works for one person will also work for another.

There's a good chance you will find something in this book that resonates with you. Just as important, you need to determine which techniques are incompatible with your personality. Read through the different methods, examine the charts, and sort through the various concepts presented in the following pages. At the very least you'll be able to eliminate some methods, and that's a start.

CHAPTER 2

The Language of Trading

In trading, large sums of money can be lost due to confusion caused by the use of imprecise language. That's why it's important to use appropriate terminology. The proper use of the following expressions removes ambiguity because they describe trading activity in precise terms.

This precise language may seem unnecessary to the untrained novice. However, to the experienced trader, who may have lost money on a trade or has witnessed a good trade get "busted" due to confusion caused by imprecise terminology, this is more than mere semantics.

Trading terminology can be confusing at times and often seems unnecessarily complicated. However, there are a few expressions that are critical to your understanding of both technical analysis and trading in general. Certain terms allow traders to express a concise thought in one or two syllables.

Trading errors can be expensive, and often there are tremendous sums of money on the line, so it's important that every party involved in the trade understands exactly what is taking place.

First, we will briefly discuss three important terms—"long," "short," and "flat." What do these terms mean?

Long—When a trader expresses an intention to go long, he or she is placing a trade that will only become profitable if the price increases. The trader wants the price to rise; if it falls, the trader loses.

Context: John is *long* ABC because he likes their new line of products.

Short—When a trader expresses an intention to sell short, he or she is placing a trade that will only become profitable if the price declines. The trader wants the price to fall; if it rises, the trader loses.

Context: Jane *shorted* XYZ just before earnings; she thinks the company might be in trouble.

The obvious question is, why don't traders simply say, "I'm going to buy stock XYZ" instead of "I'm going to go long XYZ"? In this case, the word "buy" is an imprecise term. In the world of trading, the term "buy" could mean two different things.

A trader might buy XYZ because he or she believes the price will rise. Or, a trader might buy XYZ because he or she is currently short shares of that stock. Those are two very different situations. A trader who is short a stock must buy shares if he or she wishes to exit or "cover" the short position.

Similarly, why don't traders simply say "I'm selling ABC" instead of "I'm shorting ABC"? A trader who is selling ABC might already own the shares. Perhaps this individual wishes to sell in order to exit the trade.

It's also possible that this person may wish to sell ABC short. However, there can be no confusion if a trader states that he or she is "short ABC." This trader will turn a profit if stock ABC falls, and will lose money if ABC rises.

Flat—The trader is neither long nor short. This trader has current position in the market.

The act of being flat can indicate the mere absence of a trade, but it can also represent a strategic decision. This is particularly true of short-term traders, who may wish to avoid the volatility associated with an economic report, an election, or a speech given by a central bank official. Often, such traders wait for the event to pass and then reassess the situation before reentering the market.

Context: John entered the weekend *flat* because he's going away on vacation.

There is additional terminology that is important to understand as it relates to trading. Here are some supplementary key terms:

Position—If a trader invests in XYZ in anticipation of making a profit, that trader has established a "position" in XYZ. A position can be long or short, and may involve any trading instrument—stocks, bonds, currencies, options, and so on.

One position can be used as a "hedge" against another position. This means the trader is using one position to protect or provide insurance against a potential negative move in another position.

Most hedge funds are capable of taking long and short positions simultaneously. Mutual funds and institutional traders have demonstrated a tendency to build positions over a period of weeks or months, while individual traders tend to enter and exit positions more freely.

Any position that is still in effect is referred to as an "open position"; after the trader exits that position, it is referred to as a "closed position." A position can be entered all at once, or it can be built over a series of trades.

For example, some traders prefer to initiate a position with a small trade and then add to it if the price moves in their favor. Others maintain a long-term "core" position in a stock, commodity, or currency while adding and subtracting short-term "trading" positions.

Context: John has closed his *long position* in XYZ and is planning to enter a *short position* in ABC.

Entry—The point at which the trader initiates a long or short trade or a portion of that trade. An entry can occur "at market," which means the trader is willing to accept whatever price is currently available. Or, the trader can use a "limit order," which defines a specific entry price.

Context: Jane is checking the charts to find a good *entry* point for ABC.

Stop Loss—The predetermined point at which a trader accepts a loss and exits a trade. By placing a stop, the trader attempts to define his or her risk. By accepting a small loss, the trader eliminates the possibility of a large loss.

Context: Jane placed her *stop* just beneath ABC's recent low point. If ABC reaches a new low, she'll automatically exit the trade.

Target—The predetermined point at which a trader intends to take a profit. By using a target, a trader defines the trade's potential reward. Some traders prefer to use multiple targets as a means to stay in winning positions longer.

Context: John closed half of his position at his first *target* and hopes to close the other half at the second *target*.

Time Horizon—This refers to the length of time that the trader plans to remain in the trade. A "day trader," someone who enters and exits a trading position on the same day, has a very short time horizon, while a mutual fund might have a time horizon that is measured in years.

One trader may operate within multiple time horizons, but it's important to remain consistent once the trade has been entered. It's usually a bad idea to turn a short-term trade into a long-term position just because the trade isn't working out as planned. Yet if we look into the account of an average investor, we might find unprofitable long-term positions that started out as short-term trades.

Context: John is an extremely impatient trader; he has the *time horizon* of a fruit fly.

Time Frame—This term refers to the length of time measured by each point, bar, or candle on a chart. Commonly used time frames include the weekly, daily, 240-minute, 60-minute, 30-minute, 15-minute, 5-minute, and 1-minute charts.

Context: For her *time frame,* Jane analyzes the overall situation on the daily chart before searching for trade setups on the hourly chart.

Bulls and Bears—The terms "bull" and "bear" appear frequently in trading literature, but what is the origin and significance of those terms? An upward movement is considered bullish because the attack of a bull occurs in an upward motion. An attacking bull lowers its horns and then thrusts them sharply upward.

Context: U.S. Dollar *bulls* pushed the currency to a new six-month high today.

Conversely, an attacking bear swats downward with its paws, which is why a downward move in the market is referred to as bearish. Images of these two beasts engaged in battle with one another, with the bull thrusting its horns higher while the bear swats downward from above, hang in the offices of brokers and traders around the world.

Context: The huge rally in metals prices has gold *bears* on the run.

Trend—A "trend" is a directional bias in price movement. Trends are important because they give traders an edge; if the price is moving persistently higher or lower, traders will attempt to exploit this movement by taking trades that favor the direction of the trend. The concept of trend trading is used as the basis of many popular trading strategies.

In technical analysis, an "uptrend" is represented by a series of higher low prices and higher high prices. Conversely, a "downtrend" can be accurately described as a series of lower high prices and lower low prices. Trends can remain in effect for months or years. Almost all trends end eventually, but attempting to guess when a trend will terminate can lead to hazardous trades and disappointing results.

Context: Jane established a long position in ABC because of the stock's strong upward *trend*.

In Figure 2.1, we see a sustained uptrend on the daily chart of the U.S. dollar/ Japanese yen currency pair (USDJPY) that formed in the early part of 2013. This is an upward trend because it consists of a series of higher high points (HH) and higher low points (HL).

Similarly, a downtrend consists of series of lower highs and lower lows. This concept is demonstrated in Figure 2.2, which shows shares of Herbalife Ltd. (HLF)

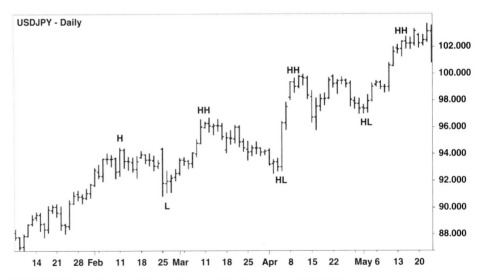

FIGURE 2.1 A Series of Higher Highs and Higher Lows in USDJPY

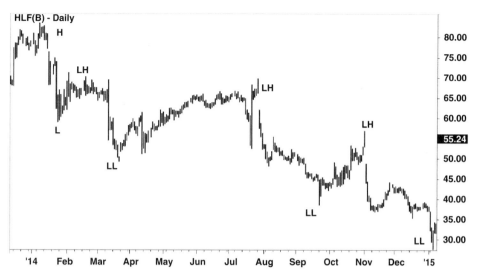

FIGURE 2.2   A Series of Lower Highs and Lower Lows in Shares of Herbalife (HLF)

forming a series of lower highs (LH) and lower lows (LL) starting in early 2014. Trends can occur in any time frame, and are not limited to long-term charts.

Context: When John noticed the prolonged *downtrend,* he knew he wanted to open a short position.

Fade: When a trader takes a position in opposition to a stock's movement, he or she is said to be "fading" that move. Possible reasons for fading a move include the following: The trader is expressing a lack of faith in the move; or believes that the market has misinterpreted a news item; or believes that the market has moved too far, too fast, and that the price is likely to return to a previous level. This term can be applied to a bullish or a bearish move.

Context: John felt the market overreacted to the strong employment report, so he *faded* the rally in the S&P 500 futures.

The more you use the terminology, the more comfortable—to the point of becoming second nature—it becomes. Most importantly, it leaves no questions about what you are doing and where you stand with your trades.

■ Final Thoughts on the Language of Trading

Trading terminology is indeed a language unto itself. The ability to understand and apply that language is critical when communicating with banks, brokers, and other market participants. In many cases, the lingo used by traders allows them to describe a situation with precision and effectiveness. It is also a means by which a trader can identify other traders.

CHAPTER 3

The Cornerstone

The concept of making money by trading the markets—not from producing goods or transporting them, but by trading shares of the companies that do so—has been around for centuries. The idea of striking it rich, or of improving one's standing in the world by the sheer force of one's intellect, is an intoxicating concept that has mass appeal.

Trading markets have often been maligned as being unfair and tilted against the "little guy," and with good reason. There are many examples of disparity in the trading markets, such as:

- The use of non-public inside information by unscrupulous individuals and companies

- The pump and dump antics of certain brokers, particularly involving penny stocks

- Analysts that tout a company to drive up its price, in order to allow their employers to sell at more favorable levels

- The use of high-frequency trading robots, which can place and cancel hundreds of thousands of orders in a millisecond

Despite these hurdles, trading is still a meritocracy in many ways. The markets do not care about your age, your skin color, or your beliefs. Markets do not care where you grew up, who your parents are, or where you went to school. The only thing that matters is the ability to extract money from the market. If you can do that on a consistent basis, you can change your life and the lives of the people who matter most to you.

Because of this strong appeal, men and women have been vying for centuries to create systems and techniques designed to anticipate market moves. This has led to a variety of concepts, many of them brilliant, some of them bizarre. Some techniques have stood the test of time, while others have faded into obscurity.

One early form of technical analysis that has survived dates back to fifteenth century Japan, where rice traders are credited with developing what we now call "candlestick charts." Today, candlestick charts are more popular than ever, and can be easily obtained by anyone. Other early forms of technical analysis failed to survive, disappearing from our collective consciousness like a lost language.

Prior to the widespread availability of personal computers and the Internet in the late twentieth century, charts were usually drawn by hand. Frequently, updated books of printed charts were popular among traders, even though the fact that they were printed on paper meant they were, by definition, outdated.

■ Dow Jones & Company

Modern technical analysis is generally recognized as beginning with Charles Dow. Mr. Dow was a journalist who worked for the Kieran News Agency, along with statistician Edward Jones and reporter Charles Bergstresser. The three men left the Kieran Agency and founded Dow Jones & Company in November of 1882.

One year later, the company began distribution of the *Customers' Afternoon Letter*, a summary of the day's financial news. The two-page publication gained popularity with Wall Street investors, as it was considered a reliable source of actionable information. The daily letter eventually became known as *The Wall Street Journal*, which officially began publication in 1889.

The partners conceived of a grouping of stocks—an index—designed to make it easy to follow the market. The first Dow Jones index began tracking the market in 1885; it consisted of eleven components, including nine railroad companies. That index was the precursor to what is now known as the Dow Jones Transportation Average. Here are its original nine rail components:

Chicago, Milwaukee, and St. Paul Railway
Chicago and North Western Railway
Delaware, Lackawanna, and Western Railroad
Lake Shore and Michigan Southern Railway
Louisville and Nashville Railroad
Missouri Pacific Railway
New York Central Railroad
Northern Pacific Railroad (preferred stock only)
Union Pacific Railway

Two non-railroad companies were also included:

Pacific Mail Steamship Company
Western Union

In 1896, it was decided to divide the stock index into two; one index for the shares of industrial companies, and the other consisting of transportation companies. This led to the creation of the Dow Jones Industrial Average, which was first calculated on May 26, 1896.

Even today, the general public refers to the Dow Jones Industrial Average as "the market," as in "the market was up 50 points today." The reason why this index is so ingrained in our consciousness is because it was the first popular grouping of stocks to gain a widespread following. With just one statistic, it became possible to ascertain the general health of the U.S. stock market.

■ The Dow Jones Industrial Average

The Dow Jones Industrial Average initially consisted of a dozen stocks, including General Electric, which remains part of that index today. Together, these stocks were considered representative of U.S. industry. The U.S. economy was much more focused on manufacturing in Mr. Dow's day, so it made sense that an index based on manufacturing and production would gain significance during that time.

It's fair to ask if this index is as relevant in the twenty-first century as it was in the nineteenth. While the Dow Jones Industrial Average is not considered a broad measure of the U.S. stock market, it has evolved in order to remain a meaningful barometer of the U.S. economy. Initially, the index consisted of the following names:

American Cotton Oil Co.
American Sugar Co.
American Tobacco Co.
Chicago Gas Co.
Distilling & Cattle Feeding Co.
General Electric Co.
Laclede Gas Co.
National Lead Company
North American Company
Tennessee Coal, Iron, and Railroad Co.
United States Leather Company
United States Rubber Company

By 1928, the Dow Jones Industrial Average had expanded to 30 companies. Over the years, dozens of names have been added and deleted, usually due to their performance and/or perceived relevance to the economy.

Today, the U.S. economy is much broader than it was in 1896, and is considered a "service economy." This means that actual services, such as repairing an automobile or cooking a meal, now make up a larger portion of the U.S. economy than manufacturing. Manufacturing can be done virtually anywhere due to automation, so it tends to occur where it can be accomplished inexpensively.

As a result, the Dow Jones Industrial Average is sometimes perceived as a narrow stock index, and professionals tend to focus on broader indices like the Standard & Poor's 500. This is somewhat unfair, as the Dow Jones Industrial Average is now a misnomer; it is no longer squarely focused on industrial stocks. Over the years, the index has diversified into the health and pharmaceutical, consumer goods, energy, technology, financial, and retail sectors, making it more representative of the true economy.

■ The Dow Jones Transportation Average

The Dow Jones Transportation Average is the descendant of the original rail-heavy index, making it older than the more prominent Dow Jones Industrial Average.

All of the goods created in U.S. factories need transport by ship, highway, or rail to their ultimate destinations. Therefore, an index was created from the companies that provided these services. The performance of these companies was considered indicative of the overall economy.

Is the Dow Jones Transportation Average still relevant? Despite the move away from manufacturing, transportation is still crucial to the U.S. economy.

This is made clear by the boom in North American energy production. In the early twenty-first century, North American output of crude oil and natural gas soared, thanks in part to advances in technology. This energy boom led to a huge increase in demand for rail transportation services, which in turn drove the transportation index to new heights. Clearly, transportation remains a relevant economic factor in the twenty-first century.

Like the Dow Jones Industrial Average, the Dow Jones Transportation Average has evolved with time. The original version predated the first powered flight, but today the index contains several airlines. In addition to railroads, which have merged into just a handful of names, the index also contains trucking, auto rental, and package delivery companies. This diversification allows the index to provide an accurate representation of the modern transportation sector.

■ Final Thoughts on the Cornerstone

When Charles Dow created his stock indices, he had no idea how significant they would become. The Dow Jones Industrial Average is so prevalent that many refer to it as "the market." Today, there are futures, options, exchange-traded funds, and a variety of other instruments that can be applied to Mr. Dow's indices.

CHAPTER 4

The Dow Theory

A reporter and journalist, Charles Dow wrote editorials that were published in *The Wall Street Journal* in which he presented his theories on predictive analysis of the stock market. Dow never formally organized his theories into a cogent whole, and never wrote a book on his findings.

The term "Dow Theory" was coined by author A.C. Nelson, who organized Dow's *Wall Street Journal* editorials into a book called *The ABC of Stock Speculation* around the time of Dow's death in 1902.

William Peter Hamilton, who became publisher of the *Journal* after Dow's passing, based his 1922 book *The Stock Market Barometer* on Dow's tenets. In 1932, Robert Rhea further refined these concepts in his work, titled *The Dow Theory: An Explanation of Its Development and an Attempt to Define Its Usefulness as an Aid to Speculation*.

Here are the basic concepts of Dow Theory:

The Averages Discount Everything. All that is known or knowable about a stock is reflected in its price. Information is acted upon, and these actions are reflected in the price of the individual stocks, and by extension, the stock averages. If an event is widely anticipated, its occurrence is likely already reflected in the indices before it happens.

Therefore, the markets don't necessarily reflect current circumstances; they often reflect anticipated future circumstances. This is why you'll sometimes see a stock market that seems completely disconnected from the current economy; at such times, the market isn't concerned with the state of the economy as it is today, but with its future condition. The notion of the price as a predictive mechanism, rather than a reflection of past or current events, is one of the lasting innovations of Dow's work.

The Market Has Three Trends—Primary, Secondary, and Minor. In today's trading vernacular, perhaps a more concise way to express this would be "the market has three time frames."

The primary trend is measured in years. The terms "bull market" and "bear market" apply to the primary trend. A secondary trend is a counter-trend, corrective movement within the primary trend that normally lasts from three weeks to three months. A minor trend refers to short-term movement within the secondary trend, and normally lasts for less than three weeks.

According to Dow Theory, the primary trend is of the greatest concern and presents the greatest opportunities. The secondary trend also creates trading opportunities, while the minor trend is usually of little consequence. The concept of trading across multiple time frames stems from this part of Dow's work.

What is a trend? As mentioned in previous chapters, an uptrend consists of a series of higher highs and higher lows, while a downtrend consists of a series of lower highs and lower lows.

■ Trends Are Persistent

Another tenet of Dow Theory that has stood the test of time is the concept of persistent trends. When the primary trend is in effect, a Dow Theory practitioner assumes that the trend will continue. This assumption stays in effect until clear reversal signals appear, such as the transportation and industrial averages together forming a series of lower lows.

Because of the persistence of trends, traders should focus on trading in the same direction as the primary trend. They should avoid trading against it, with the possible exception of short-term trades.

A trend has three phases—accumulation, public participation, and distribution.

"Accumulation" refers to buying by those "in the know." Often, this occurs after a market suffers sharp losses, and at a time when the general public has no desire to participate.

After a market has been rising for some time, the *public participation* phase begins. This occurs as the general population recognizes the existence of a bull market and decides to begin buying.

"Distribution" begins to occur as the bull market matures; this phase is often marked by wildly bullish sentiment, widespread public interest in the markets, and conspicuous representations of the bull market (on magazine covers, on television, and in movies).

■ Confirmation

"Confirmation" is another lasting tenet of Dow's work. In reference to Dow Theory, confirmation specifically refers to the relationship between the Dow Jones Industrial Average and the Dow Jones Transportation Average.

In order to confirm a bull rally, both indices must exceed a previous major high point. An excellent example of this would be if both the transports and the industrials were to reach an all-time high on the same day.

A bear move is confirmed when both indices make new lows beneath a previous major low point. If either index fails to confirm the other, the move is considered suspect.

Figure 4.1 is a comparison chart that demonstrates confirmation: The Dow Jones Industrial Average (black line) reached a new all-time closing high of 17810.06 on November 21, 2014 (point A). On the same day, the Dow Jones Transportation Average (gray line) also reached a fresh all-time closing high at 9094.16.

This confirmation creates a Dow Theory buy signal. The simultaneous new highs are considered particularly bullish. Both indices made subsequent new highs, resulting in another buy signal in December of 2014.

The length of time that passes prior to a confirmation signal is also taken into consideration. When confirmation occurs quickly, as it does in Figure 4.1, the signal is considered strong. However, if there is a considerable lag time before the confirmation occurs, the signal is considered less potent.

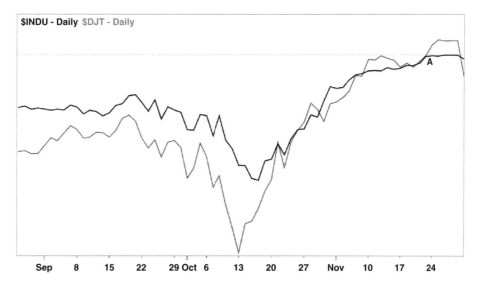

FIGURE 4.1 The Dow Jones Industrial Average (black) and the Dow Jones Transportation Average Reach Simultaneous New Highs, Resulting in a Dow Theory Buy Signal

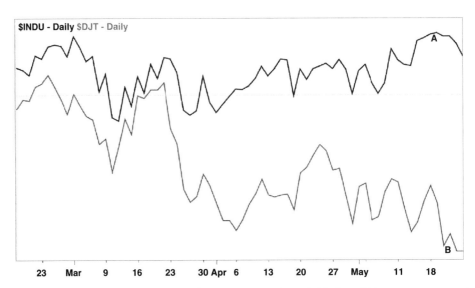

FIGURE 4.2   A Divergence Between the Dow Jones Industrial (black) and Transportation (gray) Averages

When confirmation fails to occur, it is not considered a buy or sell signal, but it can be considered a warning sign. In Figure 4.2, we see another comparison chart of the Dow Jones Industrial Average (black line) and the Dow Jones Transportation Average (gray line). Notice how the two indices are trading in tandem on the left side of the chart, and then diverge on the right.

On May 19, 2015, the Dow Jones Industrial Average closed at an all-time high of 18312.39 (point A). However, the Dow Jones Transportation Average failed to confirm this new high; in fact, the transportation index reached a six-month low just a few days later on May 22 (point B). This failure to confirm served as a warning to traders, who should have been bullish at the time, based on prior Dow Theory buy signals.

The divergence of these two indices tells us that the market wasn't as strong as it appeared to be on the surface. Weakness in the transportation index could be a sign that demand for products could be waning. However, this would not be assumed unless and until it is confirmed by price action in the industrial index.

While the divergence between the industrials and the transports in Figure 4.2 can be described as a warning sign, it's important to understand that it is *not* a sell signal. Divergence itself does not create a buy or sell signal *as it pertains to Dow Theory*.

Divergence can be used as a buy or sell signal outside of the realm of Dow Theory. For example, many traders use divergence between the MACD (moving average convergence/divergence) indicator and the price as a buy/sell indicator. However this type of divergence is unrelated to Dow Theory. We'll discuss MACD divergence in a later chapter.

When it comes to Dow Theory, there are no provisions for a neutral signal—it is always set to either buy or sell, based on the most recent signal. The most recent signal prior to the divergence in Figure 4.2 was a buy signal in December of 2014, so adherents of Dow Theory would have remained cautiously bullish.

In order to generate a Dow Theory sell signal, the Dow Jones Industrial Average would have to confirm the breakdown in the Dow Jones Transportation Average by breaking below a major low point. Both of the indices would have to break down in order to generate a sell signal, according to the theory.

■ Volume Confirmation

According to Dow Theory, volume is also used to confirm the trend. Ideally, a bull market should feature an increase in volume as prices rise, and turnover should decrease as prices fall. The opposite would be true for a bear market; volume should increase on days when the market is falling, and decrease as prices are rising.

If volume tapers off during a rally in a bull market, it could be an early indication of a trend reversal. The trend still has momentum, but buyers, particularly the institutional traders that account for much of the volume, may be losing their enthusiasm for the market. Perhaps prices have reached a point where aggressive buying is no longer warranted. This situation is sometimes referred to as a "hollow" rally.

In Figure 4.3, we see a weekly chart of the S&P 500 during a six-year bull market, starting in 2009. Note how the index's volume (bottom area of chart) begins to decrease as the index continues to soar to new heights. This could be considered an early warning that large institutional buyers are becoming reluctant to commit additional funds as prices move higher.

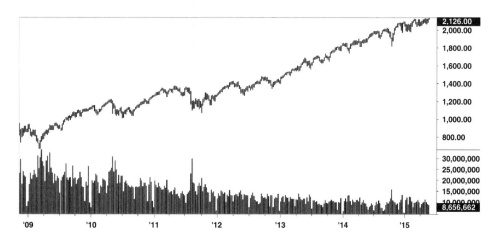

FIGURE 4.3   As the S&P 500 Rallies, Volume Begins to Decrease

The same would be true in a bear market; if prices are falling on light turnover, it could be a sign that the bear market is nearing an end. Perhaps bears are losing their desire to sell, as prices may have fallen to an area where they are now deemed attractive.

The concept of using volume as a confirmation tool applies to individual stocks as well. We'll cover volume more extensively in a later chapter.

Other Types of Confirmation

As trading markets have matured, the concept of confirmation has gained wider acceptance and taken on a broader meaning. The concept now goes far beyond the simple Dow Theory confirmation shown earlier.

For example, confirmation can occur between a stock index that consists of large companies, such as the S&P 500, and an index that is composed of smaller companies, such as the Russell 2000. If the S&P 500 reaches a new high, a simultaneous or near-simultaneous new high from the Russell 2000 confirms that the rally is broad because it encompasses both large and small companies. This is considered far more bullish than a rally that is supported by just a handful of large companies.

The concept of confirmation can also be applied across different asset classes. For example, the relationships between certain currencies and commodities can be used for the purposes of confirmation. The Canadian dollar has a positive correlation to crude oil, and the Australian dollar has a positive correlation to metals like gold and copper. This topic is covered extensively in my other books, *Forex Patterns and Probabilities* and *The Ed Ponsi Forex Playbook*.

These examples of correlation are not a part of Dow Theory, but could be considered an extension of the philosophy behind that theory.

Random Walk Theory

If you are skeptical about the principles of Dow Theory, you aren't alone. Like any predictive methodology, Dow Theory has its detractors.

One of the most notable concepts that stands in opposition to Dow Theory is the Random Walk Theory, which states that all movement in the stock market is unpredictable. This theory gained traction in 1973 with the publication of *A Random Walk Down Wall Street* by author Burton Malkiel, though the concept had been in existence for decades prior to that time.

According to the Random Walk Theory, there is absolutely no relationship between past and future price movement in the stock market, and by extension, in any market. Therefore, any attempt to trade any market by using technical analysis would be futile.

While there are certainly times when this seems to be the case, the Random Walk Theory doesn't explain the trending nature of markets. If markets are completely random, then why are price trends so prevalent and persistent?

Also, market trends are often influenced by fundamental factors; in a purely random environment this would not be the case. Take note that Dow Theory never attempts to explain why markets trend; it only acknowledges that they do.

Random Walk also fails to explain the success of many fund managers over an extended period of time. Some of the world's most successful money managers are known to be practitioners of technical analysis, such as Paul Tudor Jones II.

Supporters of the Random Walk Theory might simply credit Mr. Jones' consistent success, over decades of trading, to his good fortune. However, it's far too convenient for Random Walk supporters to claim that successful practitioners of technical analysis are simply lucky.

A Game of Chance, or a Game of Skill?

Consider the *World Series of Poker*; there is no question that in the game of poker, the cards fall in a random manner. It would be impossible to predict the order of the cards as they are dealt.

If we were to apply the Random Walk Theory to poker, we would conclude that it is impossible to win consistently at poker or at any other game in which the cards fall in an admittedly random order.

Yet every year, as the *World Series of Poker* tournament nears its end, winners from previous tournaments remain in the competition. Are these individuals consistently lucky, year after year? Or have they learned to apply a skill to a game that includes a random factor?

■ The Middle Ground

Perhaps there is a middle ground between Dow Theory and Random Walk Theory. Perhaps markets are somewhat predictable, particularly in the long run, but they are not perfectly predictable. If markets were perfectly predictable, then trading would be easy; clearly, it is not.

We have to accept the fact that there is a certain degree of randomness at work in the markets. This statement doesn't necessarily conflict with Dow Theory, which is not presented here as a panacea.

No claim has been made, here or elsewhere, that Dow Theory is a perfect predictor of market direction. However, just as it is possible to succeed consistently in a game like poker that features a random component, it is possible to succeed consistently in trading, as Paul Tudor Jones and others have done.

Random Walk assumes that we must predict the future in order to succeed, but what if that is a false premise? What if it is *not* necessary to accurately predict the future in order to succeed at trading?

Many traders will tell you that trading is more about reaction rather than prediction. That includes reaction to a set of circumstances that occur on the chart.

■ Final Thoughts on Dow Theory

Charles Dow's indices can be used in a variety of ways, and the concept of confirmation is significant among them. Confirmation can be used to determine if a bull or bear market has begun or ended. It can also be used to determine which of the three phases the trend is currently in—accumulation, public participation, or distribution.

PART II

KEY CONCEPTS OF
TECHNICAL ANALYSIS

CHAPTER 5

Common Types of Charts

A chart is simply a visual representation of price data. There are many different types of charts, and each has its advantages and disadvantages. As technology has evolved, more complex forms and elements of charting have gained popularity.

■ Price Data

Here we see price data in its raw form. These are the key pieces of information that are used in the construction of charts.

Table 5.1 shows the date, opening price, highest price reached, lowest price reached, and closing price for the Dow Jones Industrial Average from September 21, 2015 through October 9, 2015. This is the raw material from which charts are constructed. As we will see, not every chart configuration contains all of the available data.

■ Time Frames

Charts that include representations of time are usually divided into equal segments of time. A daily chart divides the data according to each trading day, an hourly chart does the same for each hour, and a five-minute chart divides price data according to five-minute intervals.

TABLE 5.1	Historical Prices of the Dow Jones Industrial Average			
Date	Open	High	Low	Close
Oct 9, 2015	17,054.69	17,110.88	17,027.23	17,084.49
Oct 8, 2015	16,904.17	17,081.28	16,859.34	17,050.75
Oct 7, 2015	16,805.42	16,963.30	16,765.00	16,912.29
Oct 6, 2015	16,774.02	16,865.09	16,746.03	16,790.19
Oct 5, 2015	16,502.10	16,798.37	16,502.10	16,776.43
Oct 2, 2015	16,258.25	16,472.77	16,013.66	16,472.37
Oct 1, 2015	16,278.62	16,348.87	16,073.82	16,272.01
Sep 30, 2015	16,057.08	16,297.60	16,057.08	16,284.70
Sep 29, 2015	16,001.76	16,118.89	15,942.37	16,049.13
Sep 28, 2015	16,313.26	16,313.26	15,981.85	16,001.89
Sep 25, 2015	16,205.07	16,465.23	16,205.07	16,314.67
Sep 24, 2015	16,257.11	16,257.11	16,016.36	16,201.32
Sep 23, 2015	16,332.81	16,355.29	16,211.98	16,279.89
Sep 22, 2015	16,477.45	16,477.45	16,221.73	16,330.47
Sep 21, 2015	16,406.10	16,578.60	16,391.88	16,510.19

Source: Google Finance

There are certain forms of charts, like point and figure charting, which contain no reference to time and therefore are not subject to time frames.

■ Line Charts

The line chart is the simplest form of charting, and is usually the first chart type that most of us encounter. It consists only of time and one price, which in most cases is the closing price.

Time is tracked on the horizontal (X) axis of the chart, and price is tracked on the vertical (Y) axis. Figure 5.1 shows a daily line chart for Amazon.com (AMZN).

Before the widespread use of personal computers, many technical analysts drew charts by hand. Line charts became popular because they were easy to create; a technician creating a daily chart only needed to obtain the dates and their corresponding closing prices. By drawing a line from each day's closing price to the next, the technical analyst could easily create a visual representation of a stock's trajectory.

Charts can be created in any time frame; just as we can draw a chart of daily prices, we can also create one from intraday prices. Figure 5.2 depicts a five-minute line chart of Amazon.com in October of 2015. It divides the day into five-minute intervals and is created from the closing price of each interval.

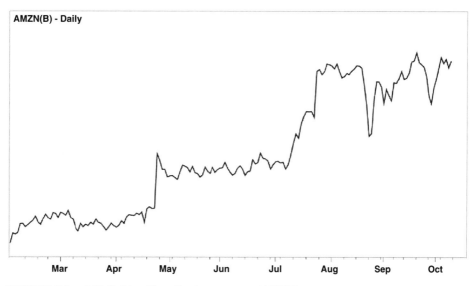

FIGURE 5.1   A Daily Line Chart for Amazon.com (AMZN)

FIGURE 5.2   A Five-Minute Line Chart of Amazon.com

Despite the wide variety of choices available, line charts are still popular. Not every chartist wants to use all of the available data at his or her disposal; many instead prefer a streamlined charting experience.

Today, line charts are most commonly used to compare the performance of two or more stocks or indices. In Figure 5.3, we see a comparison chart of the Dow Jones Industrial Average ($DJIA, black) and the Dow Jones Transportation Average ($DJT, gray) using daily line charts.

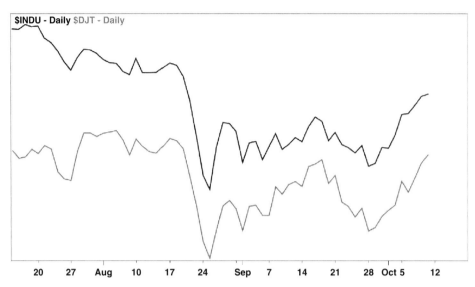

20   27   **Aug**   10   17   24   **Sep**   7   14   21   28 **Oct 5**   12

FIGURE 5.3   A Line Chart Comparison of the Dow Jones Industrial Average ($DJIA, black) and the Dow Jones Transportation Average ($DJT, gray)

■ Bar Charts

For many technical analysts, a single price isn't enough. If we look only at the closing price, we have no indication of what happened during the time frame represented. Did the price drift quietly before the close, or did a violent reversal occur before the closing price was reached? The use of line charts leaves out potentially valuable information.

To remedy this, bar charts came into use. A bar chart contains the opening, closing, high, and low prices obtained during a time period. Time is once again represented by the X axis, and price by the Y axis.

The high price is represented by the highest vertical point of the bar; conversely, the lowest point of the bar represents the lowest price reached during that time period.

A tall bar indicates that the price covered a wide trading range, and a short bar denotes a narrow trading range. The opening price is marked by a small horizontal line protruding toward the left, and the closing price is indicated by a horizontal line pointing toward the right.

Figure 5.4 depicts a daily bar chart of Apple (AAPL), showing the opening price (O), high price (H), low price (L), and closing price (C) of each day's trading.

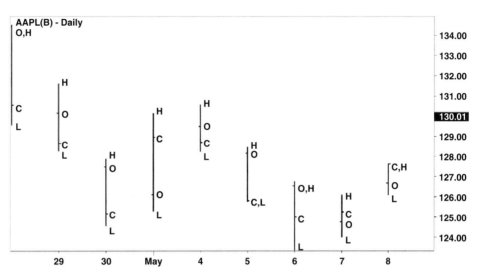

FIGURE 5.4   A Daily Bar Chart of Apple (AAPL)

Candlestick Charts

Candlestick chart patterns originated in Japan centuries ago, although the exact timing of their invention is difficult to pinpoint. Over time, this charting technique has evolved and grown in popularity.

Much of the credit for the popularity of candlestick charts is given to an eighteenth century rice trader named Munehisa Homna, who was known in his day as the "god of the markets." In addition to the popularization of candlestick patterns, Homna is believed to have written one of the earliest books on market psychology. This should come as no surprise, as market psychology is intertwined with the interpretation of candlestick charts.

However, there is considerable dispute as to Homna's importance in the development of candlestick charting, with some believing that his role was insignificant. The modern-day popularity of candlestick charts is credited to Steve Nison, an American technical analyst who published several books on the subject, including *Japanese Candlestick Charting Techniques* in 1991.

Like bar charts, candlestick chart patterns use the open, high, low, and closing prices to create a picture of price activity over a designated period of time. Instead of appearing on a bar, the price action within a time interval forms a pattern or shape. These patterns and shapes indicate whether a move is likely to continue or reverse. They can also signify indecision on the part of traders.

Reading a Candlestick Chart

As with a bar chart, the high and low price of a candlestick chart is determined by the highest and lowest point reached during a given time period. The opening and closing price, and the difference between them, is indicated within a square or rectangular box called the "body" or "real body" of the candle.

The color of the real body indicates whether the price rose or fell during a given time period. A green or white real body indicates that the opening price was below the closing price; in other words, the price rose during that time period. A black or red real body indicates that the closing price was lower than the opening price. This tells us that the price fell during the time period being analyzed.

Prices that exceed the opening and closing prices are represented by narrow vertical lines called "wicks." These lines are also referred to as "tails" or "shadows."

The various combinations of real bodies and wicks form shapes and patterns. These formations often give traders additional insights that aren't obtainable from a line or bar chart. Candlestick patterns and their meanings will be covered in later chapters.

Figure 5.5 depicts the opening, closing, high, and low prices on the daily candlestick chart of Apple. Bullish candles are shaded gray, while bearish candles are shaded black.

Note the differences and similarities between this chart and the previous one (Figure 5.4), which depicted the same price information on a bar chart.

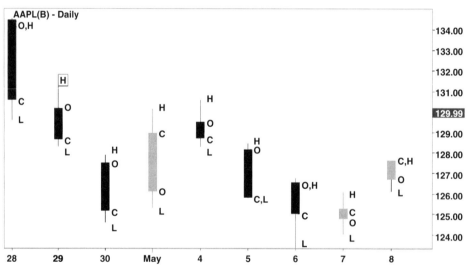

FIGURE 5.5 A Daily Candlestick Chart of Apple (AAPL)

■ Point and Figure Charts

Point and figure charting is based on changes in price only, with no consideration given to time. Some believe this paints a clearer picture of price action. Stretches of time that do not contain significant price movement are ignored and do not appear on the chart.

Detractors of point and figure charting say this technique leaves out potentially important information. Adherents to this style believe that because of their emphasis on pure price, point and figure charts make it relatively easy for traders to spot critical turning points by leaving out superfluous information.

Figure 5.6 shows a daily point and figure chart of Google Inc. Class A Shares (GOOGL). When the price on the chart is rising, this activity is depicted by a column consisting of the letter X; therefore an "X" column describes a bullish price move. Downward price movement is indicated by columns consisting of the letter O; these columns show a bearish price move.

Notice how the time intervals at the bottom of the chart are not evenly spaced. This is because time is not considered an important factor in point and figure charting. New X's and O's can only be created via price movement, and new columns can only be generated by a significant reversal in price.

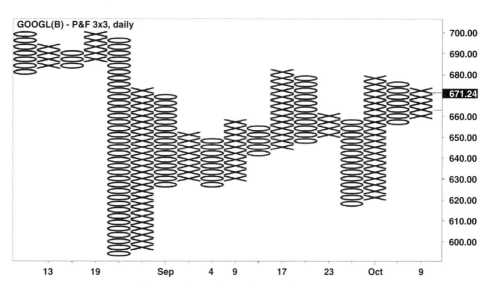

FIGURE 5.6 A Point and Figure Chart of Google Inc. Class A Shares (GOOGL)

■ The Use of Scale in Charts

As mentioned earlier, price appears on the vertical axis (Y axis) of the chart. However, there are different ways to measure price movement. We can measure a move in terms of pure price, or in terms of percentage gains or losses.

Consider this: If a stock moves from $5 to $6, it has gained $1 in price. If we measure this gain on a percentage basis, it represents a 20% increase. If a stock rises from $10 to $11, it has also gained $1 in price—but the percentage increase is only equal to 10.

If we want to measure the move in terms of price, we would use an "arithmetic" or "linear" scale. If we want to place the emphasis on percentage moves, we would use a "semi-logarithmic" scale.

An arithmetic or linear scale would treat these two price movements in exactly the same way, because both moves are equal to $1. A semi-logarithmic scale would treat these moves very differently, because they are dissimilar when considered on a percentage basis.

Figure 5.7 shows a linear chart of Apple, encompassing a five-year period from late 2009 until late 2014. Look at the prices on the Y axis and notice how they are evenly spaced. The distance from $30 to $40 appears the same as the distance from $90 to $100. The arithmetic or linear chart is based on raw price movement.

In Figure 5.8 we can view the same price information on a semi-logarithmic scale. Notice the separation of prices on the Y axis. On this chart, the distance from $30 to $40 is visibly greater than the distance between $90 and $100. The semi-logarithmic chart is based on a percentage of price movement.

FIGURE 5.7 An Apple Daily Chart, Using a Linear Scale

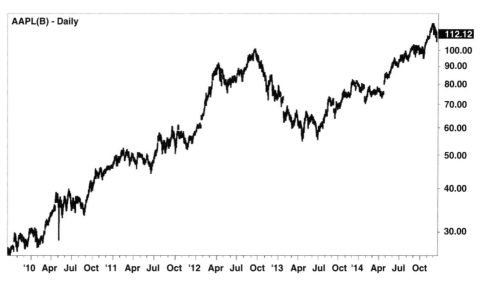

FIGURE 5.8 An Apple Daily Chart Using a Semi-Logarithmic Scale

There are no hard and fast rules regarding the usage of the arithmetic scale vs. the semi-logarithmic scale. Some traders prefer semi-logarithmic charts when analyzing longer-term price movements, and use the linear scale to analyze shorter-term price movements. Ultimately, the choice is a matter of individual preference.

■ Final Thoughts on Common Types of Charts

Each chart type offers a different window with which to view price information. Candlestick charts in particular are focused on very specific patterns, while line charts offer a more general view. Bar charts offer complete information regarding the high, low, opening, and closing prices, while point and figure charting removes time from the equation. In this sense, each chart type can be useful in its own way.

CHAPTER 6

Support and Resistance

Now that we understand the most commonly used methods of charting, let's put them to use. We'll begin with the simple concepts of support and resistance.

Imagine that you are bouncing a very heavy ball on a floor. If you bounce the ball hard enough, the floor may weaken. If you continue to bounce this very heavy ball as hard as you can, it may just break through the floor. Imagine that the ball breaks through the floor and is now one flight beneath you.

You walk down one flight of stairs to retrieve the ball. Now look up at the ceiling; it has a round hole in it. From your current perspective, it is the ceiling; but just moments ago when you were upstairs, it was the floor.

If you pick up that very heavy ball and throw it at the ceiling as hard as you can, again and again, you may weaken the ceiling. Eventually, the ball may break through the ceiling, just as it broke through the floor.

"Support" is an area where the price has shown a tendency to stop falling. Think of support as the floor beneath the market.

Why did this particular area become the "floor"? Perhaps the bulls have decided that it is a good price to take a long position, and therefore buying pressure emerges when the price reaches this area, preventing the price from falling further. Or, perhaps the price has fallen to a point where the bears are no longer comfortable selling; they'd prefer to wait in the hope of selling at a higher price. For whatever reason, the price has shown a tendency to stop falling at this point.

"Resistance" is an area where the price has shown a tendency to stop rising. Think of resistance as the ceiling above the market.

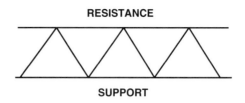

FIGURE 6.1 Support and Resistance

Why did this particular area become the "ceiling"? Perhaps the bulls no longer wish to buy once the price has reached this level, and they'd prefer to see the price drop before buying more. Or, maybe the bears have determined that this is a fair price at which to sell, and their influence exerts selling pressure at that price. For whatever reason, the price has shown a tendency to stop rising at this point (Figure 6.1).

In order to fully grasp support and resistance, we must first understand that every trade is both a buy and a sell. Think of a store; you may want to buy bread, but if the store doesn't have any, there will be no transaction. Similarly, the store owner may want to sell bread, but if nobody wants to buy it, no transaction occurs. It takes both a buyer and a seller of bread to complete the transaction.

Trading is the same way. You can't buy a stock or a currency unless an opposing party is willing to sell, and vice versa. Because there are two sides to every trade, we can make certain assumptions about the participants and their potential behavior, based on both their desire to win and their aversion to loss.

■ Support Becomes Resistance, and Vice Versa

Consider that the ceiling above you is the floor from the perspective of someone standing one flight above you, and that the floor beneath you is the ceiling to someone standing one flight below.

The example using the ball illustrates this point: Once broken, a price zone that formerly acted as support often acts as resistance, and vice versa. Because of this, technical analysts use these broken levels to locate future anticipated turning points for a stock, currency, or other trading vehicle.

Why does support become resistance, and vice versa? Let's imagine that stock XYZ stops falling every time it drops to $25 per share. Perhaps a large mutual fund or hedge fund is a buyer at that price. Individual traders notice the tendency for XYZ to rise when it reaches $25, so they too begin to buy at that price. Eventually, there are a number of bulls of various sizes that have established long positions in XYZ at $25 (Figure 6.2).

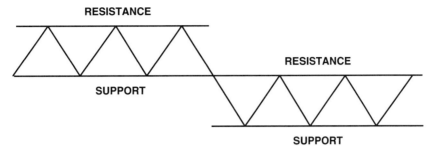

FIGURE 6.2 Support Becomes Resistance

One day, the price breaks decisively through $25, and eventually falls to $22. What can we say about the bulls who purchased XYZ at $25? We know that any traders that entered long positions in XYZ at $25 are losing money.

While the price of XYZ is influenced by a variety of factors, making future prices somewhat hard to predict, investors are somewhat easier to decipher—especially when they are losing money. In fact, if you've ever been in a losing trade, you can probably figure out how they will react.

Like all human beings, traders are ruled by the Pleasure Principle. This simply means that we are attracted to pleasure and repelled by pain. The purchase of XYZ at $25 was probably motivated by the potential pleasure of selling at a profit at higher prices.

When XYZ fell below $25, those same market participants began to experience pain. Pain is a strong motivator, and this particular brand of pain generates a fairly predictable response.

■ The Concept of Anchoring

For most of us, the fear of losing money is stronger than the desire to make money. To put it in simple terms, fear is stronger than greed. An open, losing position brings with it waves of regret. Some losing traders suddenly become religious, and start pleading with a higher power to bail them out of the situation. "Please, God," they say, "I just want to break even."

This desire to break even is strong because of a common psychological trait known as "anchoring." Buyers have mentally linked stock XYZ to the $25 purchase price, and now that's the dominant price associated with the stock in their minds.

Maybe XYZ's drop to $22 will be followed by a rally well beyond $25, or perhaps it will fall further, but all of this is secondary to the individual who has mentally anchored the stock to a particular price. The only thing that matters to this individual is that the price climbs back to $25, so that he or she can walk away without having suffered a loss.

Because of this anchoring phenomenon, some traders who purchased XYZ at $25 will now become sellers at that same price. In part due to the influence of these "anchored" traders, XYZ will encounter selling pressure when it reaches $25. The price area that once acted as support has now become resistance. To put it another way, the floor has become the ceiling.

Markets can be unpredictable, but the behavior of a losing trader is somewhat easier to predict. This sequence of events occurs because losing traders seek to avoid pain. Loss is painful, and nobody wants to lose. Certainly nobody wants to view themselves as a loser. This is one of the reasons why trading is difficult; we have to override our ingrained tendencies.

Many experienced traders who have survived in the markets have done so because they associate more pain to holding a loss than to simply closing the trade. Experience has taught them that holding on to a small loss, in the hope of breaking even, can sometimes lead to large losses. They also have learned that large losses can be much more painful than small losses. Understanding this has allowed them to overcome any desire to hold on to a losing position.

The same thing can occur from the opposite perspective; a former area of resistance can act as support. Let's assume that stock ABC has shown a tendency to stop rising when it reaches $75. Perhaps a hedge fund that is bearish on the stock has decided that $75 is a great price at which to sell ABC short.

Or, perhaps the bulls are no longer willing to purchase the stock once it climbs to that price, and are holding out for a lower price. Other traders notice ABC's tendency to fall from this price, and they begin shorting the stock at $75 as well.

Then one day, ABC breaks decisively through $75 and runs to $80 per share. Those who shorted at $75 are now faced with a decision. Should they cover their short position by repurchasing the stock, or wait for the price to fall back to $75 so they can break even?

Many professional traders would favor the former option, because they'd prefer taking a loss in ABC now rather than chancing a larger loss later. But there will always be those who choose the latter option—even among experienced professionals who should know better. Thanks to the anchoring phenomenon, the desire to break even is present even in those who are intellectually aware that it may be better to just take the loss.

Some of the traders who shorted ABC at $75 will be hoping, wishing, and praying for the stock to return to that level so they can break even. If and when it does, they'll buy to cover their short positions. The buying pressure created at $75 helps in the formation of support at that price. That $75 price point was once the ceiling, and now it has become the floor.

◾ All Levels Are Not Created Equal

It would be a mistake to attach a similar degree of significance to all support and resistance levels. Technical analysts place greater trust in a price area that has acted as support or resistance on numerous occasions over a long period of time. They place less emphasis on a price area that has been tested less frequently, or over a shorter time span.

Major Support

Figure 6.3 is an example of a major support level, since it shows that shares of Caterpillar Inc. (CAT) bounced from the $78 area on numerous occasions over a three-year period (up arrows). Each time the price reached that level, it jumped in dramatic fashion. No sustained moves below $78 occurred during that time.

At the time, $78 was considered an area of major support for Caterpillar. When support finally broke in July of 2015, the $78 area began to act as resistance (down arrow).

Because this area acted as a strong floor, with buyers entering on numerous occasions over an extended period of time, it could become a strong ceiling in the future. When the price broke through support, traders who went long at $78 became sellers when the price climbed back to that level (down arrow).

Minor Support

Compare Figure 6.3 with Figure 6.4, which depicts an area of minor support in shares of Starbucks Corp. (SBUX). The price managed several small bounces from the $39.25 (up arrows) area during a compressed time period in late 2014/early 2015.

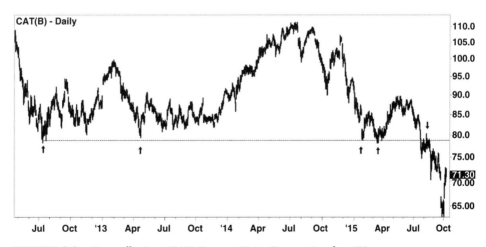

FIGURE 6.3 Caterpillar Inc. (CAT) Forms a Major Support Level at $78

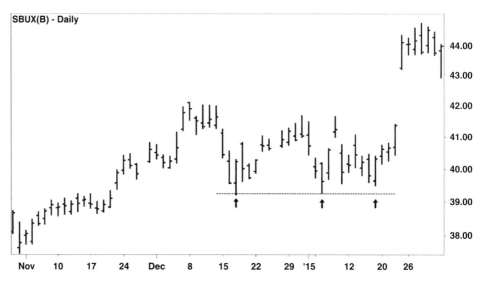

FIGURE 6.4   Minor Support in Starbucks Corp. (SBUX)

Our expectations for this support level would be very low, because the price didn't spend a great deal of time in this area. Another consideration would be that the support level was created during a year-end holiday period. Therefore, traders would assume that a minimal amount of buying and selling occurred at this level.

Remember, every trade is both a buy and a sell; it takes both a buyer and a seller to complete a transaction. Therefore, if there were few buyers at $39.25, then there were also few sellers. Since very few transactions occurred at that price, we wouldn't expect to encounter massive buying pressure from short sellers who are holding losses and seeking to break even at that level.

We also would not expect an insignificant level to become a significant level. The $39.25 area appears to be a weak floor, so if the price should break through, we would expect it to act as a weak ceiling. Perhaps there will be no reaction at all if and when the price returns to this level.

If you look closely at both Figure 6.3 and Figure 6.4, you'll notice that the price did not return to the exact same price point each time before reversing. This illustrates the fact that support is an area where buyers tend to emerge, not an exact price point.

Major Resistance

In Figure 6.5, we see an area of major resistance in shares of American International Group (symbol AIG). The price failed to break through $56.80 on at least three occasions over a nine-month period (down arrows). Notice how the attempts are spaced out; each attempt to break resistance is separated by several months. Rallies to that resistance level were soundly rejected, resulting in steep price drops.

The price finally broke through resistance in April of 2015, and rallied toward $59 (point A). This was followed by a return to the $56.80 area. While the price traded below that level, it never closed beneath $56.29 (point B). This was followed by a subsequent rally to $64 (point C).

Once again, the point is made that support isn't an exact price point. The price did manage to slip beneath support (former resistance) for a brief time, but the break above $56.80 proved to be the starting point for a new bullish trend.

Minor Resistance

Figure 6.6 illustrates an area of minor resistance on the Guggenheim CurrencyShares Japanese Yen ETF (symbol FXY). In this case, the price has been rejected on just two occasions over a period of a few days. Such an area of minor resistance could be easily broken. It is likely that only a few participants will be attempting to break even from previous trades in that area. If the price does manage to break through resistance, the resulting support level would also be considered weak.

In both Figure 6.5 and Figure 6.6, the price didn't peak at the exact same point each time. This illustrates that resistance isn't an exact price point, but an area where sellers tend to become active.

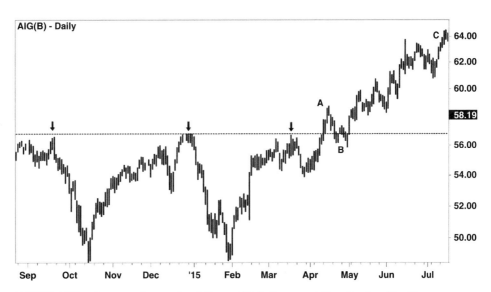

FIGURE 6.5 American International Group (AIG) Forms and Then Breaks a Significant Resistance Level

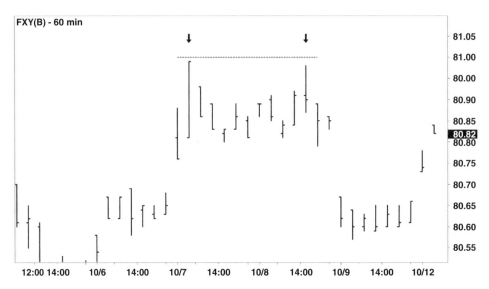

FIGURE 6.6   Minor Resistance in the Guggenheim CurrencyShares Japanese Yen ETF (FXY)

■ Pullbacks and Throwbacks

Once the price has broken through support or resistance, it often returns to the area of the breakout. The terminology used to describe this return varies, depending upon whether the breakout was bullish or bearish in nature.

If a bullish break above resistance occurs, and then the price falls back to the breakout point, the resulting downward movement is referred to as a "throwback." Figure 6.7 provides an example of a throwback; the price breaks through resistance and then is thrown back to the former resistance level, which has now become support.

Conversely, if the price breaks through support and then returns to the area of that former support level, the upward price movement following the break is referred to as a "pullback." In Figure 6.8, the price breaks through support and then pulls back toward the former support level, which has now become a resistance level.

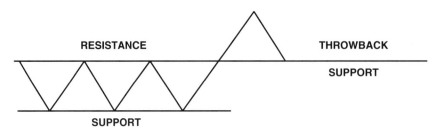

FIGURE 6.7   A Break Above Resistance Leads to a Subsequent Throwback

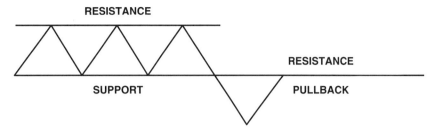

FIGURE 6.8 A Break Through Support Leads to a Subsequent Pullback

◼ Using Breaks in Support

Now that we understand the dynamics of support and resistance, let's explore different ways traders use these levels to their advantage.

The most common method is to simply sell short as the price breaks through support, but that is more easily said than done. If the trader sells at market, taking the best price available at that moment, the potential for slippage is high. Also, selling at market requires that the trader be present and paying close attention at the time of the break.

On the other hand, if the trader places an entry order beneath support in anticipation of a break lower, the price may temporarily violate the support level before rising back above it. This is known as a false break, and it will immediately put the trader in a losing position.

There is a third alternative. Let's assume that support has already been clearly broken, and we've missed the entry opportunity. Even though there is no way of knowing if the price will pull back to resistance (formerly support), we could set up a trade that "leans" against that level.

A trader does this by placing a sell order just beneath resistance (former support). If the price returns to that resistance level, a short position is entered; if it doesn't, no position is entered.

In Figure 6.9, shares of the S&P Select Financial SPDR (XLF) bounced on several occasions from $23.75 (upward arrows), indicating a level of support. Then, in August of 2015, the stock finally broke through that level, leading to a sharp sell-off.

Although there was no guarantee that the price would return to the former support level of $23.75 (now resistance), a patient trader could simply place an order to sell short at or just below that level and wait.

In this case, the trader would've been quickly rewarded for using that strategy. Just four days after the initial breakdown, the price returned to resistance. XLF reached a high of $23.79 on August 27, 2015, before suffering a reversal (point A). A second opportunity to short XLF at resistance presented itself on September 18 (point B).

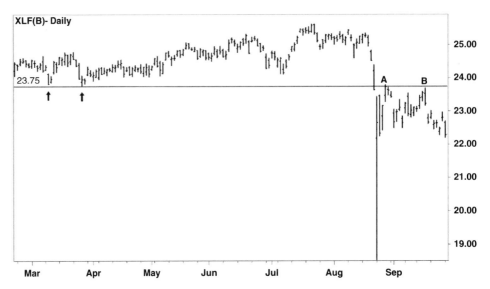

FIGURE 6.9 The S&P Select Financial SPDR (XLF) Breaks Support, Which Then Becomes Resistance

In this case, the trader assumed that a former level of support would act as resistance. If the short trade is entered and the price continues to rise above resistance, this tells us that the anticipated level of selling pressure has failed to materialize. The trader accepts that he or she is wrong and exits the trade with a small loss.

If the level in question is major—in other words, if the price has spent considerable time at that level and was rejected repeatedly before finally breaking through—there may be a significant number of traders possessing the desire to break even. This would be an important factor in determining whether to take the trade.

■ Using Breaks in Resistance

The same would be true if the price were to break through resistance. The simplest entry method would consist of going long as the price breaks out. While it is possible to catch the price as it breaks out, it can be difficult, as breakout opportunities are more easily identified in hindsight.

If a clean break of resistance occurs, and the trader misses it, he or she still has the option to place an order to buy at or just above the breakout point. There is no way of knowing whether the price will return to the breakout point, but if it does, the trader will be prepared.

If the trade is entered and then the support level fails to hold, the trade would be discarded.

In Figure 6.10, shares of Aetna Inc. (AET) encountered resistance at $85.25 on several occasions during the summer of 2014 (downward arrows). Aetna finally

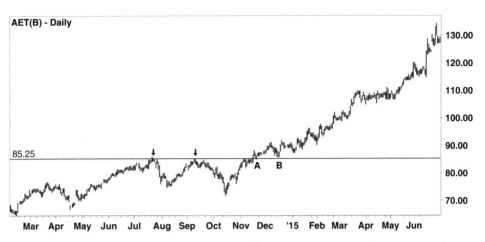

FIGURE 6.10   Aetna (AET) Breaks Resistance and Returns to Support Before Moving Higher

broke through resistance in mid-November, and was quickly thrown back to the breakout point (letter A). A second throwback occurred in December (letter B), giving investors one last chance to go long before Aetna began its run to $130.

The fact that resistance exists at a particular level is evidence that buying and selling once took place there. In this case, once resistance was broken, traders who shorted AET at $85.25 were holding a losing position and were motivated to get out—preferably at $85.25, the price at which they sold short.

Due to the anchoring phenomenon, the probability of finding buyers at $85.25 was high because that was a likely breakeven point for some short sellers. This setup was attractive because the broken area was once a significant point of resistance.

▣ Trading Between Support and Resistance

Although much emphasis is placed on trends, markets spend a significant amount of time drifting sideways. Some traders try to capitalize on this phenomenon by going long at support and/or selling short at resistance.

This is demonstrated on the 60-minute chart shown in Figure 6.11. The Great Britain pound/U.S. dollar currency pair (GBPUSD) encountered resistance on numerous occasions near 1.50 (downward arrows) and found support on several occasions near 1.47 (upward arrows). The most common approach would be to sell short near 1.50 or to go long near 1.47 in an attempt to capitalize on these levels.

In either case, the use of a target halfway between support and resistance might make sense. In this case, the halfway point would be 1.4850 (dotted line). Many traders attempt to buy at support and sell at resistance (and vice versa), but as Figure 6.11 demonstrates, the price often falls short of these targets.

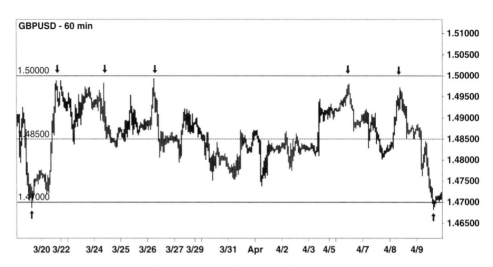

FIGURE 6.11 Support and Resistance Levels Form on the GBPUSD Currency Pair

A different approach would involve placing a buy order above 1.50 and/or a sell order below 1.47. In this scenario, the trader is anticipating a break above resistance or below support.

If the price breaks above 1.50, those who sold short at that price will now become buyers, driving the price higher. If it falls below 1.47, those who went long at that price become potential sellers. Although some false breaks may occur, the price is likely to break free at some point.

Just as a trend cannot go on forever, support and resistance levels eventually break. Some traders deal with this by combining the two concepts; they refer to the trend that preceded the sideways activity, and place orders based on the assumption that the prior trend will resume once the price breaks out.

This is a perfectly feasible strategy, as big breakouts are often preceded by tight consolidations. We will take a closer look at consolidation patterns and how to trade them in subsequent chapters.

■ Final Thoughts on Support and Resistance

Support and resistance are more than mere lines on a chart; the violation of one of these levels can create a visceral reaction among investors. Support and resistance are useful for locating turning points on the chart, and can give clues as to the pressures facing investors who are involved in a particular trading instrument.

CHAPTER 7

Trends and Trend Lines

In the examples given in the previous section, support and resistance are treated as horizontal price areas. However, the concept of support and resistance applies to non-horizontal price action as well. This becomes important when prices are moving in a clear, consistent direction. A persistent directional price movement is called a "trend."

■ Uptrends

An uptrend consists of price movement that forms a series of higher lows (HL) and higher highs (HH). In the case of an uptrend, the trend line is drawn upward beneath a series of ascending lows.

Figure 7.1 depicts a bullish trend line drawn beneath a series of higher lows on the weekly chart of the S&P 500 Depository Receipts ETF (SPY) starting in 2013.

When the price pulls back to the trend line in an uptrend, it is considered a buying opportunity. In this situation, the trend line is treated as a support level. If the price breaks through the trend line, then the trade is exited, as support is considered to be broken.

■ Downtrends

A downtrend consists of price movement that forms a series of lower highs (LH) and lower lows (LL). In the case of a downtrend, a trend line can be drawn downward above a series of descending highs.

FIGURE 7.1 A Bullish Trend Line on the Weekly Chart of the S&P 500 Depository Receipts ETF (SPY)

FIGURE 7.2 A Downtrend on the Weekly Chart of the Guggenheim CurrencyShares Canadian Dollar ETF (FXC)

Figure 7.2 depicts a downtrend on the weekly chart of the Guggenheim CurrencyShares Canadian Dollar ETF (FXC).

When the price rallies to the trend line in a downtrend, it is considered a selling opportunity. In this situation, the trend line is treated like a resistance level. If the price breaks through the bearish trend line, then resistance is considered to be broken, and any short trades that were entered are closed.

In either case, a trend line must connect a minimum of two points. A trend line that connects two points is called a "tentative" trend line; a trend line that connects at least three points is known as a "valid" trend line.

The more times the trend line has been tested (meaning that the price has come into contact with the line) without being breached, the stronger it is considered to be. Trend lines of greater duration are considered superior to those of a shorter duration.

■ Breaking the Trend Line

Sometimes the price will trade through a trend line for a short time, only to return to its original position. Such minor violations aren't considered true trend breaks. There is no firm written rule as to what constitutes a broken trend line, but many traders want to see the price close beneath a bullish trend line (or above a bearish trend line) before they consider the trend line to be broken.

Those with more stringent criteria might demand to see three consecutive closes beyond the trend line. Others use filters such as volume, as trend line breaks are considered more significant if they occur on heavy volume. We'll deal with volume in a later chapter.

One way to determine if a trend line break is significant is to observe the break on a smaller time frame. For example, in Figure 7.3 we see the price break through the bullish trend line of the E-Mini Dow Futures (@YM). This break (circled) occurs on the hourly (60-minute) chart, and it appears to be a minor violation of the trend line.

FIGURE 7.3 A Temporary Break of a Trend Line on a 60-Minute Chart of the E-Mini Dow Futures (@YM)

FIGURE 7.4   A Temporary Break of a Trend Line on a 15-Minute Chart of the E-Mini Dow Futures (@YM)

Figure 7.4 shows the same move on a 15-minute chart. Even in this time frame, the move still appears to be a minor violation. The price failed to close beneath the trend line, even on a lower time frame. The incursion was brief and therefore insignificant.

■ Consolidation

It would be incorrect to assume that the breaking of a trend line will automatically result in a new trend in the opposite direction. This is a common misconception. While the break of a trend line sometimes does result in a trend in the opposing direction, it's not uncommon for the price to simply drift sideways for an undefined amount of time, a condition known as "consolidation."

A consolidation is a period of rest that occurs after a trading vehicle has made a significant move. A chartist might say that stock XYZ is "consolidating its gains" after a strong move higher, or "consolidating its losses" after a sharp decline. While a break of a trend line doesn't necessarily indicate that a sharp reversal is about to occur, it does call the validity of the trend into question.

■ Degree or Angle of the Trend

Another consideration is the degree or angle of the trend line. Lines that are sharply inclined tend to be easier to break, as the trend could be moving at an

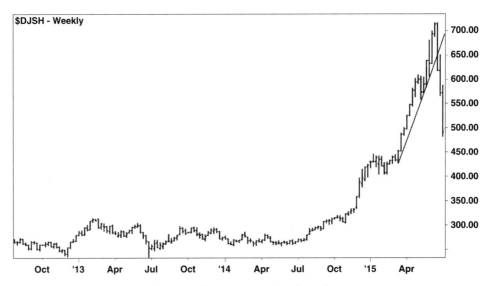

FIGURE 7.5 A Steep Trend Line in the Dow Jones Shanghai Index ($DJSH)

unsustainable pace. Chartists sometimes refer to price action of this nature as "parabolic."

Figure 7.5 depicts a steep trend line in China's stock market in early 2015, represented here on the weekly chart of the Dow Jones Shanghai Index ($DJSH). Notice how the index reverses sharply after the trend line is broken.

In mid-April of 2015, China's market regulators increased margin requirements in an effort to cool down an overheated stock market. By decreasing the buying power available to investors, officials hoped to reduce speculation in China's markets. This is a common practice when a market enters a parabolic phase.

In this case, officials feared that China's stock markets were entering a bubble. By attempting to rein in the parabolic move, China's market regulators hoped to preempt an even greater move. The longer a bubble is allowed to grow, the worse the aftermath it creates when it ultimately collapses.

Later that year, stocks fell so hard that China was forced to institute extraordinary measures to prop up its markets.

■ Sustainable Trends

Ideally, a trader would prefer a trend line that is significant yet sustainable. Lines that feature a more gradual incline tend to be easier to keep intact; however, an incline that is too gradual could also be indicative of a weak trend, and therefore might not be worth pursuing. The sweet spot is somewhere between a parabolic move and a gradual move.

■ Multiple Trend Lines

Many times, a technical analyst will encounter a chart that has more than one potential trend line. In such cases, it's acceptable to draw more than one trend line on the chart.

Since multiple trend lines can coexist on a chart, there is no "correct" trend line. However, it's very likely that there is a dominant trend line. A major trend line has more activity and/or a greater length of time associated with it than a minor trend line.

In Figure 7.6, we see two bullish trend lines on the weekly chart of electronics retailer Best Buy (BBY). The steeper of the two trend lines is easily broken, while the dominant trend line remains intact for a longer period of time.

Trend lines can intersect in a variety of ways. Some of these intersections form the basis of chart patterns, which we will examine in a later chapter.

■ Channel Lines

Earlier, we defined an uptrend as a series of higher highs and higher lows, with a trend line drawn beneath the series of higher lows. On some occasions, a parallel line can be drawn above the series of higher highs as well. These parallel lines are referred to as a bullish channel. In a bullish channel, the lower line is the trend line, and the higher line is the channel line.

FIGURE 7.6　Two Trend Lines on the Weekly Chart of Best Buy (BBY)

FIGURE 7.7 A Bullish Channel on the Weekly Chart of General Motors (GM)

Figure 7.7 depicts a bullish channel in shares of General Motors (GM). Traders may want to take bullish positions at the lower end of the channel, and exit near the upper end of the channel. In most cases they would avoid selling short, unless and until the price breaks down and out of the channel.

Similarly, a downtrend is defined as a series of lower highs and lower lows, with a trend line drawn above a series of lower highs. When a parallel trend line, known as a channel line, can be drawn beneath the series of lower lows, the result is referred to as a bear channel.

Traders would prefer to sell short near the trend line, and cover their shorts near channel line. They would most likely avoid going long in a downtrend. Figure 7.8 illustrates a bear channel on the weekly chart of the Great Britain pound/U.S. dollar currency pair (GBPUSD).

■ Using Channel Lines

A pullback to a bullish trend line drawn along a series of higher lows can be used to initiate a long position. An aggressive trader could then exit the position with a profit if and when the price reaches the upper boundary of the channel. A more conservative trader could use the center of the channel as a target. If the bullish trend line breaks, the trader would exit the position at a loss.

Similarly, a rally to a bearish trend line drawn along a series of lower highs can be used to initiate a short position. The trader could then exit the position if and when

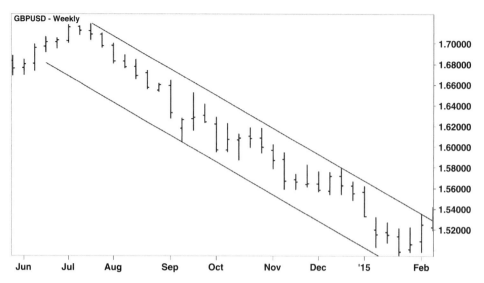

FIGURE 7.8 A Bear Channel on the Weekly Chart of Great Britain Pound/U.S. Dollar (GBPUSD)

the price reaches the lower boundary of the channel. A more conservative trader could use the center of the channel as a target. If the price breaks upward through the bearish trend line, the trader would cover the short position at a loss.

In both cases, another tactic would be to exit half of the position at the center of the channel and trail a protective stop on the remainder of the position.

■ Support Becomes Resistance

Think of a trend line as diagonal support or resistance. Just as horizontal support can become horizontal resistance, diagonal support can become diagonal resistance. We see an example of this in Figure 7.9, on the weekly chart of NASDAQ 100 E-Mini Continuous Contract (@NQ).

The bullish trend line indicates that the NASDAQ's uptrend is firmly in place. Eventually, the trend weakens and the futures contract breaks through the trend line. When @NQ attempts to climb back above the trend line, the price is rejected (arrow). The trend line has now become resistance. Similarly, a bearish trend line, once broken, will sometimes act as support.

■ Final Thoughts on Trends and Trend Lines

Support and resistance can take many forms, and a trend line could be thought of as diagonal support or resistance. Trend lines are effective tools for locating trends

FIGURE 7.9 Trend Line Support Becomes Resistance on the NASDAQ 100 E-Mini Continuous Contract (@NQ)

and determining if a trend is still in effect. A broken trend line does not necessarily lead to a reversal; sometimes the price simply drifts sideways after a trend has terminated. Steep trend lines tend to break easily, while a gently sloping trend line may show more resilience.

CHAPTER 8

Volume

When detectives are hunting for a criminal, they play close attention to that individual's height. A suspect can alter his or her appearance in any number of ways—the type of clothing worn, length and color of hair, and so on—but it is extremely difficult for a tall person to impersonate a short person, and vice versa.

Similarly, it is very difficult for large market participants to disguise their true level of interest in an investment. When mutual funds and hedge funds take an interest in a trading vehicle, they leave behind large "footprints" that are difficult to cover.

Part of our role as traders is to unlock this mystery. If we can determine what the major players are buying and selling, then we can use this information to our advantage. Technical analysts are like detectives, searching for clues left behind by large institutional traders.

■ Institutional vs. Individual Volume

Imagine that a mutual fund with $10 billion under management is considering a purchase of stock XYZ, which trades at $50. The fund manager consults with his research department and together they decide that the stock is cheap.

The manager decides to allocate 1% of the fund's assets toward purchasing the stock. One percent of $10 billion is $100 million, so at $50 per share, the fund would need to purchase two million shares of XYZ to reach its goal. The manager decides to spread this purchase out over time, because one large purchase of two million shares might drive the price sharply higher.

A trader for the fund buys a few thousand shares, and then waits to see if the price rises. If the price drops or remains stable, the trader will buy a few thousand more shares. The trader is "working the order" to obtain the best possible average price for the mutual fund. This buying could continue for weeks before the position is finally complete.

A hedge fund learns that the mutual fund is buying XYZ, and begins to establish a position in the stock. This in turn leads to more buying. Institutions compete among themselves for client funds, so word that one fund is buying XYZ might encourage other funds to do the same.

Meanwhile, individual traders are unaware that any of this is happening. However, if we look at the chart of XYZ we'll notice that the stock has a persistent bid; it's moving steadily higher on rising volume. Even on days when the market is down, the stock holds firm, as if traders are unwilling to sell. Every time XYZ dips, it seems to pop right back up.

We may not know who is buying XYZ or why its volume is rising, but that doesn't matter. All we need to understand is that somebody knows something that we don't know. We take note of the rising stock and notice the big footprints of institutional traders, expressed in the form of rising volume.

Meanwhile, a typical individual trader might buy just 1,000 shares, and then sell them at a slightly higher price. The individual trader's actions will have little or no impact on the price of XYZ.

A purchase of that size would be insignificant to the mutual fund, which must purchase millions of shares to create a meaningful position in the stock. In doing so, they drive the volume higher.

◼ Buyers vs. Sellers

On some level, every trade is both a buy and a sell, and every transaction is an agreement or an exchange between a buyer and a seller. Every price that is traded, on every chart, is created by both buyers and sellers.

When prices move higher, the reason for the move is often explained away with pat phrases, such as "there are more buyers than sellers." In reality, this might not be true. There might be one buyer and many sellers. However, if that one buyer is a hedge fund with billions of dollars under management, armed with a high degree of certainty due to its proprietary research, that single entity may overpower numerous sellers. Conceivably, one buyer might possess more money and more information than all the sellers combined.

The number of buyers or sellers is less significant than the amount of capital at their disposal and their relative levels of motivation. Instead of assuming that there are more buyers than sellers, a more accurate statement might read, "the buyers are more aggressive than the sellers" or "the buyers are more powerful than the sellers."

■ Volume Represents Commitment

Technical analysis focuses mainly on price; this is understandable, because price movement ultimately determines whether a trade is successful. It's been said that price is the ultimate indicator.

However, we should also consider just how motivated the big players might be. What is their level of commitment toward an investment? Hedge funds and mutual funds are unwilling to share this information. However, because they must establish large positions relative to individual traders, they can't help but leave clues in their wake.

We could say that a move that occurs on high volume is indicative of a high level of interest or commitment on the part of institutional traders, and a move that occurs on low volume indicates a lower level of commitment. Consider volume analysis a potential edge rather than a sure thing. The same could be said of any aspect of technical analysis.

The significance of volume applies to all asset classes, with the exception of currencies. The currency market is huge, decentralized, and open 24 hours per day. Therefore, there is no accurate way to track all of the transactions in the spot currency market. It is possible to track the volume of currency futures, and some traders use this as a proxy. However, there is no way to know at any given moment if the currency futures are presenting an accurate depiction of volume in the spot currency market.

■ High-Volume Breakouts

A bullish breakout that occurs on high volume is significant because large players are putting serious money to work. If investors are aggressively buying XYZ at $50 per share, it's because they firmly believe the stock is worth more than that price.

In technical analysis, volume is normally expressed as a series of bars, usually located at the bottom of the chart. A high bar indicates high volume, and vice versa. To determine if one time period's volume is relatively high or low, we compare it to an average created from recent time periods.

Figure 8.1 presents an example of a high-volume breakout. On January 7, 2015, Sonic Corp. (SONC) broke out to fresh highs on extremely high turnover. Over 5 million shares of SONC changed hands that day (circled); the average daily volume for the stock at the time was about one million shares per day.

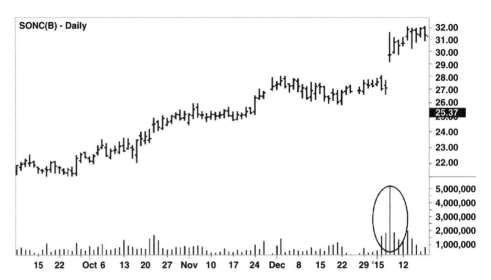

FIGURE 8.1 A High-Volume Breakout in Sonic Corp. (SONC)

Because Sonic's volume that day was more than five times its average, it's safe to say that the cash value of the shares that changed hands that day was five times the normal amount. Based on this, we may assume that institutional traders were involved in this move. After this breakout, Sonic continued to run to $36.

Something caused traders to suddenly believe that Sonic was a bargain at $28, even though that price marked the stock's all-time high up to that point. The catalyst that triggered this move was Sonic's quarterly earnings report. Note how the stock was creeping higher prior to the report. Was this a coincidence, or was Sonic's rising price giving traders a clue as to the stock's next move?

■ Volume and Trend

Volume also plays a role in trends; if volume continues to increase as a stock or market trends higher, it's an indication that the trend should continue. Perhaps volume is rising because additional buyers, acknowledging the trend, are jumping on the bandwagon.

Or, it's possible that hedge funds and mutual funds are increasing their position size as the price moves in their favor. Perhaps these funds have access to research that indicates a specific company is having a strong quarter and will beat earnings estimates. Or, they may have acquired positive information about the market as a whole or on a sector of the market.

We may not know the reasons why, but if the major players are buying as the price moves higher, perhaps we should do the same. Because they dedicate such large sums to research, there is a good chance that they know something that we don't know.

Bullish Trend Volume

Figure 8.2 depicts an example of rising volume during a bullish trend. The S&P Select Utilities SPDR (XLU) is an exchange-traded fund (ETF) that consists of utilities companies. Utilities stocks are notable for their sensitivity to interest rates. The sector began a six-year rally in early 2009 as U.S. interest rates sank to unprecedented lows. Notice how XLU's volume gradually increased as the rally unfolded, as shown on the weekly chart.

We can draw a line, very similar to a trend line, above the volume bars. This rising line depicts the steady increase in XLU's average turnover, from approximately 31 million shares per week in early 2009 to nearly 59 million shares per week by early 2015. XLU doubled in value over that time.

Accumulation

Ideally, a stock or commodity in a bullish trend should climb on high volume and pull back on light volume. This phenomenon is known as accumulation. An example of this can be found in Figure 8.3.

On the left side of the chart, the Gold Continuous Contract (@GC) is trending higher. Then the price begins to fall (circled bars). Notice how the volume drops along with the price (circled volume).

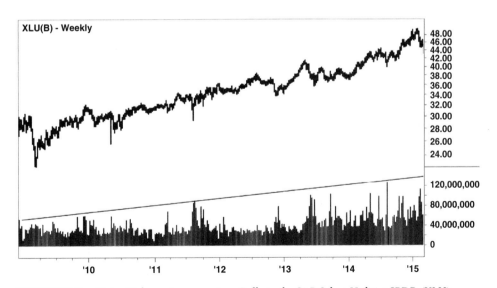

FIGURE 8.2   Rising Volume Accompanies a Rally in the S&P Select Utilities SPDR (XLU)

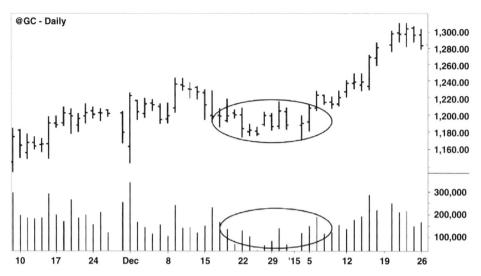

FIGURE 8.3 Signs of Accumulation in the Gold Continuous Contract (@GC)

When the price resumed its ascent on the right side of the chart, it was accompanied by an increase in volume. This example of accumulation in the gold futures contract tells us that the bulls were the more committed party at that time.

When the price fell on light volume, it was a sign that the bears had a lower level of commitment than the bulls. Therefore, it should come as no surprise that the bulls were able to overpower the bears when volume returned to the contract.

New Highs on Heavy Volume

If a stock reaches a new 52-week (one-year) high, traders would prefer that the new high be achieved on heavy volume. This is a signal of commitment from large investors, and it indicates that the trend is likely to continue. To seek out such opportunities, some traders run scans that search for stocks that are reaching 52-week highs on above-average volume.

Figure 8.4 shows Intrexon Corporation (XON) reaching a new 52-week high (arrow) on five times its average volume (circled) on January 14, 2015. Soon after this, Intrexon resumed its ascent; less than two months later, the stock traded above $50. The strategy of buying stocks as they reach new 52-week highs on heavy volume has been popular for decades.

End of the Bull Trend

Technical traders also take note of situations where a stock or commodity is rising, but its volume is decreasing as the price moves higher. This indicates a falling level of confidence on the part of buyers, and could be a warning sign that the trend is losing momentum.

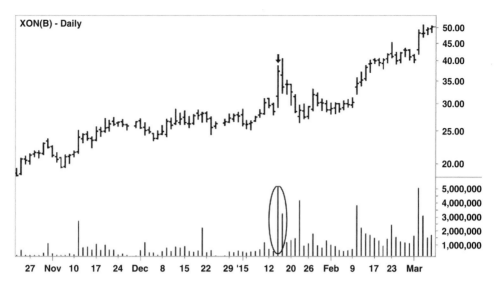

FIGURE 8.4 Shares of Intrexon Corp. (XON) Reach a 52-Week High on Heavy Volume, Then Continue Higher

For example, Figure 8.5 shows shares of Target Inc. (TGT) locked into a strong uptrend during the first half of 2013. Then in July, the volume disappears (circled) even as the stock continues to move higher. While Target's price still had upward momentum, large players appeared to be losing interest in the stock.

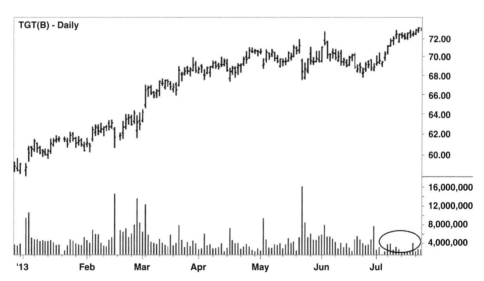

FIGURE 8.5 Volume in Shares of Target Corp. (TGT) Disappears as the Stock Continues to Rally

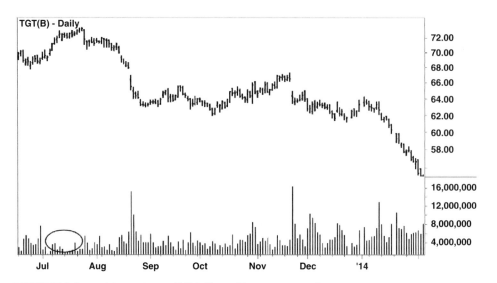

FIGURE 8.6 As Target Corp. (TGT) Shares Turn Lower, Volume Increases

In Figure 8.6, we see what happened next. Target broke its trend line in August of 2013 and declined sharply. Once the stock began to falter, the volume that had disappeared at the end of the rally suddenly returned. Volume characteristics of this nature tell us that the selling was likely driven by large institutional traders.

■ Bearish Trend Volume

What is true for the bulls is also true for the bears; in a downtrend, volume should increase as the price moves lower. Figure 8.7 demonstrates this concept.

Note the steady increase in volume in the West Texas Intermediate Crude Oil Continuous Contract (@CL) in late 2014/early 2015. As the price of WTI crude oil began to fall sharply in the fourth quarter of 2014, the bars at the bottom of the chart revealed a noticeable increase in volume.

Crude oil's volume rose from approximately 223,000 contracts per day at the start of Q3, 2014, to about 342,000 contracts per day by early 2015. Over that time, the price of WTI crude oil was cut in half.

Distribution

When a stock or commodity is in a downtrend, volume should rise during periods when the price is falling and fall during periods when the price is rising. This phenomenon is known as "distribution," and it is demonstrated in Figure 8.8, which depicts shares of Google Inc. Class C (GOOG) in a downtrend.

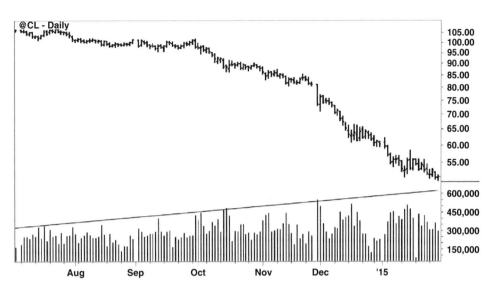

FIGURE 8.7   Volume Steadily Increases as Crude Oil Plunges

In the latter part of 2014 into early 2015, Google's price and volume were moving in opposite directions. In Figure 8.8, this phenomenon is demonstrated in three distinct segments of time.

Segment A occurs in October of 2014 and shows a steady rise in Google's volume that accompanies a decline in the stock's price. In segment B, from mid-October through mid-December, Google's volume disappears as its price rises; volume then rebounds as the price falls. Segment C, which runs from mid-December through

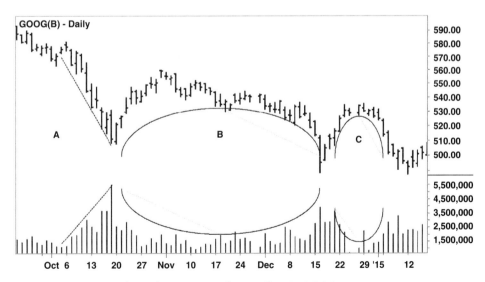

FIGURE 8.8   Signs of Distribution in Google Inc. Class C (GOOG)

early January of 2015, demonstrates a similar price/volume relationship as seen in Segment B.

In all three segments, positive movements in price are matched by negative movements in volume, and vice-versa.

End of the Bear Trend

If volume declines as the price moves lower during a downtrend, it may be an indication that the bearish move is coming to an end.

In Figure 8.9, we see Apple (AAPL) moving steadily lower from October of 2012 through April of 2013, losing more than one-third of its value. A noticeable decline in volume is visible on the right side of the chart. This decrease in volume indicated that Apple's price decline was near its end. Within days, the stock bottomed out at $55 per share. By August of 2014, Apple had reached a new all-time high.

If a stock reaches a new 52-week low, trend followers would prefer that the new low be reached on heavy volume. This is an indication that the downward move may continue.

Figure 8.10 shows mining company BHP Billiton (BHP) reaching a new 52-week low (circled) on above-average volume (arrow) in October of 2014. After a short-lived bounce, the mining stock then continued its downward trajectory. The stock eventually fell to the low 30s.

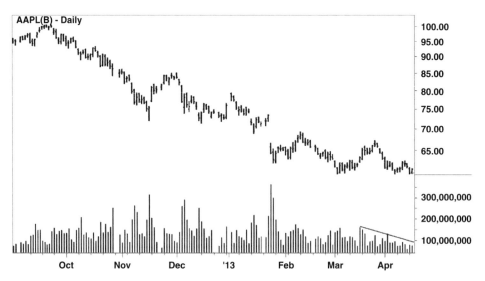

FIGURE 8.9   A Sharp Decline in Apple's Volume Marks the End of Its Downward Trend

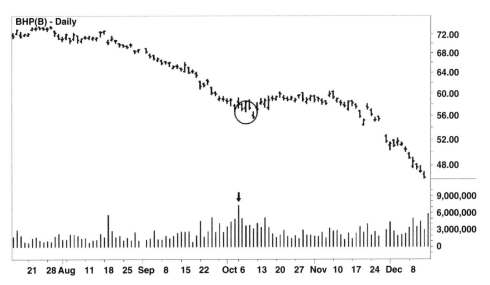

FIGURE 8.10 BHP Billiton (BHP) Hits a 52-Week Low on Heavy Volume and Then Continues Lower

■ Support, Resistance, and Volume

If a move that occurs on heavy volume inspires a greater level of confidence, then a break of support or resistance on heavy volume should do the same.

Figure 8.11 depicts a stock successfully breaking through resistance on heavy volume. Shares of Apple (AAPL) failed on several attempts to break above $78.80 in the spring of 2014 (arrows). Then in late April, Apple finally succeeded. Note how the breakout was accompanied by an increase in volume (circled). Within four months, the stock climbed above $100.

Figure 8.12 shows Amazon.com Inc. (AMZN) bouncing off of support at $380 in early 2014 (up arrows). Notice the pickup in volume as Amazon breaks support (point A).

In March, the stock rallied back to the former support level, where it encountered resistance (down arrow). Note how the volume disappeared as Amazon approached $380 (point B). The decline in volume indicated a lack of commitment on the part of buyers. Not surprisingly, Amazon failed in its attempt to break above $380.

The stock then proceeded to fall sharply, with volume gradually increasing as the price declined. After falling below $300, a decline of about 25%, volume dried up again in May (point C). This was an indication that Amazon's downtrend was about to come to an end.

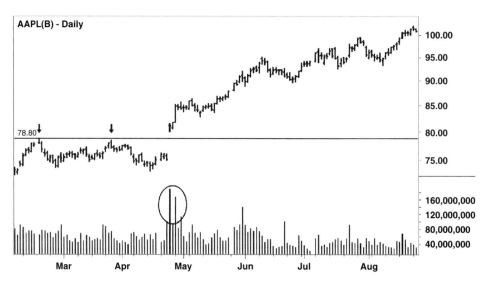

FIGURE 8.11 Apple (AAPL) Breaks Through Resistance on Heavy Volume

FIGURE 8.12 Amazon.com (AMZN) Breaks Through Support on Heavy Volume

Climactic Volume and Capitulation

Occasionally, negative sentiment for a stock or index will reach a fever pitch. At times like these, market participants exhibit herd-like behavior and engage in panic

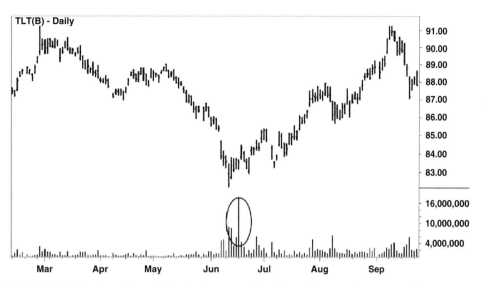

FIGURE 8.13 Capitulation Marks the Bottom in the iShares 20+ Year Treasury Bond ETF (TLT)

selling. The trading vehicle falls sharply on extremely heavy volume, as traders are willing to sell at any price.

This condition is referred to as "capitulation," and is often accompanied by what is known as climactic volume. The frenzied selling often marks a turning point in the price of a stock or index.

Eventually, sellers reach a point of exhaustion, as most of the investors who wished to sell have now exited. With the sellers out of the way and the price severely depressed, the path of least resistance now leads higher.

In Figure 8.13, we see an example of capitulation. A sell-off in the iShares 20+ Year Treasury Bond ETF (TLT) began in March of 2007. The downtrend accelerated into June, and volume began to increase as the price fell further.

Sellers finally capitulated during a series of high-volume sessions in mid-June (circled). With the sellers sufficiently satisfied, the path of least resistance for TLT was higher. Over the next three months, TLT regained all of its earlier losses.

Figure 8.14 presents another example of capitulation. Shortly after its initial public offering in November of 2013, shares of Twitter Inc. (TWTR) peaked at $74. The stock then entered a downtrend that caused it to lose more than half its value.

Then on May 6, 2014, the stock gapped lower on nearly 10 times its average daily volume (circled). After some follow-through selling the next day, the stock began to rally. Over the following four months, Twitter climbed from $30 to $55 per share.

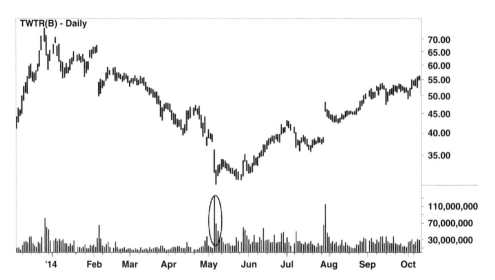

FIGURE 8.14   Capitulation Selling in Shares of Twitter (TWTR)

■ Short-Covering Rallies

Capitulation is usually associated with selling because it reflects a highly emotional and fearful state. Generally, the emotion of greed is associated with buying, and the emotion of fear is associated with selling. Because fear is considered the stronger of the two emotions, fear-driven selling, also known as panic selling, can cause markets to collapse quickly.

However, traders have also been known to engage in panic buying. Just as traders who are long are fearful of losing money due to heavy selling, shorts can also "throw in the towel" and surrender to relentless buying pressure.

A "short-covering rally" occurs when shorts panic and run for the exits. This happens when a heavily shorted stock begins to rally. Fearful of a further move to the upside, traders are motivated to "buy to cover" their short positions. This buying forces the rallying stock or commodity to move even higher, and is also considered a form of capitulation.

Figure 8.15 provides an example of a short-covering rally. In 2014, shares of heavily-shorted electronics retailer Radio Shack were in a death spiral.

Then in late August, rumors of a potential buyout began to circulate. Volume exploded to the upside as panicked shorts hurried to cover their positions (circled).

The rumors turned out to be false, and within a few days Radio Shack resumed its descent. By late 2015, the remains of Radio Shack, now trading under the name RS Legacy Group (symbol RSHCQ!), fell to two cents per share.

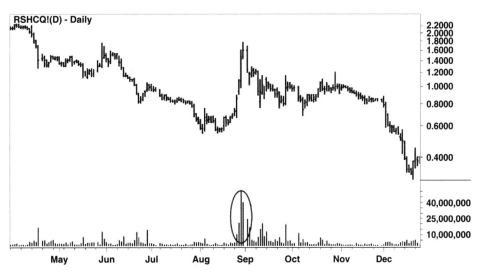

FIGURE 8.15   A Short-Covering Rally in Shares of Radio Shack

Some traders attempt to anticipate short-covering rallies before they occur. Candidates for short-covering rallies can be obtained by running a screen for heavily shorted stocks.

If a market begins to rally, it will often pull heavily shorted names along with it. As these stocks rise in price, shorts may begin to panic as they see their profits disintegrating.

Figure 8.16 depicts a simple screen for finding short-covering candidates, using the Finviz.com stock screener. We selected only two criteria: At least 20% of the

	Overview	Valuation	Financial	**Ownership**	Performance	Technical	Custom	Charts	Tickers	

Total: 51 #1   save as portfolio

No.	Ticker	Market Cap	Outstanding	Float	Insider Own	Insider Trans	Inst Own	Inst Trans	▼ Float Short
1	MOMO	3.24B	188.88M	8.00M	-	-	11.20%	51.73%	83.28%
2	PPC	6.33B	259.70M	63.88M	0.10%	-36.10%	39.30%	11.91%	68.51%
3	CMCM	4.93B	141.62M	12.00M	-	-	44.70%	3.64%	61.65%
4	ATHM	5.16B	111.25M	8.50M	-	-	69.60%	3.13%	50.75%
5	WUBA	9.29B	115.53M	11.76M	22.48%	0.00%	42.50%	13.39%	50.59%
6	QUNR	6.18B	120.14M	11.44M	28.73%	0.00%	90.10%	12.52%	47.85%
7	MNKD	2.51B	409.58M	256.80M	0.60%	-22.01%	26.50%	6.96%	43.98%
8	GME	4.73B	107.17M	104.52M	1.90%	-7.06%	-	-6.06%	43.14%
9	MYGN	2.31B	69.45M	69.14M	0.10%	0.00%	-	-1.70%	41.92%
10	JMEI	3.48B	145.19M	11.14M	-	-	31.70%	15.83%	41.78%

FIGURE 8.16   Short-Covering Screen from the Finviz.com Stock Screener

Source: Finviz.com

shares available for trading (the "float") must be held short, and the stock must have a market capitalization of greater than $2 billion. This screen produced 51 candidates for a short-covering rally.

■ Final Thoughts on Volume

Large institutional traders go to great lengths to disguise their intentions, and one of our roles as traders is to attempt to determine what those intentions may be. Volume is a tool that can be used in this manner, as a rally or plunge that occurs on heavy volume is more likely to be influenced by these institutions. By decoding the intentions of the biggest players in the market, it's possible to gain an edge in trading.

CHAPTER 9

Gaps

If volume represents commitment, then gaps represent excitement. A gap occurs when the price leaps higher or lower from the previous price, leaving an empty space, or gap, between the two prices.

Gaps occur frequently in illiquid trading instruments, due to a lack of buyers and/or sellers, and are not considered significant under these circumstances. They are less common, and therefore of greater significance, when they occur in highly liquid trading vehicles.

Gaps are rare in the currency market, especially in highly liquid currencies such as the euro and the U.S. dollar, due to the massive size of that market. However, under extreme circumstances, currency gaps can and do occur, as we will see.

■ Full Gaps and Partial Gaps

If the price gaps beyond the previous session's high or low, it is considered a full gap. In Figure 9.1, shares of Tesla Motors Inc. (TSLA) closed at $191.00 on April 2, 2015 (arrow). Tesla's high that day was $193.23 (letter A).

On the following day, Tesla opened at $198 (letter B). This is considered a full gap, because the price has opened above the high of the previous day. A vertical empty space is visible between the two bars.

If the price gaps higher or lower but fails to open beyond the previous session's high or low, it is considered a partial gap. For example, in Figure 9.2, shares of Facebook closed at $77.46 (letter A) on May 12, 2015 (arrow). Facebook's high that day was $77.89 (letter B).

On the following day, Facebook opened at $77.72 (letter C). This was higher than the previous day's close of $77.46, and therefore it's considered a gap. However,

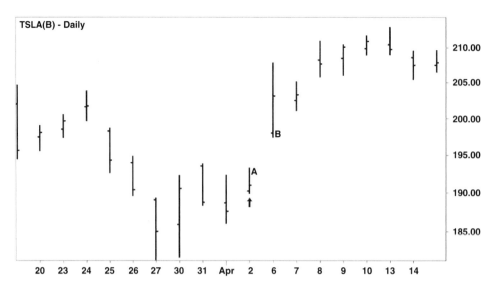

FIGURE 9.1 A Full Gap in Shares of Tesla Motors (TSLA)

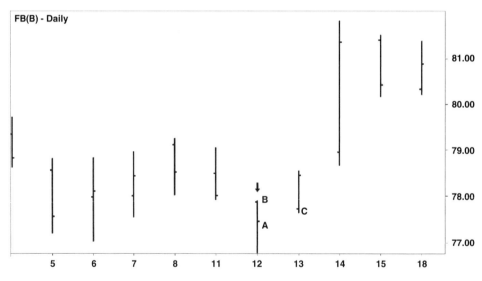

FIGURE 9.2 A Partial Gap in Shares of Facebook (FB)

the May 13 open is lower than the previous day's high of $77.89, making it a partial gap. In this case, there is no vertical empty space between the two bars.

■ Gaps in Illiquid Investments

In Figure 9.3, the PowerShares DB German Bund Futures Exchange-Traded Notes (BUNL) provides an excellent example of an illiquid investment. Note that opening

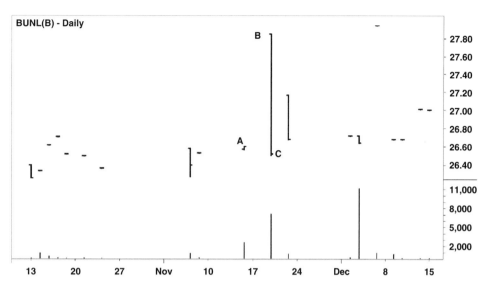

FIGURE 9.3   A Chart of an Illiquid Trading Instrument

gaps on this chart are an almost daily occurrence. On some days, no shares are traded at all. Take note of the high volatility of this investment, which goes hand in hand with its low volume.

The closing price of BUNL was $26.60 on November 14, 2014 (point A). BUNL did not trade again until a long bar appeared on November 19. The opening price of the long bar was $27.85 (point B). This represented a huge opening gap from the previous close.

However, by the session's end, BUNL had surrendered all of its gains to close at $26.52 (point C). Why did BUNL take such a wild ride, only to wind up back where it started?

Here is a likely scenario: When BUNL opened for trading on November 19, someone placed an order to buy at market. The buyer probably underestimated the depth of the market for shares of BUNL, and placed a larger order than was advisable. The price then rose until it could find enough available sellers to fill the order.

Once the order was filled, the price returned to its previous area. By the end of this sequence, the buyer had lost $1.28 per share. If that individual chooses to sell, and once again places a large market order, he or she may face a similar situation.

This demonstrates the negative qualities inherent in illiquid trading vehicles. These qualities make for dangerous trading. It can be difficult to find enough available shares to enter the trade.

It might be just as difficult to find someone to take the other side of the trade when you wish to exit. Traders sometimes get "trapped" in illiquid positions because they can't find a counterparty to take the opposing side of the trade.

■ Intraday Gaps

Some investments will gap in the middle of the trading session. These intraday gaps are particularly prone to occur during lunch hours, when many participants are away from their desks.

Due to a lack of buyers and sellers, the price must move higher to find sellers, or lower to find buyers, in order to fill market orders. Trading such instruments can lead to bad fills, as market orders may unintentionally move the market. This results in a higher purchase price for a buyer, or a lower selling price for a seller.

How can we tell if we are trading an illiquid investment? One way is to check a stock's statistics, such as its average daily volume. Many traders avoid stocks that have an average volume of less than 500,000 shares per day. Average volume is usually based on 50 trading sessions.

Another statistic worth checking is the company's market capitalization, or "market cap." The market cap of a company is the amount of money it would take to purchase all of the available shares at their current price. Some traders will avoid trading a stock if the company's market cap is less than $1 billion dollars. This is because stocks with very low market capitalizations, known as "small caps," tend to be less liquid than "large cap" stocks.

Average daily volume and market capitalization statistics are easy to obtain. Websites such as Google Finance, Yahoo Finance, and many others provide this information free of charge.

One way to determine a stock's depth is to view the buy and sell orders as they are listed on Level II. This can be tricky, as Level II contains many hidden orders, and a considerable amount of gamesmanship occurs there. On Level II, limit orders to buy or sell frequently disappear and reappear, as traders attempt to create the impression that a stock is stronger or weaker than it actually is.

Despite these hurdles, it's pretty easy to tell which stocks are liquid, and which ones are not, simply by glancing at Level II.

Let's compare the market depth of two trading instruments: Microsoft Corp. (MSFT) and the PowerShares DB German Bund Futures Exchange-Traded Notes (BUNL), using Level II data.

Notice how MSFT (Figure 9.4) is "thick" with multiple buyers and sellers, which are located at nearly every price point. Buyers are lined up in the left column, and sellers are in the right column. The number of shares they wish to buy or sell is listed in the "size" column.

According to Level II, we could buy MSFT immediately at $46.69 (right column of Figure 9.4) or sell it at $46.68 (left column of Figure 9.5). The spread between these two prices is one cent.

In comparison, few people are interested in buying or selling BUNL (Figure 9.5). While we can place large limit or market orders on MSFT without fear of moving

MSFT(B)

ID	Bid	Size	ID	Ask	Size
baty#	46.68	300	bats#(8)	46.69	1100
edgx#(8)	46.68	763	baty#(2)	46.69	300
bats#(7)	46.68	800	edgx#(16)	46.69	2100
edgx#(15)	46.67	1652	edga#(4)	46.69	400
edga#(4)	46.67	114	edga#	46.70	100
baty#(2)	46.67	200	edgx#(21)	46.70	2500
bats#(12)	46.67	1900	bats#(17)	46.70	2200
edgx#(11)	46.66	1400	baty#(2)	46.70	200
edga#	46.66	100	baty#	46.71	100
baty#(2)	46.66	200	edgx#(15)	46.71	1700
bats#(12)	46.66	2900	bats#(17)	46.71	4300
edga#	46.65	100	edga#	46.72	100
baty#	46.65	400	edgx#(16)	46.72	1800
edgx#(17)	46.65	4301	bats#(20)	46.72	2500
bats#(13)	46.65	2800	baty#	46.72	200

FIGURE 9.4 Level II Reveals Many Buyers and Sellers of Microsoft (MSFT)

BUNL(B)

ID	Bid	Size	ID	Ask	Size
edgx#(2)	25.62	200	edgx#	27.65	100
edga#(2)	25.62	200	edgx#	29.25	100
bats#(2)	25.62	200	edga#	29.25	100
baty#(2)	25.62	200	bats#	29.25	100
bats#	19.50	100	baty#	29.25	100
			edgx#	29.42	100
			edga#	29.42	100
			bats#	29.42	100
			baty#	29.42	100
			bats#	35.40	100

FIGURE 9.5 Level II Reveals a Lack of Buyers and Sellers in the PowerShares DB German Bund Futures Exchange Traded Notes (BUNL)

the market, it is only safe to place small limit orders on BUNL, which trades with a spread of $2.03.

Based on the Level II images, and assuming there are no hidden orders and that the participants actually want to buy and sell at these prices, a market order to buy MSFT for up to 3,700 shares would be filled at $46.69.

Meanwhile, a market order to buy BUNL would be filled at $27.65, and only for 100 shares. If the market order was for 200 shares, 100 shares would be filled at $27.65, and another 100 shares would be filled at the next higher price, which is $29.25. However, if we need to sell BUNL, we will only receive $25.62 per share. Because it is an illiquid trading instrument, a significant loss could occur quickly in BUNL.

■ Opening Gaps

Gaps that occur at the start of the trading day, known as "opening gaps," are the most common. Because most markets are closed for a portion of each trading day, any information or news that occurs while the market is closed is immediately reflected in the opening price. The price moves higher or lower to account for pent-up supply or demand that emerged while the market was closed.

An individual stock can be impacted by news that is specific to that company, news that affects its industry, or news that affects the market as a whole. In some cases, the opening gap could simply be a reflection of the fact that an index of which it is a component, such as the S&P 500, is bid higher or offered lower at the open.

Sometimes, activity in one or two stocks can cause an entire index to gap. Figure 9.6 provides an example of this: On January 8, 2015, an opening gap higher in the S&P 500 SPDR ETF (SPY, top of chart) coincided with an opening gap higher in Ford Motor Company (F, bottom of chart). In this case, there was significant news on Ford, a component of the S&P 500 index, which announced a dividend payout increase of 20%.

■ Breakaway Gaps

With over 1,800 companies listed on the New York Stock Exchange, and thousands of stocks available to trade on the NASDAQ, it's impossible for investors to pay close attention to all stocks at all times. Traders tend to get excited about volatile stocks that are in the news, and lose interest in stocks that are trapped in narrow ranges for weeks or months. Because of this, it's inevitable that some individual stocks will fall in and out of favor.

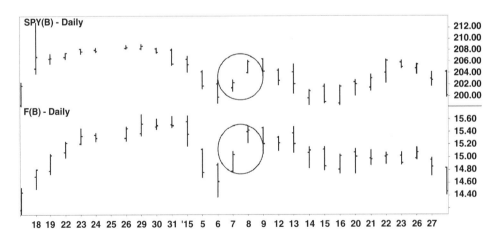

FIGURE 9.6 A Gap in Ford Helps Create a Gap in the S&P 500 SPDR ETF (SPY)

Occasionally, dormant stocks spring back to life. A strong earnings report, a shift in business practices, or a technical innovation can thrust the inactive stock back into the limelight. A stock that has been derided or ignored suddenly begins to attract interest and generate excitement. This excitement causes the price to gap higher and break out of its established range.

Many traders believe these so-called "breakaway gaps" present significant opportunities because they are symptomatic of a shift in perception. Because many participants are no longer paying attention to the stock, not all of them will immediately become aware of this change. The stock could be in for a major move, and perhaps at the beginning of a new long-term trend, as more of these formerly disinterested investors take a fresh look at the stock and climb on board.

Figure 9.7 provides an example of a breakaway gap: In December of 2011, shares of Microsoft Corp. (MSFT) were trapped in a narrow range between $25.14 and $26.19 (rectangle). Then on January 3 (arrow), the first trading day of 2012, Microsoft gapped higher, breaking the stock out of its slumber and igniting a move higher. Suddenly, Microsoft went from being ignored to being adored, and a new trend was born. By late February, the stock climbed as high as $32.

Breakaway gaps are considered more impressive when accompanied by a corresponding increase in volume (See Figure 9.8). After being trapped in a consolidation pattern for three months (rectangle), shares of Apple (AAPL) leapt higher on April 24, 2014 (arrow). The move occurred on nearly three times the average daily volume for the stock, based on the previous 50 trading sessions (circled).

FIGURE 9.7 A Breakaway Gap in Microsoft (MSFT) Ignites a Rally

FIGURE 9.8   A Breakaway Gap in Apple (AAPL) Is Accompanied by a Surge in Volume

Runaway Gaps

Unlike breakaway gaps, which represent a change in perception and perhaps a turning point, a "runaway gap" reinforces the market's current perception about a particular stock. A runaway gap occurs when a stock is already trending, either higher or lower, and then a gap occurs in the direction of the prevailing trend. A runaway gap indicates that the current trend is accelerating. Because these gaps indicate a continuation of the current trend, they are also referred to as "continuation gaps."

Several runaway gaps are shown in Figure 9.9 of United Continental Holdings Inc. (UAL) in late 2014. With shares already in a sustained uptrend, UAL gaps higher on Nov. 28, 2014 (circle A). Several days later, on Dec. 4, UAL gapped higher again (circle B). After these gaps, UAL continued to work its way higher.

Exhaustion Gaps

An "exhaustion gap" is a runaway gap that occurs after a stock, commodity, or currency has already made a significant run. It could be thought of as the last gasp of a trend.

When it occurs in an uptrend, the trading instrument has already attracted many buyers. It has also crushed the shorts, forcing them to cover. At this point, the overwhelming majority of participants trading the stock are already long.

Then, an additional bit of good news or publicity generates one final burst of excitement. This draws in investors who are afraid of missing out on what they now

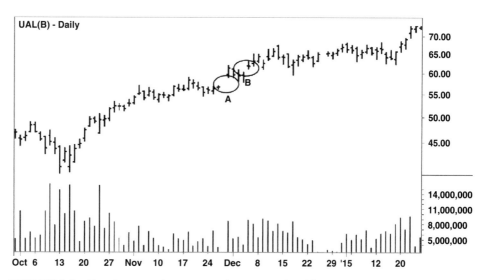

FIGURE 9.9   Two Runaway Gaps in United Continental Holdings (UAL)

perceive as a can't-miss opportunity. Unfortunately, these investors are late to the party and are entering a fresh long position at or near the top of the market.

The exhaustion gap represents a form of capitulation on the part of the buyers. The stock has now reached a point where nearly everyone who wants to own it already does, and few investors want to take the other side of the trade. With traders lined up so heavily on one side of the market, the trading instrument is ripe for a reversal.

In Figure 9.10, we see an example of an exhaustion gap. Shares of Isis Pharmaceuticals (ISIS) rally from the low $30s to the low $50s in a three-month period. The stock then gaps higher (circled) on February 21, 2014, on heavy volume (arrow). This proves to be an exhaustion gap, as the price then retraces back to $30.

Figure 9.10 brings up an important point: Although the high volume could be considered a clue, an exhaustion gap can only be identified with certainty in hindsight. At the time of the gap in Figure 9.10, there was no way to know if it was an exhaustion gap or a continuation gap. Only subsequent market activity made it clear that this was an exhaustion gap.

■ Island Reversals

An "island reversal" is really a combination of two different types of gaps. First, an exhaustion gap occurs; this is followed by a breakaway gap in the opposite direction. In between the two gaps is a series of bars or candles known as an "island," disconnected from price action on both sides by the two gaps.

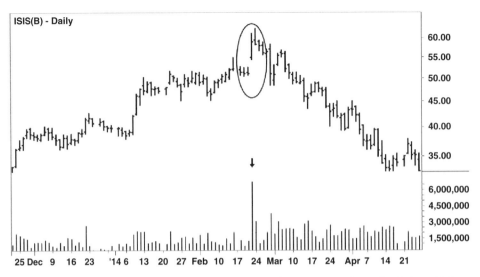

FIGURE 9.10 An Exhaustion Gap in Isis Pharmaceuticals (ISIS) Coincides with a Spike in Volume

Island gaps often mark major turning points. Figure 9.11 depicts an island reversal; starting in late 2013, shares of Whole Foods Markets (WFM) were trending lower. On May 7, 2014, WFM gapped down sharply (point A). In retrospect, this proved to be an exhaustion gap.

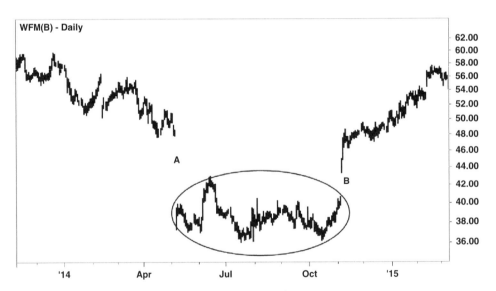

FIGURE 9.11 An Island Reversal in Whole Foods Markets (WFM)

For the next six months, the stock moved sideways. Then on November 6, Whole Foods Markets gapped sharply higher (point B). This breakaway gap proved to be the start of a new uptrend. Between the two gaps, an island is visible (circled).

The island gap represents a drastic change in perception. At first, it may have appeared to be a continuation of the downtrend, but in fact it was the last gasp of that trend. Those who shorted near the bottom were faced with a choice; either take the loss or stay short and risk being stranded on that island.

■ Gap Fills

By definition, when a price gaps higher or lower, prices inside the gapped area remain untouched. Because of this, there is a possibility that unfilled limit orders remain inside the gapped area. Because banks and brokers earn part of their income by filling orders, an unfilled order represents money left on the table.

Some traders assume that these gaps will eventually be filled, so that banks and brokers can execute those unfilled orders. It's possible that banks and brokers themselves may generate the necessary buying or selling activity to cause the gap to fill, thereby forcing the execution of those orders.

Since many gaps are eventually filled, this concept does have traction, and trading strategies have been designed with this in mind. One technique involves using the bottom of the gapped area as support, and/or the top of the gapped area as resistance.

Figure 9.12 demonstrates the use of the lower end of the gapped area as support. AT&T Inc. (T) gapped higher at the open on December 18, 2014, potentially leaving unfilled orders behind (point A).

The gap remained unfilled (dotted lines) until January 7, 2015, when the price re-entered the gapped area, causing the majority of the gap to be filled (point B).

Once the unfilled orders had been executed, the price reversed course. In this case, the lower range of the gapped area acted as support.

A similar scenario can occur when the price gaps lower. In Figure 9.13, the iShares 20+ Year Treasury Bond ETF (TLT) gapped down at the open on August 25, 2015 (point A). The gap remained unfilled until October 2, when the price rallied toward the upper end gapped zone (dotted lines), causing unfilled orders to be executed (point B). Once the orders were filled, the price resumed its downward trajectory. In this case, the upper range of the gap acted as resistance.

The intentional filling of a gap by a bank or broker isn't necessarily a nefarious deed. Banks and brokers know where their customers' orders are located, and work under the assumption that most customers would prefer to have their orders filled. While protective stops may be hit during this process, the goal of the banks and brokers is not necessarily to target stops.

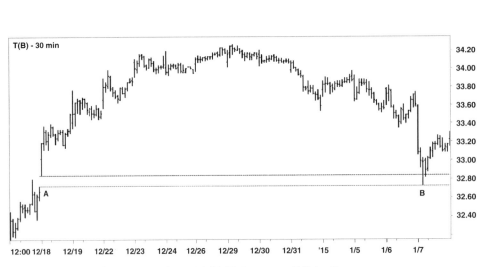

FIGURE 9.12   After a Gap Higher, AT&T (T) Returns to Fill the Gap

FIGURE 9.13   After a Gap Lowers, the iShares 20+ Year Treasury Bond ETF (TLT) Rises to Fill the Gap

■ Currency Market Gaps

Because the currency markets are decentralized, and because so much volume changes hands among a relatively small number of currencies, these markets tend to be extremely thick with buyers and sellers. However, gaps can occur. Because large gaps are rare in the currency market, they can take market participants by surprise, sometimes with devastating results.

Currency's Black Thursday

Here's a brutal example: In 2011, the Swiss National Bank instituted an exchange rate barrier at 1.20 on the euro/Swiss franc currency pair (EURCHF). Every time the euro would fall to that level against the franc, the Swiss central bank would buy large quantities of euros in order to weaken the Swiss franc and maintain EURCHF's position above the 1.20 barrier.

In early 2015, Europe was on the verge of a recession. To boost its economies, the European Central Bank announced plans to institute an asset purchase policy known as "quantitative easing," which was likely to result in a further weakening of the euro. Faced with these circumstances, the Swiss National Bank decided that it could no longer maintain the barrier at 1.20.

What happened next can be seen in Figure 9.14. At 4:30 a.m. Eastern time, on January 15, 2015, the Swiss National Bank announced that it would abandon its policy of defending the 1.20 barrier on the euro/Swiss franc currency pair (EURCHF).

Moments later, EURCHF gapped all the way from 1.20 to 1.04—a massive and unprecedented move. As a result of the Swiss National Bank's actions, years of pent-up selling pressure had been unleashed in a matter of seconds.

Traders who were long were blown out as the EURCHF exchange rate gapped far beyond all protective stops, resulting in huge negative balances in some trading accounts.

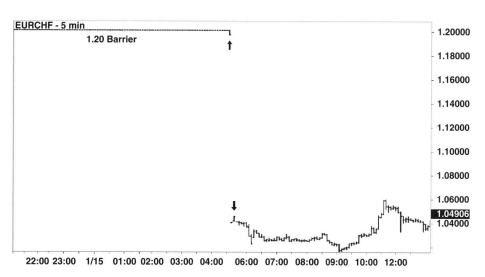

FIGURE 9.14   A Massive Gap Lowers in the Euro/Swiss Franc (EURCHF) Currency Pair

Other traders who were short EURCHF at the time had what was likely their best trading day ever. Because the currency market is heavily leveraged, some traders who were short saw their accounts swell by over 1,000% overnight.

However, not everyone was so lucky. Unable to cope with sudden losses, several currency brokers immediately went out of business. Others were rescued or purchased for pennies on the dollar. Several hedge funds also were badly damaged, with one fund becoming worthless overnight.

To many in the retail currency trading industry, the events that transpired on January 15, 2015, represented the end of an era. That date became known in the forex industry as Black Thursday, which is also the term used to describe the U.S. stock market crash of October 24, 1929, which began the Great Depression.

Currency's Black Wednesday

This is not to be confused with Black Wednesday, which refers to the events of September 16, 1992. On that date, currency trader George Soros broke the Bank of England by selling over $10 billion worth of British pounds, which helped cause that currency to collapse.

Just as with the Swiss franc in 2015, the collapse of the British pound in 1992 was the result of an official policy that defied market forces and ultimately failed.

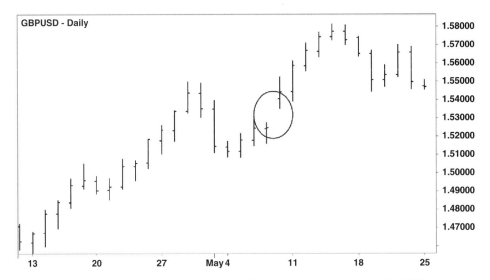

FIGURE 9.15   An Election Causes a Gap in the British Pound/U.S. Dollar (GBPUSD) Currency Pair

Currency Election Gaps

A less dramatic example of a currency market gap is depicted in Figure 9.15. That gap occurred on May 8, 2015.

On that day, the British pound gapped sharply higher against the U.S. dollar and other currencies after the results of a general election were announced. Gaps such as this one in the Great Britain pound/U.S. dollar currency pair (GBPUSD) are rare, because of the highly liquid nature of the currency market.

Notice how there are no other gaps visible in Figure 9.15. The gap of 158 pips in GBPUSD was unusually large by currency market standards. Still, it was only about one-tenth the size of the EURCHF gap depicted in Figure 9.14.

■ Final Thoughts on Gaps

A gap occurs when the price moves abruptly higher or lower, leaving behind an area where no trades were executed. Because of this, unfilled orders are often left behind in the gapped area. If the price gaps beyond the previous session's high or low, it is considered a full gap. If the price gaps higher or lower but fails to open beyond the previous session's high or low, it is considered a partial gap. Gaps commonly occur when a market opens. Illiquid trading vehicles have a higher tendency to gap than liquid trading vehicles.

PART III

PRICE PATTERNS

CHAPTER 10

Reversal Chart Patterns

A technical chart pattern consists of a specific combination of lines and/or arcs that appear on a chart. In most cases, the lines and arcs form shapes that are believed to indicate a bullish or bearish directional bias. Chart patterns occur in all forms of trading; the same sequences of lines and arcs that appear in stock and index charts can also be found in the charts of currency pairs and futures contracts.

Most patterns fall into one of two categories:

1) Reversal chart patterns indicate that the price is about to change direction.
2) Continuation chart patterns indicate that the price should continue in its current direction.

When it comes to price patterns, location is of key importance. In fact, it could be said that a chart pattern is defined not only by its shape, but by the price action that precedes it.

A pattern that hints at a continuation of the current move is useless if there is no existing trend that can be continued. Likewise, without a trend to reverse, a chart pattern that hints at a price reversal loses its meaning. *All patterns must be viewed within the context of the price action that preceded that pattern's formation.*

Chart patterns occur in all different chart types and time frames; they are just as likely to appear on a five-minute line chart as they are on a monthly candlestick chart. Because these patterns can occur in any time period, they are considered "fractal" in nature.

The passage of time has not altered these line and curve combinations. Much has changed in the world over the past hundred years, but the same patterns that can be found today are visible in hand-drawn charts from decades ago. In fact, some candlestick charting patterns are centuries old.

Human beings have an unfortunate tendency to see what we want to see. Because of this, it can be difficult to treat all chart patterns with 100% objectivity. There are even those who question whether the patterns discussed here actually exist, as if they are purely the result of the mental gymnastics of the observer.

Because we tend to see what we want to see, it might be a good idea to avoid searching for specific patterns. Instead, examine charts without expectations, looking for nothing in particular, and wait for a pattern to reveal itself. A good pattern should be fairly obvious; it should stand out. If it takes more than a few seconds to identify the pattern, it might not be a useful example of that formation.

■ Patterns Are Imperfect

A novice might expect that every occurrence of a chart pattern will lead to the anticipated result on every occasion. Those who do may become disillusioned when they realize this is not the case. Every experienced trader has witnessed the failure of a chart pattern; and the longer you trade, the more failures you will see. If these patterns are flawed, then why use them at all?

If any aspect of technical or fundamental analysis worked consistently and flawlessly, trading would be an easy game indeed. If that were the case, this book and any book written about trading would be very short, consisting only of the one thing that always does the trick. There would be no need to delve into other areas.

Anything that works more often than not has value. From the perspective of both the gambler and the trader, any situation that offers better than 50–50 odds of a positive outcome should be exploited.

Have you ever noticed that casinos don't offer games that favor the gambler? Often, the odds on a given game of chance favor the casino by only a slight margin. Yet a casino empire can be built via the consistent exploitation of slightly favorable odds. Since that's the case, shouldn't traders also search for situations that give them an advantage?

That's why it's important that we manage our expectations. Chart patterns aren't the key to an unbeatable advantage, and their use won't automatically result in a bonanza of trading profits. They are simply used in an attempt to gain an edge.

■ Reversal vs. Continuation Patterns

As mentioned earlier, chart patterns can be grouped into two main categories— reversal patterns and continuation patterns. Reversal patterns tend to be more dramatic and impactful than continuation patterns, making them a natural starting point for this section of the book.

Trends can continue for long periods of time, and because of this both traders and investors tend to become complacent. The reversal of a trend provides a jolt to these complacent market participants, shocking them into action and creating an opportunity for those looking to take the other side of the trade.

■ The Head and Shoulders Reversal Pattern

We noted earlier that an uptrend is defined as a series of higher highs and higher lows. As long as this pattern remains intact, the uptrend is valid.

Eventually, every uptrend will cease making higher highs. When lower highs and lower lows are introduced into a series of higher highs and higher lows, it forms the basis for one of the most notorious reversal patterns in existence—the "head and shoulders" pattern.

The head and shoulders is a bearish reversal pattern that consists of three main parts: the left shoulder, the head, and the right shoulder. The pattern begins as a series of higher highs and higher lows—the classic definition of an uptrend.

That sequence is altered when a low point is formed that has the same approximate value as the previous low. The left shoulder and head of the pattern are now fully formed; this is the first sign that a change in trend may be imminent.

The price rallies from this low point, but instead of resuming the sequence of higher highs, a lower high occurs. Often, this lower high is similar in value to a prior high point that is now the peak of the left shoulder. Then the price slides back to the previous low for a third time, forming the right shoulder. The pattern is now complete. See Figure 10.1 for what the structure of this pattern looks like.

As we can see in Figure 10.1, the pattern of highs within the head and shoulders are thus: high, higher high, and lower high. The three lows should be similar in

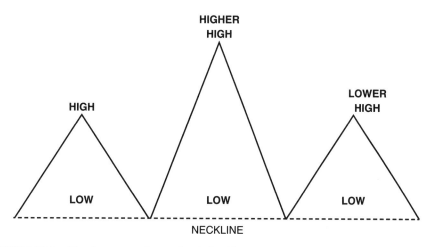

FIGURE 10.1   The Structure of a Head and Shoulders Pattern

value and represent an area of horizontal support. A line is drawn across the three lows; this is known as the "neckline" of the pattern.

An uptrend consists of higher highs and higher lows, while a downtrend consists of lower highs and lower lows. Think of the head and shoulders pattern as the transition point between these two opposing trends. The left side of the pattern represents the end of the uptrend (the final higher high), and the right side of the pattern represents the beginning of the downtrend (the first lower high).

Take a look at the massive head and shoulder pattern in Figure 10.2, on the weekly chart of the British pound/Japanese yen currency pair (GBPJPY). Note that the pattern itself took over a year to form after several years of dominance by the British pound over the Japanese yen.

As you view Figure 10.2, keep in mind that the location of any reversal pattern is critical, and that a pattern is defined by the price action that precedes it.

The head and shoulders is located in the upper right corner of the chart (L-H-R). The pattern was preceded by a massive, multi-year rally, as GBPJPY climbed from below 150 to above 250. The location of the head and shoulders within the uptrend validates the pattern, as any reversal pattern requires a prior trend that must be reversed.

Once the pattern was completed, a shocking reversal occurred. The British pound was crushed beneath the weight of the strengthening Japanese yen. Fortunes were both made and lost as GBPJPY surrendered seven years' worth of gains and fell back below 150.

Volume Considerations

Volume is also an important consideration of the head and shoulders pattern. If a higher high occurs on expanding volume, that is considered healthy and normal in

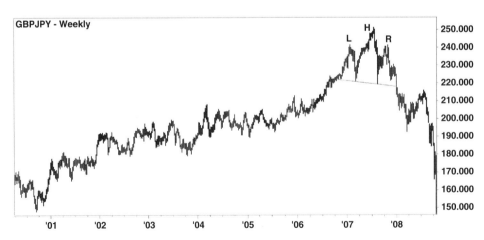

FIGURE 10.2 A Head and Shoulders Pattern in the Weekly Chart of GBPJPY

an uptrend. The same can be said of a throwback that occurs on lighter-than-average volume.

However, in an ideal scenario, the head and shoulders pattern sees volume diminish on each successive peak. The higher high that forms the peak of the head should ideally occur on lower volume than the previous high, which formed the left shoulder. Volume should diminish further on the third peak, as the right shoulder forms.

This demonstrates a lack of enthusiasm on the part of the bulls, who are losing their will to continue buying at higher prices. If and when the neckline breaks, that break should occur on high volume.

Figure 10.3 shows volume falling as the pattern forms. Shares of Apple (AAPL) rallied in the second half of 1999, but the rally came to an end in March of 2000, which also represented the peak of the head and shoulders pattern (H).

Note that in general, the volume beneath the head and shoulders pattern (rectangle) is low compared to the rally that preceded it. Volume is extremely low on the first bounce from the neckline (arrow). Once the neckline was broken, volume began to increase as the price moved lower.

The example is imperfect because the volume on the second bounce from the neckline is higher than the first. The slanted neckline (dotted line) does not negate the pattern and is perfectly acceptable.

The neckline is the focal point for traders who wish to use this pattern to their advantage. Since the price advances upward from the neckline on several occasions during the formation of any head and shoulders pattern, we can assume that some traders were buying at that level.

What can be said of those who took long positions on the neckline and are still in the trade? We know that those buyers, along with any buyers who entered at higher

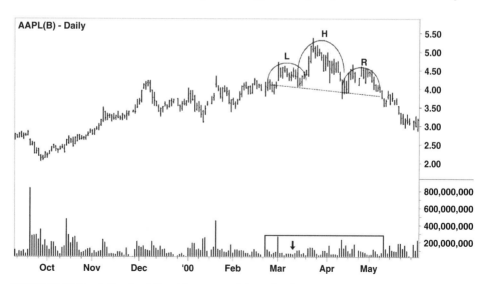

FIGURE 10.3 A Head and Shoulders on Apple's Daily Chart

levels and are also still in the trade, will be holding losing positions if the neckline should break. These losing traders will be motivated to sell, which should help push the price lower.

Aggressive traders will close long positions and/or sell short as the price breaks through the neckline, without waiting to see if the price will close beneath the neckline. Other traders, wishing to avoid a false break, will allow the price to close below the neckline before initiating a short position. This is considered a safer method of entry, but it isn't always feasible because the price can move sharply once the break occurs. A trader who waits for the price to close beneath support may find the price has moved far beneath the neckline, creating a less than ideal risk/reward scenario.

Second Chance Entry

A more conservative entry approach for a short trade would be to wait for the price to close beneath the neckline, and then place an order to sell short just below the neckline. The assumption is that the neckline, which was the major support level of the pattern, should now act as resistance should the price manage to rally back to that level. There is no guarantee that the price will rally back to the neckline, but if it does, the trader is now presented with a "second chance" opportunity to sell at resistance within the context of a head and shoulders breakdown.

The second chance entry for a head and shoulders pattern is illustrated in Figure 10.4. In late summer of 2012, Apple began to form a head and shoulders pattern. Then on October 8, the stock gapped down through neckline support (dotted line). This break of the neckline was the first opportunity to sell short.

If we extend the neckline to the right, we see the price rally into the neckline's extension on October 16 and 17 (arrow). The neckline, formerly support, now acts

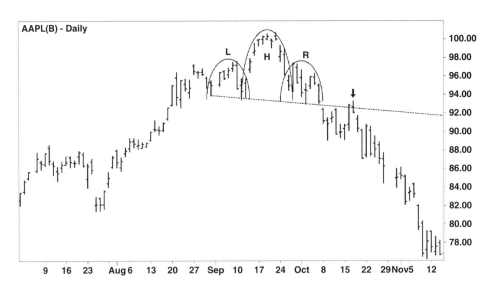

FIGURE 10.4 Apple Head and Shoulders with a Second Chance Entry

FIGURE 10.5 A Head and Shoulders on the Dow Jones Shanghai ($DJSH) Average Leads to Multiple Entry Opportunities

as resistance, and the stock's advance is halted at that point. For traders who missed the initial breakdown, the rally to the neckline is the second chance to sell short.

Figure 10.5 also illustrates the second chance concept, but in this example multiple opportunities to sell short are visible. The stage was set when the Dow Jones Shanghai Index ($DJSH) formed a head and shoulders pattern (L-H-R, circled) after a massive rally in 2015.

The index broke through the neckline (dotted line) in late June. On the following three consecutive trading days, the index climbed to the neckline's extension, only to fall back each time (first arrow).

In late July, the index rallied to just beneath the neckline's extension, creating another shorting opportunity (second arrow). Then in mid-August, the $DJSH rallied to the neckline's extension one more time.

There are two takeaways from Figure 10.5. First, you may get more than one second chance to enter a trade.

Second, considerable time may pass before a second chance entry opportunity presents itself. In a situation such as this, it might be helpful for a trader to set automatic alerts to inform him or her if the price has returned to the vicinity of the entry point.

Measuring Techniques

If a head and shoulders breakdown occurs, how far should we expect the price to fall? Traditional technical analysis uses a simple measuring technique to create a general price target by measuring from the peak of the head to the neckline. The assumption is that the price will decline by an equivalent amount.

For example, if a stock has formed a head and shoulders pattern that measures from $50 (head) to $40 (neckline), the height of the pattern is $10. The assumption is that once the price breaks the neckline at $40, it should fall another $10. In this case, the target would be $30.

Traders who use multiple targets may wish to expand on this concept by measuring from the head *and* from the right shoulder to the neckline. Since the head is always higher than the shoulders, doing so will result in two separate targets.

For example, if the right shoulder is located at approximately $45 and the neckline is $40, the resulting target would be $35. Now the trader has two targets, $35 and $30. The trader could close half of the position at each target.

Why Measure?

The measurement technique is simple, but does it make sense? Is there any real basis to justify the use of this technique, or does it just provide an easy solution to an otherwise difficult problem?

Keep in mind that prior to the introduction of personal computers and the widespread use of the Internet, most charts were hand-drawn. Early technical analysts needed a simple method to determine targets and stops, and didn't have the ability to rigorously test their strategies. That's why we consider all targets that involve measuring techniques to be general targets. Measuring techniques should be used as a guideline, in conjunction with other methods of creating stops and targets.

Variations on the Head and Shoulders Pattern

A fairly common variation on this pattern is one that contains multiple heads and/or shoulders. In some cases, the head and shoulders pattern forms as it normally does but fails to break the neckline; instead, it forms a second or even third right shoulder. The fact that this version of the pattern has multiple right shoulders doesn't invalidate its meaning.

Figure 10.6 presents an interesting example of this phenomenon. The U.S. dollar/Japanese yen currency pair (USDJPY) formed a huge head and shoulders pattern spanning the years 2001 through 2003.

At the time of its formation, the left shoulder (L) must have appeared as a double top. The head also looks similar to a double top (H), as does the original right shoulder (R). We'll cover double tops later in this chapter.

Instead of breaking the neckline after the formation of the right shoulder, the pattern formed two additional right shoulders (R2, R3) before finally breaking down in September of 2003.

At the time, Japan's central bank, the Bank of Japan, was engaged in a policy of currency intervention designed to prevent USDJPY from falling to lower levels.

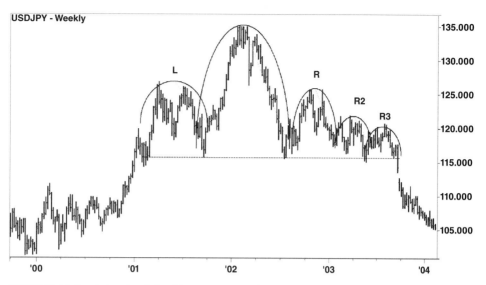

FIGURE 10.6 A Head and Shoulders on USDJPY's Weekly Chart Features Three Right Shoulders

When USDJPY falls, Japan's exports to the U.S. become less profitable. When the Bank of Japan ceased the pursuit of this policy, USDJPY fell sharply, causing the neckline to break.

Island Head and Shoulders

A less common version of the pattern is the "island head and shoulders." In this version of the pattern, the price has gapped up prior to the formation of the head and shoulders. After the head and shoulders is fully formed, the pattern ends with a gap down. This leaves the pattern itself disconnected from the rest of the chart—hence, the term "island."

An example of this odd version of the head and shoulders pattern appears in Figure 10.7. After a multi-year rally that saw the stock's value increase by over 600%, shares of Whole Foods Market Inc. (WFM) gapped sharply higher on May 8 of 2013, on approximately 4X average volume (point A).

The stock continued to rally, reaching what was at the time an all-time closing high above $65 in October of 2013, which proved to be the head of the pattern. The stock then began to trend lower, forming a series of lower highs and lower lows. This resulted in a messy but clearly visible head and shoulders pattern with a slightly downward sloping neckline.

Then on May 7, 2014, almost one year to the date of the gap higher, WFM suffered a huge gap down on nearly 10X its average volume, thus completing the pattern (point B).

FIGURE 10.7   An Island Head and Shoulders in Whole Foods Markets (WFM)

■ Inverse Head and Shoulders Pattern

Most chart reversal patterns have an inverse version, and the head and shoulders pattern is no exception. The inverse head and shoulders begins as a series of lower highs and lower lows—the classic definition of a downtrend.

In this case, after the formation of a lower low, a high point occurs that is not lower, but equal to the previous high. This "equal high" breaks the pattern of lower highs. As the price falls away from this level, a higher low is formed, preferably on light volume. The price returns to the area of the previous high for a third time, forming the neckline, which is also resistance.

The pattern is completed when the price closes above this neckline, turning an area of former resistance into support. Those who shorted at or below the neckline and are still in the trade are now holding losing positions; they may feel the need to cover short positions, forcing the price higher still. See Figure 10.8 for the structure of this pattern.

After the pattern is complete, some traders go long as the price breaks above the neckline, while others wait for the price to close above it. The disadvantage to the latter method is that the price may close far above the neckline, creating an unfavorable risk/reward setup.

After the price has broken out, conservative traders will wait for a throwback to the neckline, a former resistance area that should now act as support before entering the trade. However, there is no guarantee that such a throwback will occur, or that a second chance entry will become available.

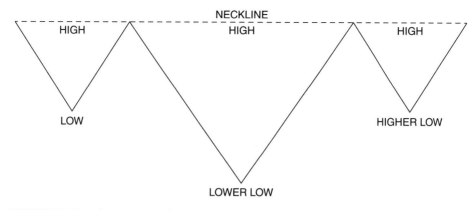

FIGURE 10.8 The Structure of an Inverse Head and Shoulders

All of the variations of the bearish head and shoulders pattern are similarly valid in their bullish, inverted versions. Multiple heads and/or shoulders sometimes appear, but these occurrences do not alter the meaning of the pattern.

Price objectives can be determined using the simple measuring technique described earlier in this chapter. Some analysts believe that volume should fall on each successive rally to the neckline, although strict adherence to this condition would disqualify a large percentage of the setups. Ideally, the break above the neckline should occur on high volume.

Figure 10.9 shows an inverted head and shoulders pattern on a 60-minute chart. After a brief sell-off, the Gold Continuous Contract (@GC) formed a small inverted head and shoulders pattern in October of 2014. The pattern marked a short-term bottom, as gold then rallied.

FIGURE 10.9 An Inverted Head and Shoulders on the Gold Continuous Contract Hourly Chart

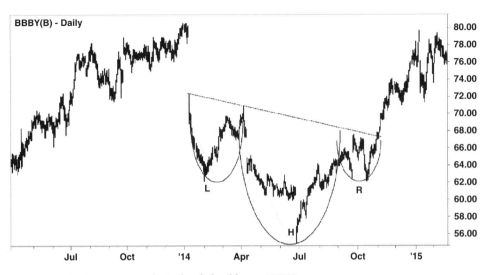

FIGURE 10.10   An Inverted Head and Shoulders in BBBY

Figure 10.9 brings up an interesting point; not every pattern offers a large potential return. A small pattern, such as the one in Figure 10.9, yields a less ambitious target than a similar pattern of greater size. The same can also be said of a pattern that forms over a short period of time; the inverted head and shoulders depicted in Figure 10.9 formed over just three days.

Because the inverted head and shoulders in Figure 10.9 was relatively small and occurred on a 60-minute chart, the pattern was appropriate for traders with a short time horizon. Investors should consider the size of the pattern and the length of time that went into its formation before taking action.

Compare this to the example of an inverted head and shoulders in Figure 10.10, which shows shares of Bed Bath and Beyond (BBBY) plunging just days after reaching an all-time high in January of 2014.

This pattern appears on a daily chart, as it formed over a longer period of time. After ten months, the formation was complete and BBBY broke out to the upside. Two months later, the stock was trading near its old highs.

■ Head and Shoulders Continuation Pattern

Our initial discussion of the head and shoulders pattern placed a heavy emphasis on location. It was made clear that a bearish head and shoulders reversal pattern should be located in an uptrend, and a bullish inverted head and shoulders pattern should occur in a downtrend.

However, you may encounter situations where the shape of a head and shoulders forms within a downtrend, or the shape of an inverted head and shoulders appears

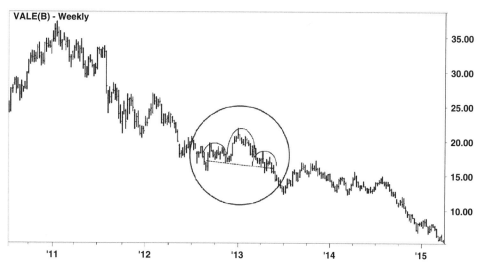

FIGURE 10.11　A Continuation Head and Shoulders in VALE S.A. (VALE)

within an uptrend. What, if any, is the meaning of these patterns when they appear in this context? They are considered continuation patterns.

Figure 10.11 provides an example of a head and shoulders continuation pattern. Brazil-based mining company VALE S.A. (VALE) was already in a downtrend when the shape of a head and shoulders pattern appeared. After the pattern was completed, VALE broke through the neckline, causing the downtrend to resume. When it occurs in this context, the head and shoulders is considered a bearish continuation pattern, not a reversal pattern.

Similarly, an inverted head and shoulders, which is a reversal indicator when it appears in a downtrend, is considered a continuation pattern when it appears within an uptrend.

In Figure 10.12, Waste Connections (WCN) was clearly in an uptrend when the shape of the inverted head and shoulders pattern appeared. The price failed to cross above the neckline after the right shoulder was completed. Subsequently, a second right shoulder formed (R2).

In April of 2014, the breakout succeeded; by June of that year, WCN reached an all-time high.

Because the inverted head and shoulders pattern appeared in an uptrend, and not after a sell-off, it was considered a continuation pattern.

■ Double Top Pattern

If we understand the concept of a head and shoulders pattern, the bearish double top pattern should be easy to comprehend.

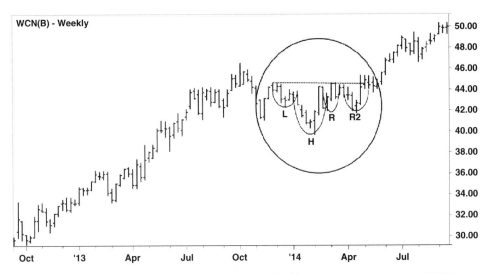

FIGURE 10.12 A Continuation Inverted Head and Shoulders in Waste Connections (WCN)

First, a stock, currency, or commodity must form a series of higher highs and higher lows—the definition of an uptrend. The sequence is disrupted when the price finally fails to reach a higher high; instead the price is only able to match its previous high. The chart now resembles twin mountain peaks; the two peaks do not have to be perfectly symmetrical. Ideally, volume on the first peak is higher than it is on the second peak.

The focal point of this pattern is the "valley" that lies between the peaks. That low point is considered the support level of the pattern. If and when the price falls beneath that low, traders use it as a signal to sell because the next likely move is lower. Figure 10.13 shows the structure of this pattern.

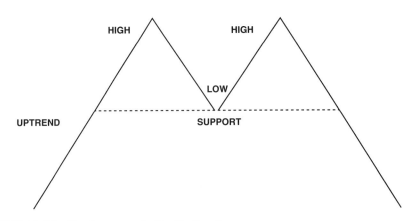

FIGURE 10.13 The Structure of a Double Top Pattern

When support breaks, several courses of action become available. Aggressive traders will short immediately, while more conservative traders will wait for the price to close beneath support, in order to avoid being caught in a false break.

There is a downside to the conservative approach; it's possible that by the time that candle closes, the price will have moved far beneath support.

After the break occurs, some traders will place a sell order just beneath the former support level, which should now act as resistance. These traders hope for a "second chance" to sell short after the breakdown. This is similar to the tactic that a trader might employ in the case of a head and shoulders breakdown.

In Figure 10.14, shares of semiconductor company Altera Corp. (ALTR) sky-rocketed from 2009 through early 2011, forming a series of higher highs and higher lows. A double top pattern then formed (circled), leading to a sell-off. Altera lost one-third of its value before recovering.

In order to determine price targets for double tops, a measurement technique similar to the one described in the head and shoulders pattern is utilized. Traders simply measure from the height of the double top pattern down to support. The assumption is that a similar-sized drop will occur after the price has breached support.

For example, if the twin peaks of the double top are located at approximately $75, and the support between the peaks is located at $70, then the height of the pattern is $5. The assumption is that once support at $70 breaks, the price will move lower by an additional $5, to $65.

This concept is illustrated in Figure 10.15. After a significant rally, shares of Continental Resources (CLR) formed a slightly asymmetrical double top pattern from June through September of 2014.

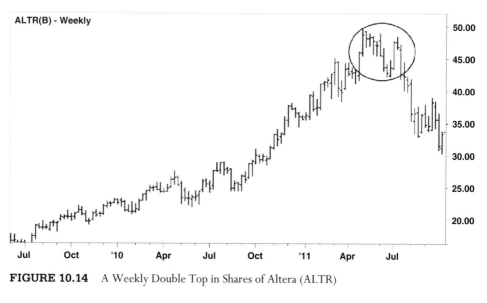

FIGURE 10.14 A Weekly Double Top in Shares of Altera (ALTR)

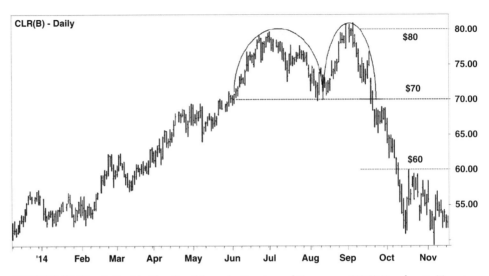

FIGURE 10.15 A Double Top Breakdown in Continental Resources (CLR) Reaches Its Target

The support level of the pattern was approximately $70, and the top of the formation was just above $80, giving the pattern a height of roughly $10. If we subtract $10 from the former support level of $70, the measuring technique gives us a target of $60. That target was easily achieved after CLR's breakdown. In this case, no second chance entry occurred.

■ Double Bottom Pattern

The bullish double bottom pattern is simply the inverse of the bearish double top formation. The price has formed a downtrend, consisting of a series of lower lows and lower highs. At some point, the price fails to make a lower low; instead the low price approximately matches the previous low. The two lows need not be exactly the same. Figure 10.16 shows the structure of this pattern.

The focal point of this pattern is the high that rests between the two lows; this area is now considered resistance. If the price breaks above resistance, the pattern is complete and the breakout has occurred.

Aggressive traders will go long as the price breaks out, while more conservative traders will wait for the price to close above resistance, in order to avoid being caught in a false break. After the break occurs, traders who missed the initial move could place a buy order just above the former resistance level, which should now act as support. These traders hope to buy on a throwback to the former resistance level, in order to get a second chance entry.

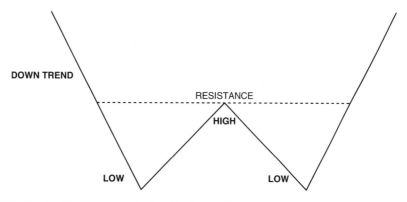

FIGURE 10.16   The Structure of a Double Bottom Pattern

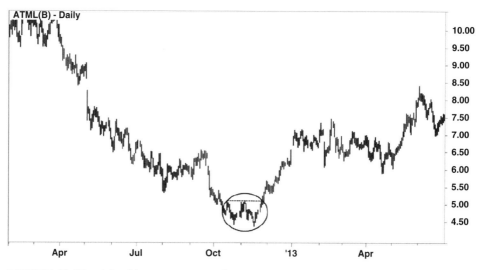

FIGURE 10.17   A Double Bottom in Atmel Corp

In Figure 10.17, after losing over half of their value, shares of Atmel Corp. (ATML) formed and broke out of a double bottom. The breakout occurred in late November of 2012, leading to a gain of over 50 percent.

Price targets for double bottoms can also be created via the measuring technique. Figure 10.18 zooms in on the double bottom presented in Figure 10.17 to show the process of creating the target.

The low point of the pattern is $4.37, and the resistance level is $5.11. This gives the pattern a height of $0.74. The height of the pattern is then added to the breakout point to create a target of $5.85. The target was achieved in under a month, and the price continued to rally afterward.

FIGURE 10.18   A Close-Up of the Atmel Double Bottom, with Target

■ Triple Top Pattern

This bearish pattern is a slightly more elaborate version of a double top, and it's analyzed in exactly the same way. In Figure 10.19, three relatively symmetrical tops are visible on the daily chart of MetLife Inc. (MET).

The upper boundary of the pattern is approximately $58, and the support level is located in the vicinity of $54, giving the pattern a height of $4. Subtract $4 from $54 to create a target price of $50.

FIGURE 10.19   A Triple Top Pattern in Shares of MetLife (MET)

Is a triple top pattern superior to a double top? The formation isn't necessarily better or worse; it's simply based on the number of tops. A double bottom may actually be a triple bottom when applied to a different time frame, and vice versa. Of greater concern than the number of tops is the size of the pattern and the amount of time that went into its formation.

■ Triple Bottom Pattern

This is the bullish version of the triple top pattern. In Figure 10.20, the S&P Select Energy SPDR (XLE), an exchange-traded fund that consists mainly of large-cap energy stocks like Exxon Mobile Corp. (XOM) and Chevron (CVX), was routed in the second half of 2014.

The price drop was due to the widespread introduction of new, more efficient crude oil drilling techniques, which led to a glut of supply. In June of 2014, the price of a barrel of West Texas Intermediate (WTI) crude oil was over $100; by January of 2015, the price had fallen to $45. The sharp sell-off in crude oil led to a general decline in energy-related stocks.

After a sharp sell-off, a triple bottom pattern began to form on XLE's daily chart in December of 2014. The pattern's resistance level was approximately $81, and its lower boundary was near $72, giving the pattern a height of $9. Adding the height of the pattern to the resistance level created a price target of $90.

By February of 2015, the price of WTI crude oil had climbed back to nearly $55. Optimism was building that low prices would force oil drillers to reduce output. XLE responded by breaking above $81.

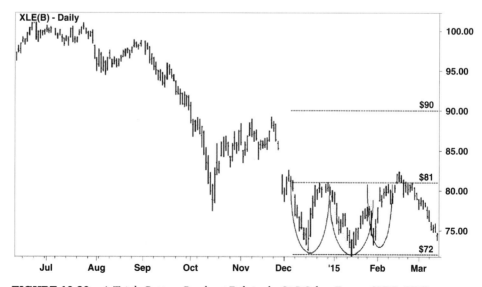

FIGURE 10.20 A Triple Bottom Breakout Fails in the S&P Select Energy SPDR (XLE)

However, the breakout failed just a few days later as crude oil sank back below $50. Traders who went long on the breakout lost money on the trade as XLE fell back below $81.

This is an example of a failed pattern. One should never get the impression that technical analysis will work flawlessly on every occasion. If any aspect of technical analysis were foolproof, then technicians would only focus on that one area.

■ Diamond Reversal Patterns

The diamond pattern is generally used as a reversal pattern, although it can also appear as a continuation pattern. Because of this discrepancy, traders typically wait for the price to break out of a diamond pattern before attempting to determine which role it will assume.

The diamond pattern is really a combination of two patterns; it begins as a broadening formation or megaphone pattern (this will be covered in Chapter 12), and resolves into a symmetrical triangle. The diamond gets its name from the shape that is created by the combination of the two patterns. It's not necessary for the lines that form the diamond to be perfectly symmetrical.

Diamond patterns can be difficult to spot, because the shape isn't obvious until the pattern is nearly complete.

Bullish Diamond Reversal

In the bullish diamond reversal pattern, a steep downtrend resolves into a diamond-shaped consolidation. When the price breaks through the upper boundary of the diamond, the area of former resistance becomes support. The trader has the option of buying the breakout, waiting for a close above the trend line, or buying a throwback back to the former resistance level.

In Figure 10.21, shares of Netflix Inc. (NFLX) declined sharply in March of 2014. Beginning in April, the stock began to consolidate into a pattern that eventually took the shape of a diamond. In mid-May, Netflix broke out of the consolidation and quickly regained the territory it lost during March.

Bearish Diamond Reversal

In the bearish diamond reversal pattern, a steep uptrend resolves into a diamond consolidation. When the price breaks through the lower boundary of the diamond, that area of former support becomes resistance. The trader has the option of selling the breakdown, waiting for a close beneath the trend line, or shorting a rally back to the former support level, which should now act as resistance.

In Figure 10.22, the S&P 500 Index ($INX) rallied sharply in early 2011 before consolidating into a diamond pattern. The upper range of the diamond is just above

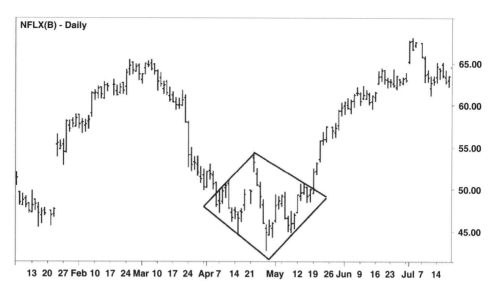

FIGURE 10.21 A Bullish Diamond Reversal in Shares of Netflix Inc. (NFLX)

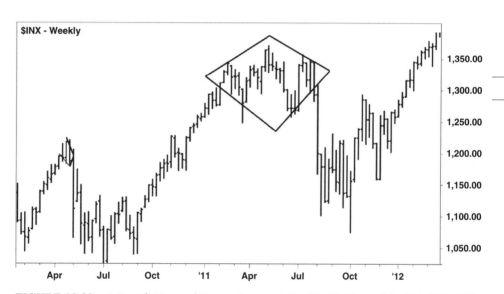

FIGURE 10.22 A Bearish Diamond Pattern Appears in the Weekly Chart of the S&P 500 ($INX)

1,350, and the lower range is approximately 1,250. This gives the diamond a height of approximately 100 points.

A sell signal occurred when the price broke out of the pattern at approximately 1,300. A target price can be created by subtracting the height of the pattern (100 points) from the entry point (1,300), which generates a target of approximately 1,200. That target was easily achieved during the first weekly bar after the breakdown.

The most important thing to remember about reversal patterns is this: In order for a reversal pattern to have meaning, it must be preceded by a trend or a significant directional move. Otherwise, there is nothing to reverse.

■ Final Thoughts on Reversal Chart Patterns

A reversal pattern indicates a high degree of likelihood that the current trend is about to change. This makes reversal patterns useful in creating trade entries and exits. All price patterns must be viewed within the context of the price action that preceded that pattern's formation. Without a trend to reverse, a chart pattern that hints at a price reversal loses its meaning.

CHAPTER 11

Continuation Patterns

We've already reviewed a number of patterns that indicate a reversal is about to take place. However, there are many patterns that suggest the opposite is about to occur. The following patterns indicate that the price will continue trending in its current direction.

After a period of trending, a market will often pause. This pause is known as a "consolidation." On many occasions, these consolidations form specific shapes and patterns known as "continuation patterns."

Let's take a closer look at continuation patterns—what they are, what they mean, and how we might use them to our advantage.

■ Triangles

Symmetrical Triangle

A triangle consists of two opposing trend lines. Imagine that a series of lower highs appears on a chart, simultaneously coexisting with a series of higher lows. The result would be two trend lines that move toward each other.

This formation is known as a "symmetrical triangle" and has no directional bias. This is because both the bulls and bears are demonstrating strength. The bulls are making purchases at consistently higher levels, and the bears are selling at consistently lower levels.

Symmetrical triangles are assumed to be continuation patterns; in other words, the price should continue moving in the direction established prior to the formation of the symmetrical triangle. In these cases, the triangle itself is merely a consolidation that occurs within the trend.

However, the pattern itself shows that both bulls and bears have a similar degree of control, so the psychology behind the symmetrical triangle seems to say that neither the bulls nor the bears can boast a significant advantage.

In Figure 11.1, which features the daily chart of Amazon.com Inc. (AMZN), we see a pattern of lower highs (H, LH) and higher lows (L, HL). Together, the two trend lines create a symmetrical triangle.

In this case, the triangle resolves to the downside when the pattern of higher lows is broken. Notice how the price bounced from the $285 area (arrow), which had acted as support earlier when the initial low (L) was created.

Bullish Ascending Triangle

Unlike the symmetrical triangle, the ascending triangle pattern has a clear directional bias. In this pattern, the bulls show their power by forming a series of higher lows. Because the bulls are willing to make purchases at consistently higher prices, they are considered the aggressive party.

Meanwhile, as the bulls push higher, the bears are unable to create momentum in the opposite direction. Instead, the bears form a horizontal resistance level. This indicates that the bears are simply trying to stand their ground as the bulls thrust toward them from increasingly higher levels.

The assumption is that the aggressive party, in this case the bulls, will eventually overcome the passive bears and push through resistance.

FIGURE 11.1 A Symmetrical Triangle Appears in Amazon.com

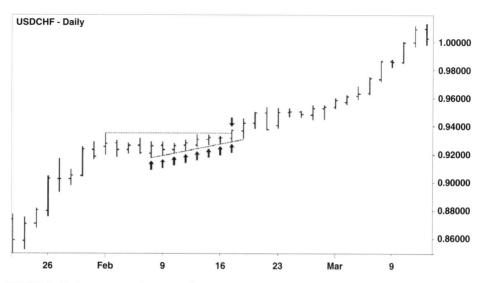

FIGURE 11.2 An Ascending Triangle in USDCHF

Figure 11.2 provides an example of an ascending triangle. The U.S. dollar/Swiss franc currency pair (USDCHF) was trending higher in early 2015. At the beginning of February, USDCHF began to consolidate into a sideways pattern.

For eight consecutive sessions, USDCHF's low of the day exceeded the previous day's low (up arrows). While the bulls were able to create a series of higher lows, the bears struggled to contain the USDCHF exchange rate beneath .9350 (horizontal dotted line).

Finally, on February 17, 2015, the bulls were able to push USDCHF above .9350 (down arrow). In an ascending triangle, a buy signal is created when the price breaks above the horizontal resistance line.

The breakout allowed the uptrend that had started prior to the ascending triangle consolidation to resume. The subsequent rally pushed USDCHF 700 pips higher within one month's time.

Like other patterns, ascending triangles sometimes offer second chance entries. This is illustrated in Figure 11.3, as shares of USG Corp. (USG) formed an ascending triangle.

In June of 2012, USG rallied from below $14 to nearly $21. Then in July, the stock had difficulty breaking above $21 on several occasions (down arrows). That resistance area became the horizontal line of the triangle.

After falling back to nearly $15, the stock began to climb in August, forming a series of higher lows (HL). An ascending trend line is clearly visible as the stock climbed back toward resistance. Then in early September of 2012, USG broke through the upper end of the triangle, creating a buy signal.

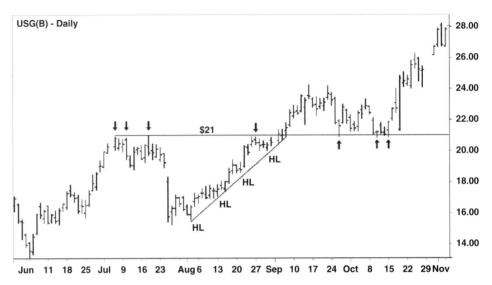

FIGURE 11.3   USG Forms an Ascending Triangle, Creating Multiple Buying Opportunities

After a short rally. USG retreated to the former resistance level of $21, which then became support (up arrows). On at least three occasions, USG bounced higher from support, giving traders numerous opportunities to get long before the stock finally rocketed higher.

Once again, measuring techniques can be used to determine a price objective after the breakout occurs. In this case, the measurement occurs from the widest point of the triangle. The measurement of the triangle can be somewhat subjective, since what constitutes the widest point depends upon where one believes the triangle originated.

In Figure 11.3, the low end of the triangle is approximately $15, while the resistance level is $21. This gives the triangle a height of $6. In order to obtain the target, add $6 to the former resistance (now support) area of $21 for a result of $27. That price target was achieved less than two months after the initial breakout, which was followed by numerous "second chance" entries.

Aggressive traders can buy the breakout, while a more conservative approach would be to go long after a daily bar or candle closes above resistance. Since the broken resistance level should now act as support, conservative traders can wait for pullback to the breakout area for a second chance at entering a long position.

As mentioned earlier, patterns are defined not only by their shape, but by the price action that precedes them. This is also true of the ascending triangle; many traders believe that their chances of success are enhanced when using the ascending triangle within an uptrend.

Bearish Descending Triangle Pattern

This is the inverted version of the ascending triangle; in this case, the bears demonstrate their superior firepower by pushing the price to a series of lower highs. Meanwhile, bulls can only form a horizontal support level, indicating a lower level of commitment than the bears.

The assumption here is that the passive bulls will eventually be overrun by the aggressive bears. This bearish pattern is considered more effective when it appears within an overall bearish trend, although this is not a requirement.

In Figure 11.4, the Dow Jones Transportation Average ($DJT) formed a series of lower highs during April and May of 2015. Bears were willing to sell at progressively lower levels (H-LH-LH). Meanwhile, bulls fought to maintain support at approximately 8,530 (dotted horizontal line), but were unable to push the index higher.

In late May, support was broken; soon afterward, the 8,530 area began to act as resistance (down arrows). This created numerous opportunities to short the transportation index, which finally plunged in mid-August.

Flags and Pennants

Imagine a person running up flights of stairs. He runs up five flights and is temporarily out of breath. So, he hunches over, breathing heavily for a few minutes, until he is ready to resume. Then he runs up five more flights of steps.

FIGURE 11.4 A Descending Triangle Forms in the Dow Jones Transportation Average ($DJT), Creating Multiple Selling Opportunities

In essence, this is what happens during flag and pennant patterns. The price makes a sharp directional move and then consolidates the move by "resting." The period of rest is frequently expressed in the form of shapes called "flags" and "pennants." The expectation is that after the flag or pennant is completed, the prior trend will resume.

Bull Flag Pattern

A bull flag pattern begins with a sharp, almost vertical bullish movement. This move indicates that the bulls are the dominant party. This initial bullish move is known as the "flagpole."

This initial thrust is followed by mild reversal, which slopes gently in the opposite direction. This second move indicates that the bears are unable to muster an equivalent response. The bear move forms a shape that is bounded by two parallel lines, resembling a flag.

Consider the implications of those two movements; the first move shows the bulls are firmly in charge, and the mildly bearish reaction to this move merely confirms this fact.

What is expected to happen next should come as no surprise. The dominant party, in this case the bulls, are expected to take control. As a result, the price is expected to continue moving higher.

How much higher? A measuring technique is used to determine the bull flag's price target. The first step is to measure the height of the flagpole. Then, if and when the price breaks out of the consolidation, traditional technical analysis assumes that a move of equal magnitude will occur.

Therefore, if the flagpole measures $2 in height, the assumption is that the price will move higher by another $2 if and when it breaks out of the consolidation. In a currency trade, a flagpole measuring 50 pips would generate a target of an additional 50 pips above the point of the breakout from the flag itself.

Figure 11.5 actually contains two examples of a bull flag pattern. In the first example, shares of PacWest Bancorp (PACW) thrust higher in late 2014, from a low of $37.63 on October 15 (letter A) to a high of $41.08 on October 21 (letter B). This initial thrust of $3.45 represents the flagpole.

PacWest then consolidated its gains, forming the flag itself. The low point of the flag is $39.75, the October 27 low (letter C). If we add $3.45 to the low point of $39.75, the resulting target price is $43.20, which was reached on November 3, 2014.

After reaching that target, another flag formed. The flagpole of the second formation was created by the move from $39.75 (letter C) to $43.33, the November 3 high. This gave the second flagpole a height of $3.58.

FIGURE 11.5 Several Bull Flags appear in the Chart of PacWest Bancorp (PACW)

The low point of the second flag is $42.20. Add the length of the flagpole ($3.58) to this figure to create a target of $45.78. That target was reached on November 7, 2014 (letter F).

Bull Pennant Pattern

The bull pennant pattern is similar to the bull flag pattern. Like the bull flag, it begins with a sharp thrust higher, followed by a mildly bearish consolidation. In this case, the consolidation is shaped differently from the flag; instead of two parallel lines, the consolidation resembles a small symmetrical triangle.

While the shape is slightly different, the meaning is unchanged—the bulls are firmly in charge here, and when given an opportunity to respond, the bears can do little about it. Once the price breaks out of the pennant, the bulls are expected to reassert their dominance.

Figure 11.6 shows a bull pennant formation in shares of Springleaf Holdings Inc. (LEAF). On February 20, 2015, Springleaf, a company that specialized in making subprime loans to consumers, jumped higher on above-average volume (letter A). The move was due to a rumor that the company was about to purchase OneMain Financial Holdings, the subprime consumer lending arm of investment giant Citigroup.

The February 20 move is similar to the "flagpole" found in a flag formation. The initial thrust runs from the February 20 low of $33.68 to the February 24 high of $40.56. This gives the flagpole a height of $6.88.

Over the following week, LEAF entered the consolidation phase of the pennant formation. Note how the two lines of the pennant converge, demonstrating a

FIGURE 11.6 Springleaf Holdings (LEAF) Explodes Out of a Bull Pennant

tightening range. Notice also the decline in volume during the consolidation period, which is considered normal in this situation (letter B).

Then on March 3, Citigroup officially announced it had agreed to sell OneMain Financial to Springleaf. The bull pennant pattern was successfully completed when LEAF made a dramatic move, gapping higher on extremely heavy volume on the day of the announcement (letter C).

Targets for the bull pennant are created in a similar manner as with the bull flag: first by measuring the initial thrust, and then adding that amount onto the consolidation.

As previously noted, the initial thrust is measured from $33.68 to $40.56, a move of $6.88. The vertex of the pennant is approximately $38.15. If we add $6.88 to that price, a target of $45.03 is created. That target was easily achieved, as the March 3 high was $52.48.

Bear Flag Pattern

The logic of the bull flag can also be applied to a bearish move. A bear flag pattern begins with a sharp thrust lower, indicating that the bears are aggressive. This initial thrust is the flagpole.

Given an opportunity to reply, the bulls can only manage a mild response, in the form of a gently rising consolidation bounded by two parallel lines. If and when the price breaks downward from the consolidation, a move equivalent to the size of the flagpole is anticipated.

Figure 11.7 provides an example of a bear flag in the currency market that occurred in October of 2015. After a rally, the euro/Great Britain pound (EURGBP) currency pair started trending lower on the 240-minute (four-hour) chart. This time frame is

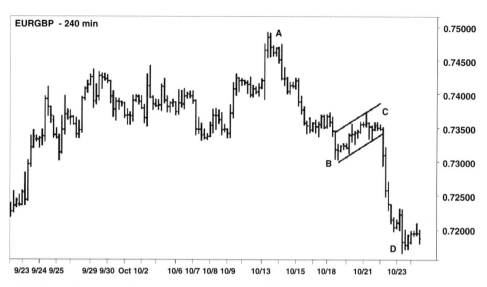

FIGURE 11.7 A Bear Flag Pattern Appears in the EURGBP Currency Pair

commonly associated with the currency markets, which are open 24 hours per day during the trading week.

First, the bears took charge as the EURGBP currency pair fell from approximately .7500 (point A) to .7300 (point B), a move of 200 pips. This was followed by a weak response from the bulls, causing EURGBP to climb to .7370 (point C).

According to standard measuring techniques, a break lower from the bear flag should generate an additional 200-pip move. If we subtract 200 pips from .7370, a target of .7170 is created (point D). That target was achieved on October 23.

The catalyst for the plunge in the euro, which was hard-hit across the board at the time, was a speech by European Central Bank Chief Mario Draghi. Mr. Draghi discussed the expansion of a stimulus program, causing stocks to rally and the euro to plunge.

Bear Pennant Pattern

The bear pennant is similar to the bear flag with one major difference—the shape of the consolidation after the initial move resembles a symmetrical triangle rather than a flag. Otherwise, the patterns are similar, as is the method used for determining a target price.

In Figure 11.8, a head and shoulders pattern is visible in shares of Procter & Gamble (PG) in late 2014. The neckline broke in spectacular fashion, creating a large gap down on January 27, 2015.

Consider that gap part of the move prior to the formation of the bear pennant. Even though it isn't visible on the chart, the gap represents a sharp thrust lower, similar to a flagpole.

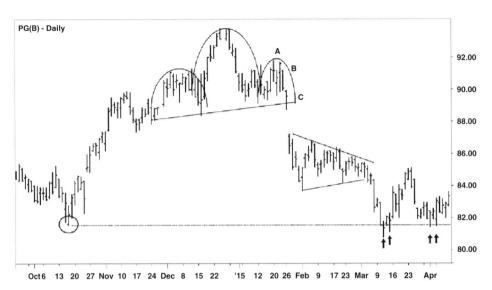

FIGURE 11.8   A Bear Pennant Follows a Head and Shoulders in Procter & Gamble (PG)

Procter & Gamble then consolidated its losses by forming a series of lower highs and higher lows. This pattern represents the consolidation portion of the pennant. Then in early March, Procter & Gamble broke down from the pennant, leading to another sharp move lower.

Where does the move prior to the consolidation begin? It is necessary to answer this question in order to measure the move, which in turn will allow us to create a target price. It's obvious that a major move occurred, but what price should mark its starting point?

After the neckline was broken, the price gapped down from just under $90. However, the two prior candles indicate that the price was already moving in that direction before the gap occurred.

There are three possible points from which we can measure the move prior to the formation of the consolidation:

1) From the height of the right shoulder, which is approximately $92 (point A).
2) From the second bar prior to the gap lower. As mentioned earlier, the last two bars prior to the gap indicate that the price was already moving lower. In this case, the measurement would begin from approximately $91 (point B).
3) From the start of the gap itself, which is approximately $89.50 (point C).

Also, notice how the price found support in October of 2014 after a throwback to $81.57 (circle, dotted horizontal line). Procter & Gamble bounced several times from that area after falling from the bear pennant. The stock rebounded from that level again on several other occasions in March and April of 2015 (arrows).

■ Wedges

Bullish Wedge

A bullish wedge, also referred to as a falling wedge, is a continuation pattern that slopes downward, in the opposite direction of a prior bullish trend. In this sense, it's similar to a bull flag pattern, in which the flag itself slopes in the opposite direction of the trend.

While the pattern contains a series of lower highs and lower lows, each subsequent low barely exceeds the previous low, causing a line drawn beneath those lows to slope gently lower. This contrasts with a line drawn above the lower highs, which forms a steeper slope.

The two resulting lines converge at an angle. As these lines draw nearer to each other, a move in the direction of the prior trend is anticipated.

In Figure 11.9, the PureFunds ISE Cyber Security ETF (HACK) is shown trending higher soon after its initial public offering. The ETF climbed to an all-time high of $27.62 in late December of 2014 (point H).

This was followed by a series of lower highs (LH) and lower lows (LL), with the highs falling at a more dramatic angle than the lows. As the two lines draw closer, HACK blasts out of the pattern on heavy volume. The move occurred soon after a series of widely publicized computer hacking scandals.

Bearish Wedge

A bearish wedge, also known as a rising wedge, is a continuation pattern move that slopes upward, in the opposite direction of a bearish trend. In this sense, it's similar

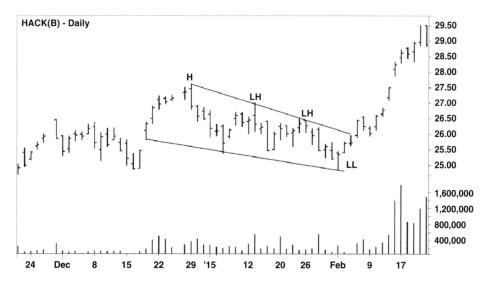

FIGURE 11.9 A Bullish Wedge Appears in HACK

to a bear flag pattern, in which the flag itself slopes in the opposite direction of the trend.

The pattern contains a series of higher highs and higher lows; the line drawn above the highs slopes gently higher, while the line drawn beneath the higher lows forms a steeper slope. As the two resulting lines converge, the price resumes its downward trend.

In Figure 11.10, the Australian dollar/Japanese yen currency pair (AUDJPY) is shown trending lower in January of 2015. On two separate occasions, a rising wedge forms, leading to a sharp sell-off in the direction of the predominant trend.

Bullish Rectangle

A bullish rectangle occurs when, after moving higher in an uptrend, the price forms a sideways consolidation, which is bounded by clear levels of support and resistance. The area of consolidation resembles a box or a rectangle.

In theory, this consolidation is similar to a symmetrical triangle. The main difference is, the converging trend lines of the symmetrical triangle are replaced by the parallel lines of the rectangle. As with the symmetrical triangle, it is assumed that the price is merely taking a breather before resuming its ascent.

For example, in Figure 11.11, the U.S. Dollar Index ($DXY) has formed an uptrend on the hourly chart. The index then formed a rectangular sideways consolidation, featuring clearly defined horizontal support and resistance lines. Eventually, the dollar index broke out of the rectangle and resumed its uptrend.

Rectangles can occur in a variety of time frames. In Figure 11.12, shares of Cheesecake Factory (CAKE) rallied for several years before forming a large

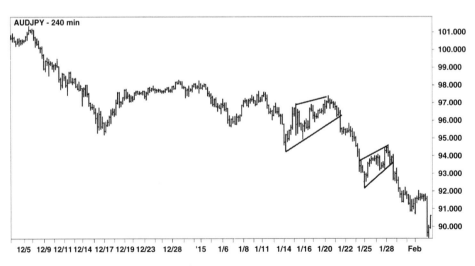

FIGURE 11.10 Several Bearish Wedges Appear in AUDJPY

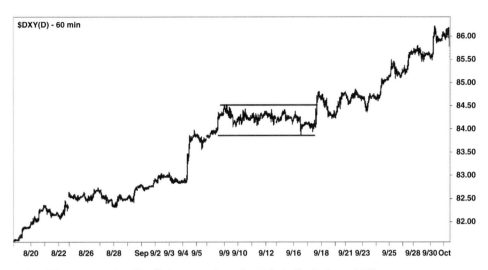

FIGURE 11.11   A Small Bullish Rectangle in the U.S. Dollar Index ($DXY)

FIGURE 11.12   A Large Bullish Rectangle Forms in Shares of the Cheesecake Factory (CAKE)

rectangle pattern. After consolidating for over a year, CAKE exited out of the top of the pattern, just as 2014 drew to a close.

The stock then climbed for one month, reaching an all-time high before the rally stalled. After a brief retreat, CAKE resumed its rally to reach another all-time high.

Can the support and resistance levels that border the rectangle be used as entry and exit points? While these levels can be used in this way, one should take note of the size of the pattern and the length of time involved in its creation.

When playing a bounce off of support or resistance, small, tight rectangle consolidations present a smaller potential reward than large rectangles. Placing trades within small consolidations can be dangerous because, at some point, the price is likely to break out.

Take note again of Figure 11.11, which features the U.S. Dollar Index. This rectangle lasted for less than two weeks; during that time, the price remained in a tight range, making it less than ideal for range bound trading.

The rectangle pattern that occurred on Cheesecake Factory's chart in Figure 11.12 was much broader and longer in duration, making it a better candidate for placing trades within the pattern.

Also, keep in mind that a trader who sells at resistance within an uptrend is fighting against that trend, and is likely to get smoked if the trend reestablishes itself. In an uptrend, it would be perfectly acceptable to buy at support within the consolidation, as this entry would be in harmony with the trend. Likewise, it would be acceptable to sell short at resistance within the rectangle if the pattern appears in an established downtrend.

Bearish Rectangle

A bearish rectangle occurs when the price forms a sideways consolidation after trending lower. The consolidation area is bounded by clear levels of support and resistance, and resembles a box or a rectangle. This consolidation merely represents a pause in the action prior to the resumption of the downtrend.

In Figure 11.13, shares of Valeant Pharmaceutical International (VRX) fell sharply in September of 2015, amid accusations that the company engaged in deceptive accounting practices (point A). During the first three weeks of October, the stock

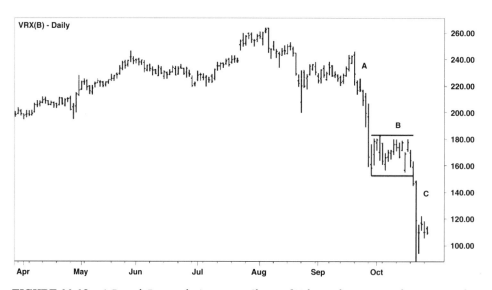

FIGURE 11.13 A Bearish Rectangle Appears in Shares of Valeant Pharmaceutical International (VRX)

consolidated its losses into a rectangle pattern (point B). On October 20, the stock broke out of the lower boundary of the triangle, and on October 21, the stock plunged again (point C). At the time of this writing, it was unknown if the accusations were true or false.

■ Final Thoughts on Continuation Patterns

Continuation patterns indicate a high degree of likelihood that the price will continue moving in its current direction. When it comes to price patterns, location is of key importance. It could be said that a chart pattern is defined not only by its shape, but by the price action that precedes it. Triangles, flags, and pennants are common examples of continuation patterns.

CHAPTER 12

Additional Chart Patterns

So far, we've covered reversal chart patterns and continuation chart patterns. However, there are some technical patterns that don't fit easily into either category, yet are just as important. The following technical patterns could be described as possessing some of the qualities of both reversal and continuation patterns.

■ The Cup with Handle Formation

What is the "cup with handle" formation? It's a bullish pattern that was identified by William O'Neal and popularized in his 1988 publication *How to Make Money in Stocks*. The book was often given as a gift to subscribers of O'Neal's *Investors' Business Daily* (also known as *IBD*).

IBD started as a popular daily newspaper that featured its own brand of analysis along with market news and other features. In the days before the Internet gained popularity, professionals who favored fundamentals usually had a copy of *The Wall Street Journal* on their desks, while technically oriented pros favored *IBD*.

As the name implies, the cup with handle pattern consists of two separate parts: the cup and the handle. The cup resembles a single rounded bottom, but with a caveat. Unlike a double bottom or a triple bottom, it is not required that the cup with handle pattern appear in a downtrend.

The cup's rounded bottom is supposed to indicate a "shaking out" process. It gives bears and uncommitted longs an opportunity to sell the stock. When the process of eliminating these "weak hands" has been completed, the price is expected to climb back to the starting point of the cup, completing the first portion of the pattern.

The handle is simply an "echo" of the cup. It often resembles a smaller version of the cup itself. The handle represents one last chance to shake out the weak hands before the stock begins to move higher.

Here are some general guidelines for the cup with handle pattern:

The cup should be at least seven weeks in duration. There is no time limit on how long the cup can be.
Ideally, the handle retracement is equal to just 15 to 25 percent of the depth of the cup.
The process of forming the handle should take at least five days.
The breakout from the handle should occur on high volume.
The buy point is ten cents above the highest point of the handle.

Again, these are some general guidelines. Please refer to Mr. O'Neal's work for a complete set of rules.

Figure 12.1 shows an example of a cup with handle pattern. Shares of biotech company Celgene (CELG) formed a cup starting in February of 2014 (letter A). By early June, the cup was complete (letter B).

This was followed by a tightly formed handle, which did not enter deeply into the range of the cup (letter C). In mid-June of 2014, Celgene blasted out of the formation on high volume (circled). The stock quickly shot to $90, a new all-time high, and reached $140 by the following year.

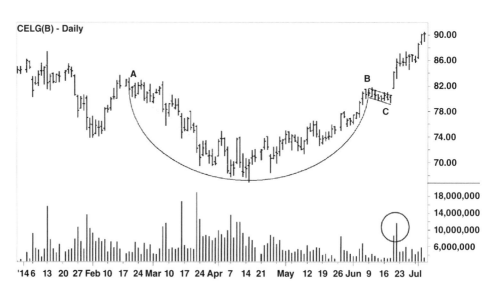

FIGURE 12.1   A Cup with Handle Pattern in Celgene Corp. (CELG)

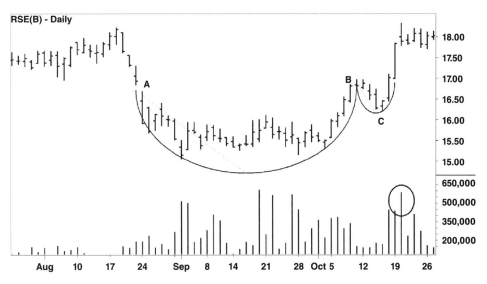

FIGURE 12.2 A Cup with Handle Formation in Rouse Properties (RSE)

Another example of the cup with handle pattern is demonstrated in Figure 12.2. After a decline in August of 2015, shares of Rouse Properties Inc. (RSE) began to form a cup (letter A). By early October, the cup was completed (letter B). RSE then formed a handle that resembles a smaller version of the cup (letter C). Then in mid-October, Rouse Properties shot out of the handle and raced higher on heavy volume (circled).

■ Fractal Cup with Handle

In late November of 2013, a cup with handle pattern was noticed on the daily chart of Hewlett-Packard Co. (HPQ). Upon first glance, it appeared to be a typical example of the pattern.

As Figure 12.3 indicates, the cup portion of the pattern was about three months in duration. The handle appeared to equal less than one-third of the depth of the cup. The price had recently shot out of the handle, on November 27, 2013 (arrow).

Zooming out on the daily chart, it became apparent that this was no ordinary cup with handle. The cup itself was the handle of a larger cup that had started forming in early 2012. It was a cup with handle pattern within a larger cup with handle pattern—a fractal cup with handle, as depicted in Figure 12.4.

This unusual formation was presented to my colleague at *Real Money Pro,* the legendary hedge fund manager and financial TV host Jim Cramer.

Mr. Cramer's work is oriented toward fundamental analysis, and he noted that the fundamentals of the company seemed quite promising. Jim decided to feature

FIGURE 12.3   A Cup with Handle in Shares of Hewlett-Packard (HPQ)

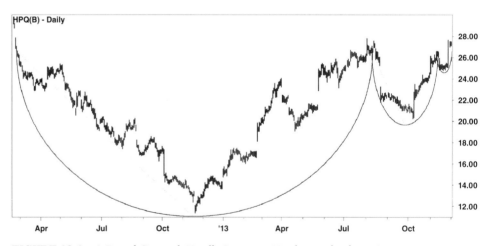

FIGURE 12.4   A Fractal Cup with Handle Pattern in Hewlett-Packard (HPQ)

Hewlett-Packard on the technical analysis segment of his popular TV show, *Mad Money with Jim Cramer*, on December 3, 2013.

Keep in mind that Hewlett-Packard had already risen sharply that year. However, the stock had performed poorly in the three previous years, falling 18.27% in 2010, 38.81% in 2011, and 44.68% in 2012. Apple's products were dominating the computer space, driving competitors like Hewlett-Packard to their knees.

Then a sharp turnaround in 2013 caused HPQ to rise by over 96%. How could anyone possibly recommend a stock that had already nearly doubled in price?

I tuned in to Mr. Cramer's show and awaited *Off the Charts*, a regular segment that focuses on technical analysis. Jim pulled up the fractal cup and handle chart and highlighted my analysis. He gushed over the stock's inexpensive valuation; at the time HPQ traded at just 7✕ the following year's anticipated earnings. Jim finished with a flourish:

> "The charts, as interpreted by Ed Ponsi, and the fundamentals, as interpreted by me, are in total agreement. Hewlett-Packard appears to be going higher. I think it's a screaming buy, buy, buy!"

The following day, Hewlett Packard gapped higher, which is not unusual when a stock is featured in a positive light on a national television program. Once the excitement faded, the stock did too, drifting back to the vicinity of the breakout point.

The stock drifted sideways into the December holidays. Then, at the start of 2014, Hewlett-Packard took off like a rocket. Over the next 12 months, the tech giant gained 43.42%, outpacing the indices.

In retrospect, both the technicals and the fundamentals were right on the money. Figure 12.5 depicts a weekly view of Hewlett-Packard's fractal cup with handle, along with the impressive rally that followed.

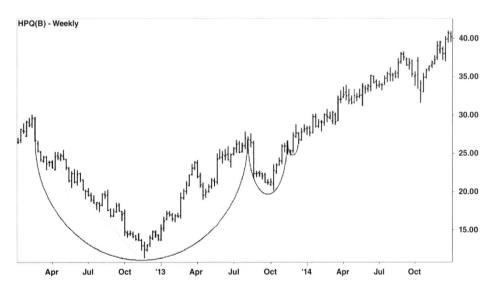

FIGURE 12.5   The Aftermath of a Fractal Cup with Handle in Hewlett-Packard (HPQ)

■ Respect Both Technical and Fundamental Analysis

Trading legend Jim Cramer could have easily dismissed my analysis of Hewlett-Packard, since he's a fundamental analyst. Instead, he kept an open mind. Even though he's not a technical analyst, he respected the technicals and used them in conjunction with his own analysis.

In much the same way, we as technical analysts should also respect fundamental analysis. Even though we believe that the chart contains all of the necessary information, I've learned over the years that some of the best traders pay close attention to any edge they can acquire, be it technical, fundamental, or something unrelated to either discipline.

Some of the best trades I've ever witnessed came as a result of a combination of technical analysis and fundamental analysis. The two disciplines should not be viewed as unrelated; instead, I like to think of technical analysis and fundamental analysis as two separate sides of the same coin.

■ The Broadening Formation

Technical analysis is useful, but it isn't perfect. Why is it that there are no perfect patterns or techniques?

One reason is that markets change. Even if you could create the perfect trading system, one that would've been successful in the past, markets are in a constant state of flux. Because of this, tactics that worked in the past sometimes become ineffective, and strategies that failed in the recent past sometimes regain their effectiveness.

In addition, not all patterns are helpful or useful. One technical formation in particular depicts a market that is difficult to trade, particularly if you are a trend follower. This pattern is known as the "broadening formation."

The broadening formation consists of a series of higher highs and lower lows, and presents a very frustrating scenario for trend traders. An example of this pattern appears in Figure 12.6, which features the daily chart of the U.S. Dollar Index ($DXY) during a four-month span in 2013.

In Figure 12.6, the U.S. dollar broke out to a new high, then broke to a new low, then reversed to form a higher high, and then reversed again to form a lower low, before reversing yet again to create another higher high.

The pattern resulting from this activity is called a broadening formation, and is also known as a megaphone pattern. For traders who follow trends, this pattern is a nightmare.

FIGURE 12.6 A Broadening Formation in the U.S. Dollar Index ($INX)

Currency traders who were following a breakout system most likely went long when the price broke to new highs, and then flipped to a short position when the price turned and broke to new lows. Then the pattern repeated itself. If the trader were following a strict, nondiscretionary system, he or she would've taken every entry, both long and short.

Using such a strategy on the broadening formation in Figure 12.6 would've resulted in a series of losses. Perhaps it is a coincidence, but several major currency hedge funds went out of business at the end of 2013.

For example, FX Concepts was a $14 billion currency hedge fund, the largest of its kind in its day. The fund ran into a difficult stretch of trading in 2013. By the end of that year, FX Concepts had closed its doors, citing a lack of assets.

Soon thereafter, a company named QFS Asset Management also closed its currency hedge fund.

Hedge funds are notoriously secretive. While it's not known what led to the demise of several major currency hedge funds in 2013, it is true that the U.S. dollar, as the world's dominant reserve currency, is a component of the majority of currency trades.

Is it possible that currency hedge fund traders, many of whom adhere to a trend-following philosophy, were undone by the broadening formation in the U.S. Dollar Index shown in Figure 12.6?

If successfully identified, a broadening formation can be traded via a "reversion to the mean strategy." This simply means that instead of attempting to trade with the trend, a trader "fades," or trades against, strong moves.

Or, we can simply leave the broadening formation alone, which is exactly what many traders choose to do.

■ Final Thoughts on Additional Chart Patterns

There are some chart patterns that are difficult to classify. Some of these patterns contain elements of both reversal patterns and continuation patterns, while others do not fall clearly into either category. In spite of this, there are several useful patterns that can be described as a neither reversal nor a continuation pattern.

PART IV

CANDLESTICK PATTERNS

CHAPTER 13

Candlestick Charting Patterns

Candlestick charts have exploded in popularity in recent years. They contain the opening, high, low, and closing prices of a given period of time, just as a bar chart does, but they also contain something more—a window into the emotions of the participants involved.

Not every candlestick that appears on a chart has a deep meaning, but the shapes and patterns that they form, both individually and collectively, often tell a useful story. It is a story about price and about the emotions and reactions that changes in prices tend to generate among traders.

While prices can be capricious and difficult to forecast, human nature is somewhat more predictable. We all understand the feelings associated with winning and losing. Candlestick charts reveal these emotions as they are shared by market participants, more clearly than any other charting technique.

We can divide candlestick patterns into three categories:

1. Those that suggest a reversal of the current price direction
2. Those that suggest a continuation of the current price direction
3. Those that indicate indecision on the part of market participants

Reversal patterns tend to be the most dramatic, conspicuous, and useful of these formations, so we'll begin there.

◼ Candlestick Reversal Patterns

In trading, there has always been a fascination with getting in and out at the best possible price. Traders love to brag that they "printed the bottom" when buying, meaning that they purchased at the lowest price possible. Less fortunate market players may bemoan the fact that they "top-ticked" a trade, meaning that their purchase occurred at the highest possible price.

While luck, or the lack of it, does play a role in catching extreme price points, certain candlestick patterns provide useful indications that a stock, currency, or index has peaked or bottomed. Reversal candlestick patterns reveal the "pressure points" that cause participants to turn from bear to bull, or vice versa.

For information on the terminology of candlesticks ("real body," "wicks," etc.), please review Chapter 5, Common Types of Charts.

The Hammer Pattern

The hammer is a bullish reversal candlestick pattern. It is a single-candle pattern, consisting of a small real body that rests on top of a long wick. As a rule of thumb, the hammer's lower wick should be at least twice as long as its body. There should be no upper wick on top of the body, although a small upper wick is considered acceptable. The color shading of the real body is unimportant; it can be either white or black.

When analyzing the hammer pattern, the most important factors are its location and the intensity of the move that preceded its formation. A hammer that forms after a sharp, sustained bearish move is best suited to usher in a bullish reversal. Conversely, a hammer that follows a weak downward move is not expected to generate a sharp move higher.

In Figure 13.1, we see a hammer pattern (circled) on the weekly chart of the iShares Dow Jones U.S. ETF (IYY). The pattern occurs on the weekly chart after a significant drop in price, and marks a major turning point on the chart.

What emotions occur within a hammer pattern? Let's assume that the price has been declining for days, as shown in Figure 13.1. The bears are having their way. At one point during the formation of the hammer, the price reached the bottom of the wick; this tells us that the bears were winning yet again. Imagine how good it must have felt to be a bear as the price fell to a new low.

Then something dramatic happened. The price turned and began to rally sharply. Imagine the disappointment of the bears who sold during the creation of the wick, only to have the price turn against them with a vengeance.

Imagine the pain of someone who sold short at the bottom of the wick, only to watch the price reverse. There is no question that this trader lost money; it's only a matter of how much.

Even traders who have been short for days are now watching their gains erode, and wondering if they too should run for cover. The hammer creates a wave a negative emotion among the once-happy bears.

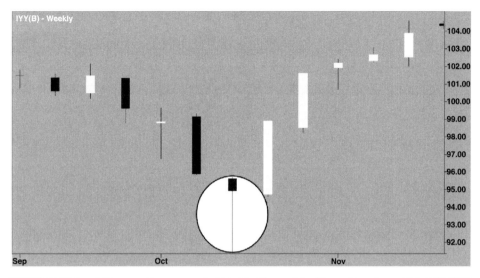

FIGURE 13.1 A Hammer Pattern on the Weekly Chart of the iShares Dow Jones U.S. ETF (IYY)

Pay special attention to the length of the wick; hammers that possess long wicks are indicative of sharp and violent reversals. The length of the wick could be considered a measurement of the emotion that the move itself generates.

When you see a hammer pattern, imagine someone placing his or her hand on a hot stove and getting burned: the longer the wick of the hammer, the hotter the stove.

If you've ever placed your hand on a hot stove and gotten burned, what is the one thing that you are unlikely to do immediately afterward? The thing that you are least likely to do is to put your hand back on that burning stove again.

When you see the hammer pattern, you know that sellers were burned. You know that the least likely thing that those sellers will do is to sell again, and risk getting burned once more.

By indicating that a group of sellers has been removed from the equation, the hammer pattern tells us that the path of least resistance is higher.

A Matter of Degree

Not all hammer patterns are created equal; in fact, this is true of most candlestick patterns. We shouldn't place equal emphasis on two hammers that are likely to generate two different levels of response. Let's take a look at two instances where a hammer marked a bottom to illustrate this point.

Figure 13.2 depicts the daily movement of the S&P 500 during September and October of 2014. Note that the hammer pattern (circled) is preceded by a very sharp move lower, which creates a setup for an equally sharp reversal.

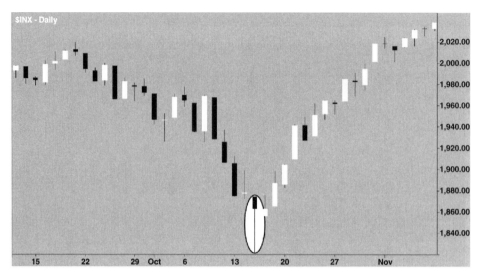

FIGURE 13.2   A Hammer Pattern on the Daily Chart of the S&P 500 Index ($INX)

Note also how the bearish black candles that precede the hammer are long and close at or near their lows. This indicates that the bears were firmly in control. The wick of the hammer itself is very long, which informs us that a dramatic intraday reversal has occurred.

Based on these factors, the odds of a sharp reversal were very high, and that's exactly what occurred. Figure 13.2 provides an almost ideal example of what traders want to see when they find a hammer pattern.

Compare the hammer in Figure 13.2 to those found in Figure 13.3, which depicts two hammers (circled) in the S&P 500 daily chart in September of 2011. Both of the hammers in Figure 13.3 led to rallies. However, the price action that preceded each of those hammers was mild. Therefore, it should come as no surprise that the ensuing rallies were also mild in nature.

During the formation of those two hammers, the price remained within a previously established trading range. There was no violent upheaval, and therefore there was no sharp swing in the emotions or the expectations of the market participants.

Therefore, it should come as no surprise that the two hammers in Figure 13.3 failed to generate significant market movement. This comparison demonstrates why we should always view candlestick patterns within the context of their surroundings.

Final Thought on Hammers

In Figure 13.3, one of the hammers has a black body, and one has a white body. The color shading of the body of a hammer pattern can be either color. However, some

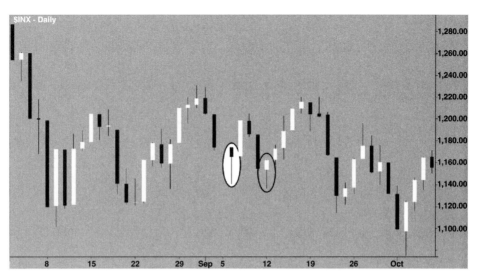

FIGURE 13.3   Two Small Hammers Lead to Minor Rallies in the S&P 500 Index ($INX)

traders express a preference for a hammer with a white body, because this indicates that the candle closed at or near its high.

Bullish candles that close at or near the high of the session hint at continuation. If a bullish candle closes at or near its high, traders are likely to believe that the move will continue, since buyers have shown no sign of relenting.

If buyers had chosen to take profits, the selling would've pushed the price beneath its highs. The fact that buyers don't wish to take profits means they believe the price is headed higher.

Shooting Star Pattern

Nearly every bullish candlestick pattern has a mirror-image bearish version. If the hammer indicates a bullish reversal when it appears in a downtrend, then it must have a counterpart that signals a bearish reversal when it appears in an uptrend. That candlestick pattern is called a "shooting star."

A shooting star is simply the bearish version of the hammer pattern. It consists of a long wick on top of a small real body. The shading of the real body is considered insignificant. Figure 13.4 depicts a shooting star pattern on the weekly chart of Merck & Co. (MRK).

The shooting star only has meaning when it appears in an uptrend. Since the shooting star is essentially the opposite of a hammer, this candlestick indicates that the bulls have suffered a reversal: the longer the wick on top of the shooting star, the greater the amount of pain felt by the bulls.

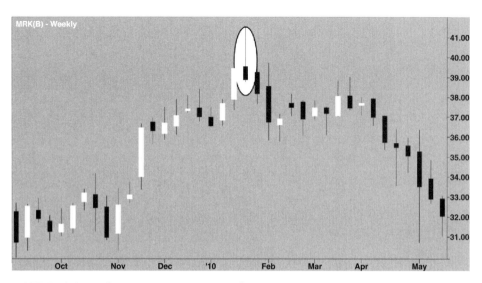

FIGURE 13.4   A Shooting Star Pattern in Merck & Co. (MRK)

With the bulls in retreat, time is likely to pass before they decide to lower their horns and charge again. With a contingent of bulls now removed from the equation, the shooting star tells us that the path of least resistance is lower.

Final Thought on Shooting Stars

The color shading of the real body of a shooting star pattern can be either white or black. However, some traders express a preference for a shooting star with a black body, because this indicates that the candle closed at or near its low.

Bearish candles that close at or near the low of the session hint at continuation. If a bearish candle closes at or near its low, traders are likely to believe that the move will continue, since sellers have shown no sign of relenting.

If sellers had chosen to take profits, their buying would've pushed the price above its lows. The fact that sellers didn't wish to take profits means they believe the price is headed lower.

Hanging Man Pattern

Without proper context, the shape of the hammer loses its meaning. In fact, the very same shape that comprises the bullish hammer pattern is considered bearish when it appears in an uptrend.

When the pattern forms under these circumstances, it is known as a "hanging man" pattern. As with the hammer, the hanging man consists of a small real body located on top of a long wick. There should be little or no wick on top of the real body, and the color shade of the body is considered unimportant.

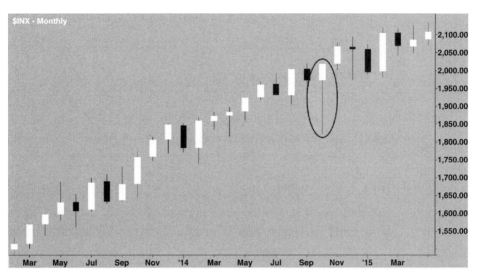

FIGURE 13.5 A Failed Hanging Man Pattern on the Monthly Chart of the S&P 500 Index ($INX)

Figure 13.5 provides an example of a hanging man pattern on the monthly chart of the S&P 500 in October of 2014. In this case, the market ignored the bearish pattern and continued moving higher.

The hanging man pattern is considered a sign of trouble for the bulls. The uptrend remains intact, but the appearance of a strong bearish contingent, which has the ability to push the price to the bottom of the wick, means that the bulls could soon encounter significant resistance.

Questioning the Assumption behind the Hanging Man Pattern

While the hanging man is considered bearish, there are those who have questioned that assumption. Consider what transpired in Figure 13.5; prior to the formation of the hanging man, the market was in full rally mode. Bulls were having their way with the market.

Then, during the formation of the hanging man candle, a significant sell-off occurred, and the price fell to the bottom of the wick. The bears were gaining the upper hand. However, the bears' victory proved to be short-lived, as it was followed by a sharp and vicious reversal.

Any bearish trader who sold short during the formation of that wick found their gains quickly ripped away. For the bears, it was a fleeting victory, followed by a resounding defeat. This would seem to have the effect of discouraging, rather than encouraging, bearish traders.

The hanging man did reveal the existence of a contingent of bears, as well as the fact that they were willing to take action. However, the events that transpired by the completion of the pattern would seem to favor the bulls, according to some observers.

Inverted Hammer Pattern

Just as the shooting star is the bearish opposite of a hammer pattern, the inverted hammer is the bullish counterpart of the hanging man pattern. An inverted hammer looks exactly like a shooting star; the only difference is its location. While a shooting star is significant when it appears in an uptrend, an inverted hammer is considered meaningful when it occurs in a downtrend.

As shown in Figure 13.6, a steep drop in shares of Tesla Motors (TSLA) led to the formation of an inverted hammer pattern in May of 2014. The candle marked a short-term bottom, as it was followed by a rally that recaptured most of the territory lost during the previous sell-off.

The inverted hammer is considered to be a bullish pattern for the same reasons that the hanging man pattern is considered to be bearish. Therefore, as with the hanging man, there will be those who question the assumptions attached to this pattern.

Bullish Engulfing

Bullish engulfing is a two-candle bullish reversal pattern. It consists of a black candle followed by a white candle that opens below the low of the black candle. The white candle should have both a lower low and a higher high than the black candle that preceded it. It completely "engulfs" the previous candle, negating the price action of that candle.

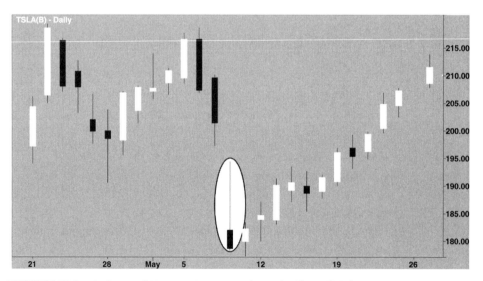

FIGURE 13.6 An Inverted Hammer Pattern on the Daily Chart of Tesla Motors (TSLA)

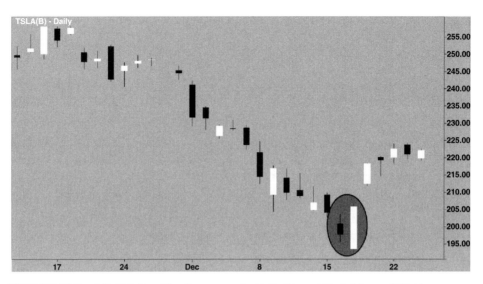

FIGURE 13.7 A Bullish Engulfing Pattern on the Daily Chart of Tesla Motors (TSLA)

Bullish engulfing is also known as an "outside" candle pattern. It is only considered significant when it appears in a downtrend.

An example of bullish engulfing appears in Figure 13.7. Shares of Tesla Motors (TSLA) were caught in a downtrend in late 2014. The downtrend was halted when a bullish engulfing pattern appeared.

A bullish engulfing pattern essentially contains the same price action as a hammer with a white body. The main difference is that the price action that occurs in the hammer, a single candle pattern, is spread out over two candles.

The psychology involved in a bullish engulfing pattern is similar to that of a hammer. All seems well for the bears, who are having their way with the market. Then the downtrend is disrupted by a white candle, which completely engulfs the previous black candle.

Once the white candle has been completed, every short position that was taken during the previous black candle is now facing a loss. Because of this, some shorts may consider covering their losing positions, which requires that they buy. The resulting buying pressure helps push the price higher.

Bearish Engulfing

Bearish engulfing is a two-candle bearish reversal pattern. It consists of a white candle followed by a black candle. The black candle should gap higher to open above the high of the white candle. It should also have both a higher high and a lower low than the candle that preceded it. In other words, the black candle completely "engulfs" the white candle.

Just as with bullish engulfing, this is known as an "outside" candle pattern. Bearish engulfing is only considered significant when it appears in an uptrend.

FIGURE 13.8 Two Bearish Engulfing Patterns on the Weekly Chart of Sonic Corp. (SONC)

In Figure 13.8, shares of fast-food restaurant Sonic Corp. (SONC) rallied sharply from late 2014 through early 2015. The stock peaked in March of 2015, after forming a bearish engulfing pattern on its weekly chart (point A). After a sell-off, the stock attempted to rally again. Then a second bearish engulfing pattern formed, leading to a deeper sell-off (point B).

A bearish engulfing pattern is essentially the same as a shooting star pattern with a black body. The main difference is that the price action contained in the shooting star, a single candle pattern, is spread out over two candles.

The psychology involved in this pattern is also similar to that of a shooting star. All seems well for the bulls, who are enjoying an uptrend. Then the trend is disrupted by a black candle, which completely engulfs the previous white candle.

Once the black candle has been completed, every long position that was taken during the previous white candle is now faced with a loss. Many of these losing traders may exit their long positions by selling, which lends additional strength to the bearish reversal.

Piercing Line

The piercing line pattern is a two-candle bullish reversal pattern. It consists of a black candle followed by a white candle. The piercing line pattern is only considered significant when it appears in a downtrend.

The white candle should open below the low of the previous candle, just like bullish engulfing. It should also close above the midpoint of the body of the candle

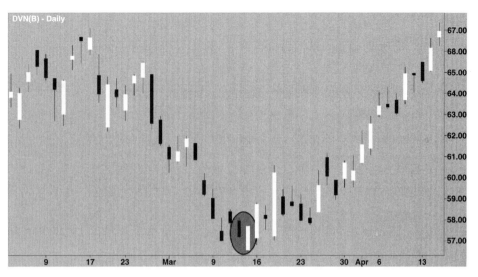

FIGURE 13.9   A Piercing Line Pattern Forms on the Daily Chart of Devon Energy (DVN)

that preceded it, but not above its high. In other words, it doesn't completely "engulf" the previous candle.

Figure 13.9 provides an example of the piercing line pattern. Devon Energy (DVN) was in a downtrend in late February/early March of 2015. Then a piercing line pattern formed in mid-March (circled), putting a halt to the stock's decline and igniting a rally.

A piercing line pattern is essentially the same as a hammer with a black body. The main difference is that the activity contained in the hammer, a single candle pattern, is spread out over two candles.

The psychology of the piercing line pattern is slightly different from bullish engulfing, because not every trader who sold short during the first candle is holding a loss. Those traders who sold short on the upper part of the black candle—the portion of the first candle above the high of the second candle—are still holding profitable positions.

Therefore, the urgency for short covering that is created by a piercing line pattern is less intense than the urgency created by a bullish engulfing pattern.

Dark Cloud Cover

The dark cloud cover pattern is a two-candle bearish reversal pattern. It consists of a white candle followed by a black candle. The black candle should open above the high of the white candle that preceded it. The dark cloud cover pattern is only considered significant when it appears in an uptrend.

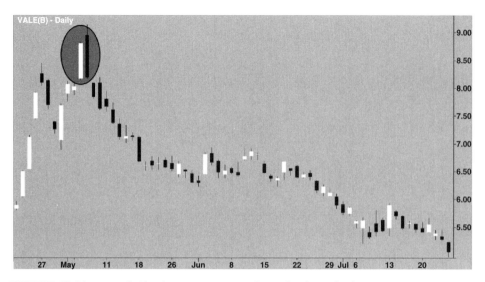

FIGURE 13.10 A Dark Cloud Cover Pattern on the Daily Chart of Vale S.A. (VALE)

The second candle of the pattern should close below the midpoint of the body of the candle that preceded it. Because it fails to close beneath the low of the first candle, it doesn't completely engulf the previous candle.

A dark cloud cover pattern is essentially the same as a shooting star with a white body. The main difference is that the activity contained in the shooting star, a single candle pattern, is spread out over two candles.

Figure 13.10 depicts a dark cloud cover pattern in shares of Brazilian mining company VALE S.A. (VALE).

The psychology of the dark cloud cover pattern is slightly different from bearish engulfing, because not every trader who went long during the first candle of the pattern is holding a loss. Those traders who went long on the lower part of the white candle—the portion of the first candle below the close of the second candle—are still holding profitable positions.

Therefore, the urgency for exiting long positions that is created by a dark cloud cover pattern is less intense than the urgency created by a bearish engulfing pattern.

Morning Star Pattern

The morning star is a reversal pattern that is effective in a downtrend. It consists of three candles. It begins with a long bearish candle, followed by a small-bodied candle, which is in turn followed by a long bullish candle.

The second candle should close beneath the low of the first candle in the pattern. The small body of the second candle represents indecision at a major turning point. If the second candle is a "doji" – a small candle in which the opening and closing prices are virtually the same – the pattern is referred to as a morning doji star.

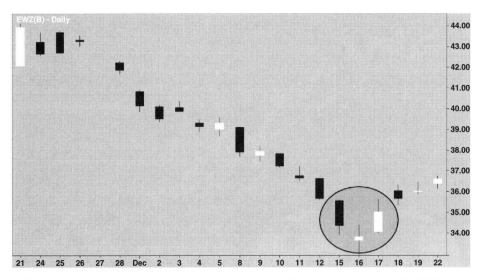

FIGURE 13.11 A Morning Star Pattern in the iShares MSCI Brazilian Capped ETF (EWZ)

The third candle of the morning star pattern should close above the midpoint of the first candle. When this happens, the three candles together simulate the piercing line pattern.

The morning star pattern is considered more effective if the third candle closes above the high of the first candle. When this occurs, the effect of the pattern is similar to a bullish engulfing pattern.

Figure 13.11 depicts a morning star pattern in the iShares MSCI Brazilian Capped ETF (EWZ).

Bullish Abandoned Baby

A bullish abandoned baby pattern is similar to a morning star with a few exceptions. The price should gap from the first candle to the second, and again from the second candle to the third. The wicks or shadows of the second candle should not overlap any portion of the first or third candles.

Figure 13.12 shows a bullish abandoned baby pattern in the U.S. Oil Fund ETF (USO). Unlike Figure 13.11, no portion of the three candles within the pattern overlap.

Evening Star Pattern

The evening star is a reversal pattern that is effective in an uptrend. It consists of three candles. It begins with a long bullish candle, followed by a small-bodied candle, which is in turn followed by a long bearish candle.

The second candle should close above the high of the first candle in the pattern. The small body of the second candle represents indecision at a major turning

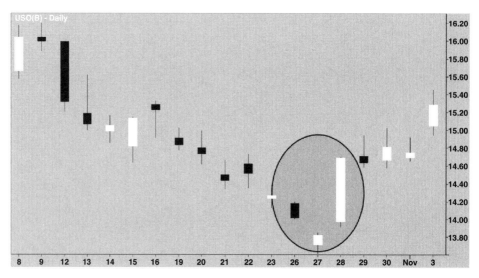

FIGURE 13.12 A Bullish Abandoned Baby Pattern in the U.S. Oil Fund ETF (USO)

point. If the second candle is a doji star, the pattern is referred to as an evening doji star.

The third candle of the evening star pattern should close below the midpoint of the first candle. When this happens, the three candles together simulate the dark cloud cover pattern. The evening star pattern is considered more effective if the third candle closes below the low of the first candle. In this case, the pattern would be similar to a bearish engulfing pattern.

Figure 13.13 depicts an evening star pattern in shares of Wells Fargo (WFC).

Bearish Abandoned Baby

A bearish abandoned baby pattern is similar to an evening star with a few exceptions. The price should gap from the first candle to the second, and again from the second candle to the third. The wicks or shadows of the second candle should not overlap any portion of the first or third candles.

Figure 13.14 shows a bearish abandoned baby pattern in the ProShares Ultrashort Bloomberg Crude Oil ETF (SCO). Unlike Figure 13.13, no portion of the second candle overlaps the first or third candles.

Three White Soldiers Pattern

This is a bullish reversal pattern that appears in a downtrend. After a series of bearish candles, three consecutive long bullish candles form. Each of the three bullish candles opens above the previous candle's low, usually in the middle of the previous candle's range, and closes above the previous candle's high. This indicates that the trend has changed and the bulls have now assumed control.

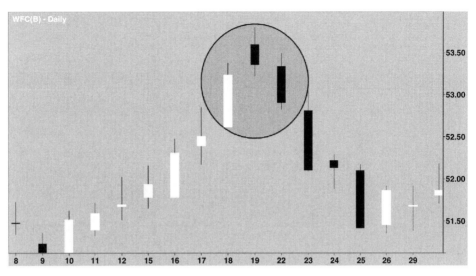

FIGURE 13.13   An Evening Star Pattern in Shares of Wells Fargo (WFC)

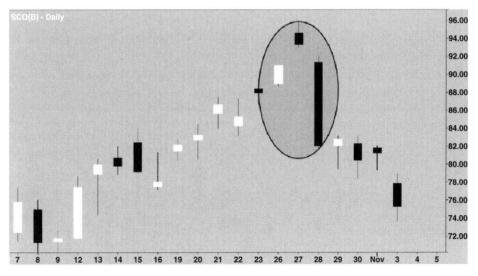

FIGURE 13.14   A Bearish Abandoned Baby Pattern in the ProShares Ultrashort Bloomberg Crude Oil ETF (SCO)

Figure 13.15 depicts a three white soldiers pattern in shares of Buffalo Wild Wings (BWLD) that led to a significant rally in the stock.

Three Black Crows Pattern

This is a bearish reversal pattern that appears in an uptrend. After a series of bullish candles, three consecutive long bearish candles form. Each of the three bearish

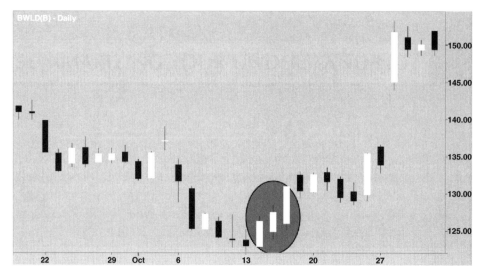

FIGURE 13.15   A Three White Soldiers Pattern Appears in Shares of Buffalo Wild Wings (BWLD)

candles opens below the previous candle's high and closes beneath the previous candle's low. This indicates that the trend has changed and the bears have now gained control.

Figure 13.16 depicts a three black crows pattern in the daily chart of Yelp Inc. (YELP). The pattern ignited a significant sell-off in the stock.

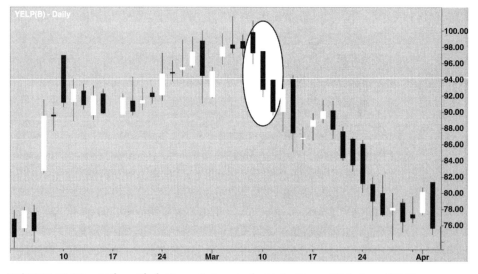

FIGURE 13.16   A Three Black Crows Pattern in the Daily Chart of Yelp Inc. (YELP)

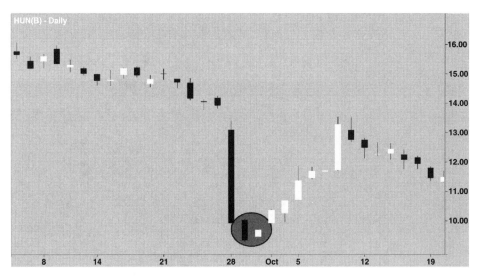

FIGURE 13.17 A Bullish Harami Pattern on the Daily Chart of Huntsman Corporation (HUN)

Bullish Harami Pattern

The bullish harami is a two-candle reversal pattern that appears in a downtrend. The first candle is a long bearish candle. This is followed by a small-bodied candle that gaps higher into the mid-range of the first candle. The second candle fits easily within the range of the first candle.

Figure 13.17 provides an example of a bullish harami pattern. Shares of Huntsman Corporation (HUN) sold off sharply in September of 2015. The stock found its bottom when a bullish harami formed on September 29 and 30, leading to a significant reversal.

Bearish Harami Pattern

The bearish harami is a two-candle reversal pattern that appears in an uptrend. The first candle is a long bullish candle. This is followed by a small-bodied candle that gaps lower into the mid-range of the first candle. The second candle fits easily within the range of the first candle.

A bearish harami can be seen in Figure 13.18. Shares of American Tower Corp. (AMT) rallied in October of 2015. The stock formed a bearish harami on November 2 and 3 of that year, leading to a sharp reversal.

The term "harami" means "pregnant" in Japanese, and when looking at the harami pattern it's easy to think of the first candle as the mother and the second as the baby. The psychological impact of the harami pattern is considerably less jarring than those of a long-wicked shooting star or a bearish engulfing candle.

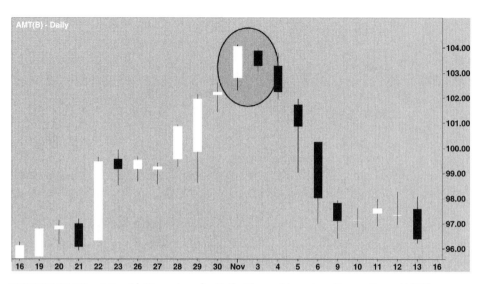

FIGURE 13.18 A Bearish Harami on the Daily Chart of American Tower Corp. (AMT)

If you were in a position, and the price gapped mildly in the opposite direction but failed to follow through, you probably wouldn't feel compelled to exit your position. However, even though the pattern doesn't elicit a dramatic response, it could still be the catalyst for a change in trend.

Bullish Belt Hold

The bullish belt hold is a single candle reversal pattern. It is similar to a hammer; both appear in a downtrend, and both signal a trend reversal. Here is the main difference: In the hammer pattern, the price travels lower, and then reverses, while the candle is open.

The bullish belt hold pattern is different in that it gaps sharply lower and then reverses. The same activity that takes place in a hammer has occurred. The main difference is that with the bullish belt hold pattern, the price opens sharply lower, instead of moving lower after the open.

The opening price of the bullish belt hold is also the low of the session. As with the wick of a hammer, the longer the size of the bullish belt hold's body, the more significant the reversal is considered to be.

Figure 13.19 demonstrates a bullish belt hold pattern in shares of Barnes Group Inc. (B). The price gaps sharply lower and then begins to rally. The $33 opening price for Barnes was also the low of the day.

Bearish Belt Hold

The bearish belt hold is a single-candle reversal pattern. It is similar to a shooting star pattern; both appear in an uptrend, and both signal a trend reversal. Here is

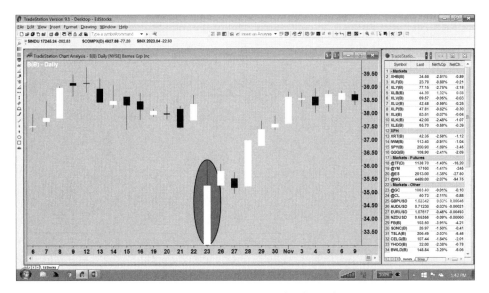

FIGURE 13.19 A Bullish Belt Hold Pattern on the Daily Chart of Barnes Group Inc. (B)

the main difference: In the shooting star pattern, the price travels higher, and then reverses, while the candle is open.

The belt hold pattern is different in that it gaps sharply higher and then reverses. The same activity that takes place in a shooting star has occurred. The main difference is that in the bearish belt hold pattern, the price opens sharply higher, instead of moving higher after the open.

The opening price of the bearish belt hold is also the high of the session. As with the wick of a shooting star, the longer the size of the bearish belt hold's body, the more significant the reversal is considered to be.

We see an example of a bearish belt hold in Figure 13.20. Shares of Affymetrix Inc. (AFFX) opened sharply higher on July 23, 2015. The opening price of $11.81 was also the stock's high price of the day. Following the appearance of the bearish belt hold, the stock sold off sharply.

Bullish Counterattack Lines

This is a two-candle reversal pattern that occurs in a downtrend. The first candle of the pattern is bearish, and moves in the direction of the trend. The second candle begins with a gap lower, but the price manages to fight its way higher, and eventually closes at the same price as the previous candle's close.

In Figure 13.21, we see an example of bullish counterattack lines. Shares of Isis Pharmaceuticals (ISIS) were in a downtrend in August of 2010. On August 23, a black candle formed. That candle closed at $7.78. The following day, ISIS gapped lower but then began to rise, to close once again at $7.78.

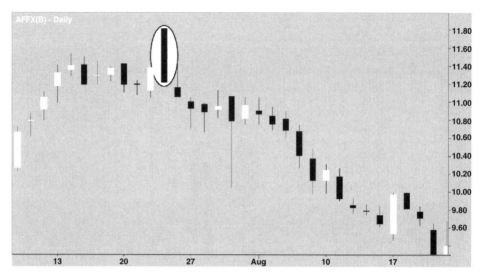

FIGURE 13.20   A Bearish Belt Hold on the Daily Chart of Affymetrix Inc. (AFFX)

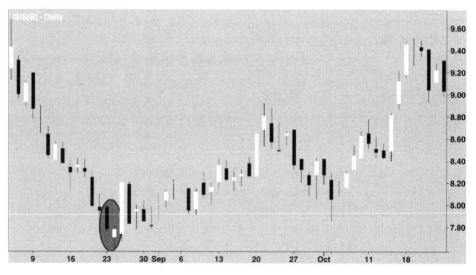

FIGURE 13.21   Bullish Counterattack Lines on the Daily Chart of Isis Pharmaceuticals (ISIS)

Because it consists of a bearish candle followed by a bullish candle, and the two candles have similar closing prices, this pattern is also referred to as "bullish meeting lines."

Bearish Counterattack Lines

This is a two-candle reversal pattern that occurs in an uptrend. The first candle of the pattern is bullish and moves in the direction of the trend. The second candle

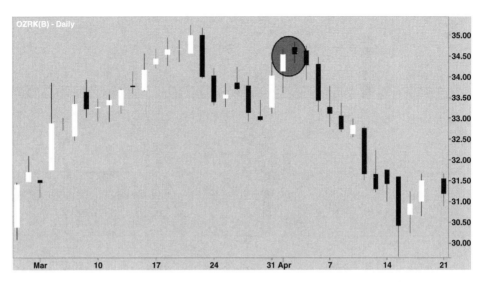

FIGURE 13.22 Bearish Counterattack Lines Form on the Daily Chart of Bank of the Ozarks (OZRK)

begins with a gap higher, but the price fades lower and eventually closes at the same price as the previous candle's close.

Figure 13.22 provides an example of bearish counterattack lines. On April 1 of 2014, shares of Bank of the Ozarks (OZRK) formed a bullish candle that closed at $34.54. The following day, the stock gapped higher, but faded to close at $34.54 once again.

In this case, the candlestick pattern was followed by a steep downtrend. Note that the bearish counterattack lines formed during the second peak of a double top pattern.

Because it consists of a bullish candle followed by a bearish candle, and because the two candles have similar closing prices, this pattern is also referred to as "bearish meeting lines."

Bullish Tweezer Bottom

This is a two-candle reversal pattern that appears in a downtrend. First, a bearish candle forms, closing at or near the low of the session. The second candle tests the previous candle's low again before moving higher. By successfully testing the same area twice, the price has encountered buying pressure, making the path of least resistance higher.

An example of a bullish tweezer bottom can be found in Figure 13.23. Shares of Flamel Technologies (FLML) were in a steep downtrend in September of 2015. On September 28, the stock fell sharply once again and closed near its low of $14.96. Then on September 29, the stock formed an identical low of $14.96. The stock subsequently rallied to nearly $20.

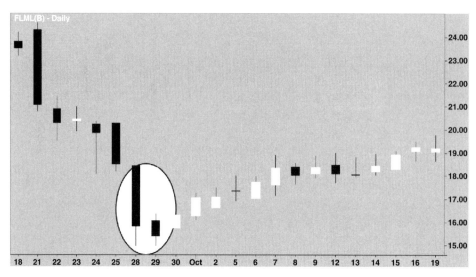

FIGURE 13.23   A Bullish Tweezer Bottom on the Daily Chart of Flamel Technologies (FLML)

Bearish Tweezer Top

This is a two-candle reversal pattern that appears in an uptrend. First, a bullish candle forms, closing at or near the high of the session. The second candle tests the previous candle's high again before pulling back. By successfully testing the same area twice, the price has encountered selling pressure, making the path of least resistance lower.

An example of a bearish tweezer top appears in Figure 13.24. The euro/U.S. dollar currency pair (EURUSD) formed a small uptrend on its 240-minute (four-hour) chart in late August of 2015. A bullish four-hour candle closed at 1.1388, followed by a bearish four-hour candle that closed at approximately the same price. The tweezer top then led to a decline in the EURUSD exchange rate.

■ Complex Candlestick Reversal Patterns

Up to this point, we've reviewed reversal patterns that consist of a few candles at most. Now let's look at several candlestick reversal patterns that could conceivably consist of many candlesticks. The following patterns share similarities with commonly used Western technical patterns.

Bullish Tower Bottom Pattern

This is a multiple candle reversal pattern that appears in a downtrend. It begins with one or more bearish candles. This is followed by a series of small-bodied candles that result in little price movement. The bullish tower bottom pattern is an indication that the downtrend is losing energy.

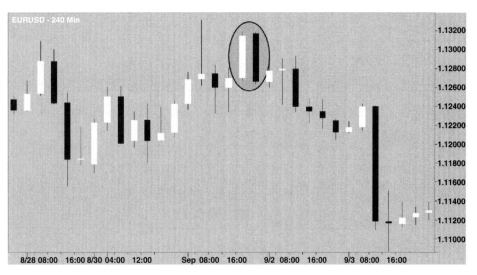

FIGURE 13.24 A Bearish Tweezer Top on an Intraday Chart of the Euro/U.S. Dollar (EURUSD)

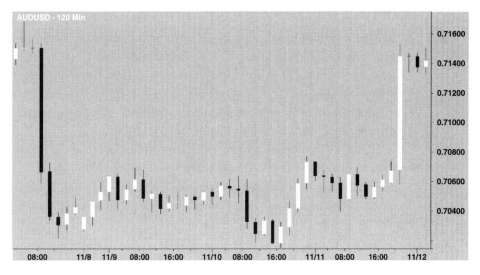

FIGURE 13.25 A Bullish Tower Bottom on an Intraday Chart of the Australian Dollar/U.S. Dollar (AUDUSD)

Finally, one or more bullish candles form, causing the price to rise and complete the pattern. The finished pattern resembles an upside-down tower.

In Figure 13.25, we see an example of a bullish tower bottom on the 120-minute (two-hour) chart of the Australian dollar/U.S. dollar (AUDUSD). AUDUSD fell sharply and then drifted sideways, forming a series of small-bodied candles. Eventually, the price broke higher, completing the pattern.

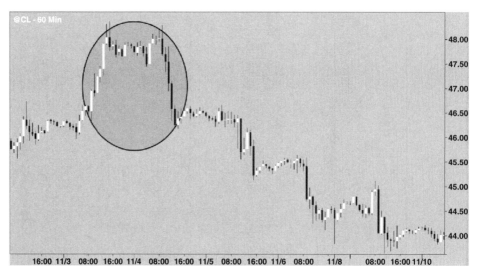

FIGURE 13.26 A Tower Top Pattern on the Hourly Chart of the Crude Oil Continuous Contract (@CL)

Bearish Tower Top Pattern

This is a multiple candle reversal pattern that appears in an uptrend. It begins with one or more bullish candles. This is followed by a series of small-bodied candles, which result in little price movement. This is an indication that the trend is losing energy.

Finally, one or more bearish candles form, completing the pattern. The finished pattern resembles a bridge or tower.

Figure 13.26 depicts a tower top pattern on the hourly chart of the Crude Oil Continuous Contract (@CL). In early November of 2015, crude oil rallied sharply. This rally was followed by a series of directionless, small-bodied candles. Then crude oil broke sharply lower, completing the pattern and leading to a sell-off.

Bullish Fry Pan Bottom Pattern

This is a multiple candle reversal pattern that appears in a downtrend. After a group of bearish candles, a series of small-bodied candles forms, indicating a loss of momentum. The downtrend flattens into a pattern resembling a rounded bottom. After a period of consolidation, the price gaps higher, indicating a change in direction and momentum.

An example of a bullish fry pan bottom appears in Figure 13.27. Shares of RPC Inc. (RES) were in a downtrend in April of 2012. The trend gradually devolved into a series of small-bodied candles. Then on April 25, the stock gapped higher, completing the pattern (arrow) and leading to a sharp reversal.

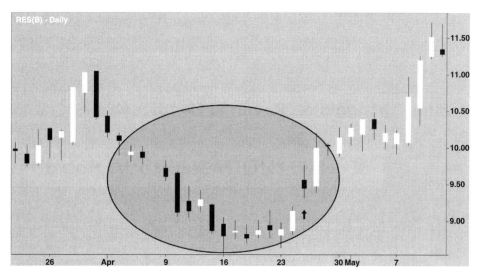

FIGURE 13.27 A Bullish Fry Pan Bottom on the Daily Chart of RPC Inc. (RES)

Bearish Dumpling Top Pattern

This is a multiple candle reversal pattern that appears in an uptrend. After a group of bullish candles, a series of small-bodied candles forms, indicating a loss of momentum. The uptrend flattens into a pattern resembling a rounded top. After a period of consolidation, the price gaps lower, indicating a change in direction and momentum.

An example of a bearish dumpling top pattern appears in Figure 13.28. Shares of Whole Foods Markets (WFM) were trending higher in early 2015. Then the

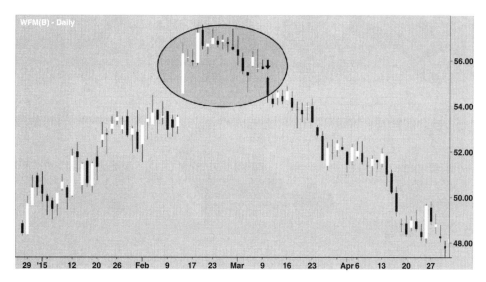

FIGURE 13.28 A Bearish Dumpling Top Pattern on the Daily Chart of Whole Foods Markets (WFM)

trend began to lose momentum, leading to a series of small-bodied candles. The stock gapped lower on March 10 (arrow), completing the pattern and igniting a downtrend in the stock. In this case, the pattern marked a significant short-term top.

■ Final Thoughts on Reversal Candles

Reversals in price can be very significant, and because of this there are many candlestick formations that inform the trader of an impending change in the direction of the price.

However, candlesticks can do much more than just advise investors of potential price reversals. A separate set of candlestick formations known as "continuation patterns" inform the trader that the price will continue in its current direction. We'll study those patterns in the following chapter.

CHAPTER 14

Continuation and Indecision Candlestick Patterns

While reversal candlestick patterns garner the most attention, there are certain useful patterns that indicate whether the current trend will continue. There are also patterns that indicate indecision. This chapter will examine both of these types of candlestick patterns.

■ Continuation Candlestick Patterns

There are ten different continuation candlestick patterns, all of which can be used to determine the longevity of current trends.

Rising Three Methods Pattern

The rising three methods pattern is a multiple-candle pattern. It's a continuation pattern that appears in an uptrend. It is usually depicted as consisting of five candles, but this is not a requirement.

First, a long bullish candlestick appears in an uptrend, indicating strength on the part of the bulls. This is followed by a series of small-bodied candles that move in the opposite direction.

It is preferable if the small candles stay within the range of the first candle. This series of small-bodied candles represents the bears fighting back, but they are only able to muster a weak response against the powerful bulls.

The final candle in the pattern is a long bullish candlestick, which closes above the highs of the previous candles in the pattern. Any traders who sold short when the bears attempted to gain control are now losing money. The bears have been defeated, and the price is now free to move higher.

The rising three methods pattern is similar in some ways to a bull flag, a continuation chart pattern.

Figure 14.1 shows a rising three methods pattern in Alcoa (AA). Notice that the uptrend was established before the formation of the pattern, and that the trend continued afterward.

Bullish Mat Hold Pattern

This is a variation on the rising three methods pattern. It is basically the same as rising three methods with one exception. If the second candle of the rising three methods pattern (the first small body) gaps above the high of the first candle in the pattern, it is known as a "bullish mat hold pattern."

Otherwise, it is similar to the rising three methods pattern in both structure and psychology. Like rising three methods, the bullish mat hold consists of a strong bullish thrust, followed by a weak rebuttal by the bears, followed by yet another strong bullish thrust.

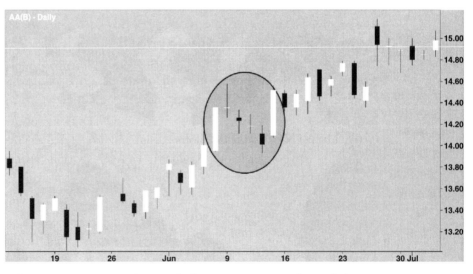

FIGURE 14.1   A Rising Three Methods Pattern Appears in Shares of Alcoa (AA)

Falling Three Methods Pattern

The falling three methods pattern is a multiple-candle pattern. It's a continuation pattern that appears in a downtrend. It is usually depicted as consisting of five candles, but this is not a requirement.

First, a long bearish candlestick appears in a downtrend, indicating strength on the part of the bears. This is followed by a series of small-bodied candles that move in the opposite direction.

It is preferable if the small candles stay within the range of the first candle. This series of small-bodied candles represents the bulls fighting back, but they are only able to muster a weak response against the powerful bears.

The final candle in the pattern is a long bearish candlestick, which closes beneath the lows of the previous candles in the pattern. Any traders who went long when the bulls attempted to gain control are now losing money. The bulls have been defeated, and the price is now free to move lower.

The falling three methods pattern is similar in some ways to a bear flag, a continuation chart pattern.

Figure 14.2 shows a falling three methods pattern in the Great Britain pound/U.S. dollar currency pair. Notice that the downtrend was established before the formation of the pattern, and that the trend continued afterward.

Bearish Mat Hold Pattern

This is a variation on the falling three methods pattern. It is basically the same as falling three methods with one exception. If the second candle of the falling three

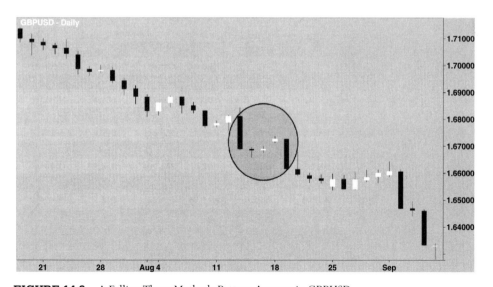

FIGURE 14.2   A Falling Three Methods Pattern Appears in GBPUSD

methods pattern (the first small-bodied candle) gaps below the low of the first candle in the pattern, it is known as a bearish mat hold pattern.

Otherwise, it is similar to the falling three methods pattern in both structure and psychology. Like falling three methods, the bearish mat hold pattern consists of a strong bearish thrust, followed by a weak rebuttal by the bulls, followed by yet another strong bearish thrust.

Bullish Separating Lines

This two-candle pattern is significant within an uptrend. The first candle begins with a gap higher, then fades to form a bearish black candle. A second candle then gaps to the same opening price as the first, but then proceeds to move higher, in the direction of the dominant trend.

Both candles have the same opening price but move in opposite directions—hence the name "separating lines." The bullish second candle completely negates any bearish impact of the first candle. Any traders who sold short during the first candle are now holding a losing position, and may be forced to cover. With these former sellers effectively removed from the equation, the path of least resistance is higher.

Figure 14.3 depicts bullish separating lines on the daily chart of Sirius XM Holdings (SIRI) in October of 2012. On October 2, SIRI gaps higher to open at $2.60, but the price then fades into a black candle. On October 3, SIRI again gaps higher to open at $2.60; only this time the price rallies to form a white candle. The second candle negated the price action of the first candle, indicating that the trend would continue higher.

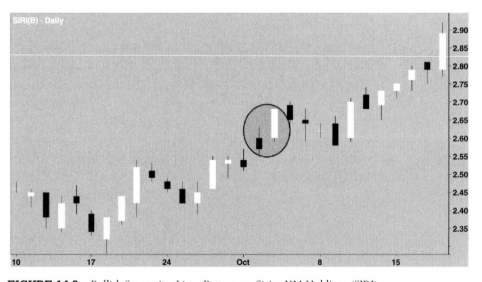

FIGURE 14.3 Bullish Separating Lines Pattern on Sirius XM Holdings (SIRI)

Bearish Separating Lines

This two-candle pattern is significant within a downtrend. The first candle begins with a gap lower, but then the price rises to form a bullish white candle. A second candle then gaps to the same opening price as the first, but then proceeds to move lower, in the direction of the dominant trend.

Both candles have the same opening price, but move in opposite directions—hence the name "separating lines." The bearish second candle completely negates any bullish impact of the first candle. Any traders who went long during the first candle are now holding a losing position and may be forced to sell. With these former buyers effectively removed from the equation, the path of least resistance is lower.

Figure 14.4 demonstrates the bearish separating lines pattern on Alcatel Lucent (ALU) in March of 2014. On March 12, ALU gaps lower to open at $4.04, but then rallies to form a white candle. Then on March 13, ALU again gaps lower to open at $4.04, only this time the price falls, forming a black candle. The second candle negated the price action of the first candle, indicating that the downtrend would continue.

Rising Window Pattern

In an uptrend, a new candle opens with a gap above the previous candle's high. In candlestick parlance, this gap is called a "window." There are no overlapping wicks or shadows in the window, as it is an area in which no trades have occurred. The window itself acts as support in the event of a throwback.

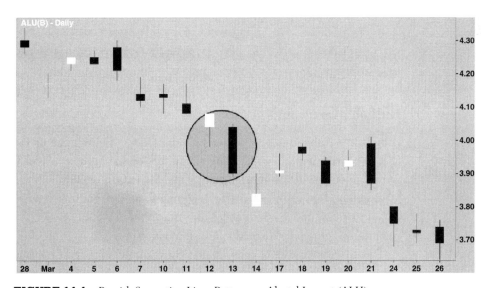

FIGURE 14.4 Bearish Separating Lines Pattern on Alcatel Lucent (ALU)

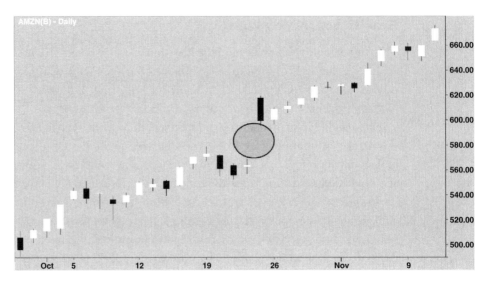

FIGURE 14.5 A Rising Window Pattern in Shares of Amazon.com (AMZN)

Figure 14.5 shows a rising window pattern in shares of Amazon.com (AMZN). The rising window served as an indication that the stock would continue to rally.

Falling Window Pattern

In a downtrend, a new candle opens with a gap beneath the previous candle's low. In candlestick parlance, this gap is called a "window." There are no overlapping wicks or shadows in the window, as it is an area in which no trades have occurred. The window itself acts as resistance in the event of a pullback.

In Figure 14.6, two falling window patterns (circled) can be seen on the daily chart of Priceline.com (PCLN) in September of 2014. Both patterns indicated that the downtrend would continue.

Bullish Marubozu

A bullish Marubozu is a single long candlestick with no upper or lower wicks that acts as a continuation candle. The candle has opened at the low of the session and moved in one direction until closing at the high of the session.

In Figure 14.7, Apple (AAPL) is shown in an uptrend on its weekly chart. The rally lost steam in early 2014, leaving the trend in doubt. However, the rally was reignited when Apple formed a bullish Marubozu (circled) in April of 2014.

This Marubozu candle tells us that the bulls are firmly in control, and that the price is likely to continue moving higher. The fact that the price is able to close on its high shows a lack of willingness on the part of the bulls to take profits. Why

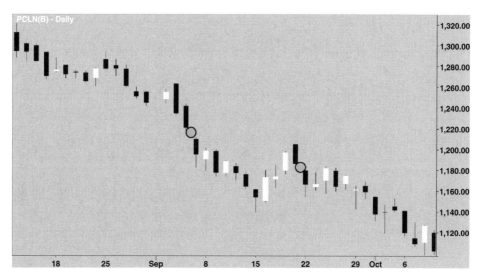

FIGURE 14.6 Two Falling Window Patterns on the Daily Chart of Priceline.com (PCLN)

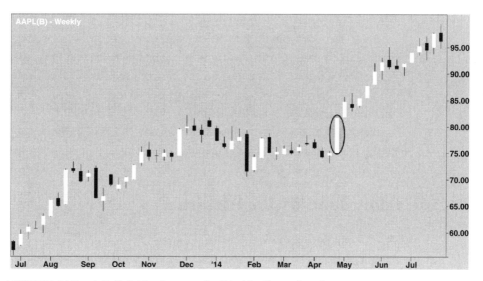

FIGURE 14.7 A Bullish Marubozu on the Weekly Chart of Apple (AAPL)

would profitable bulls be unwilling to take profits? Because they are acting on the belief that there is more upside to come.

Bearish Marubozu

A "bearish Marubozu" is a single long candlestick with no upper or lower wicks that acts as a continuation candle. The candle has opened at the high of the session and moved in one direction until closing at the low of the session.

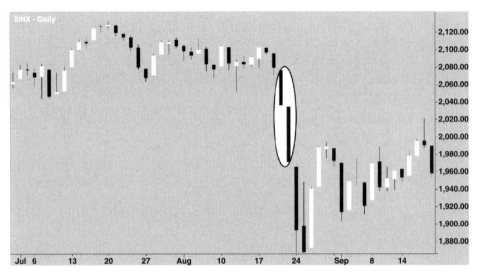

FIGURE 14.8 Two Consecutive Bearish Marubozu Candles on the Daily Chart of the S&P 500 Index ($INX)

This Marubozu candle tells us that the bears are firmly in control, and that the price is likely to continue moving lower. The fact that the price is able to close on its low shows a lack of willingness on the part of the bears to take profits. Why would profitable bears be unwilling to take profits? Because they are acting on the belief that there is more downside to come.

Figure 14.8 shows two consecutive bearish Marubozu candles on the daily chart of the S&P 500 Index ($INX) in August of 2015.

■ Indecision Candlestick Patterns

Not all candlesticks or candlestick patterns hint at a directional change or a continuation of the current direction. Some candlestick formations indicate indecision on the part of traders. Let's examine different varieties of this type of candle.

The Doji Pattern

When the closing price of a stock, currency, or commodity is equal or nearly equal to its opening price, the resulting candle is referred to as a "doji." A doji candle has no real body; it consists of a horizontal line that indicates the price range of the measured time period, and a vertical line that represents both the opening and closing price.

The doji is often mistakenly referred to as a reversal candle. In truth, it only indicates indecision. While indecision *could* lead to a reversal, when viewed alone it

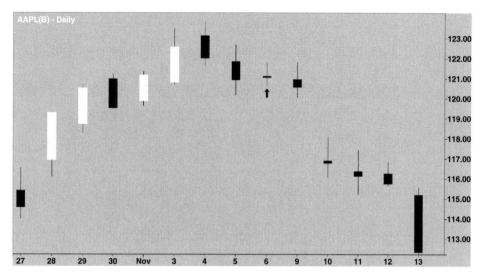

FIGURE 14.9 A Doji Forms on the Daily Chart of Apple (arrow)

is neither a reversal candle nor a continuation candle. It simply indicates that a battle between bulls and bears has ended in a draw.

In Figure 14.9, a doji is visible on the daily chart of Apple (arrow). In this case, it marked a short period of indecision after a rally and prior to a sell-off.

The Dragonfly Doji

A dragonfly doji has similar opening and closing prices, which occur at the upper end of the candle's range. It also has a long bottom shadow or wick, indicating that a push lower by the bears was rejected.

The meaning of the dragonfly doji depends on its context. For example, if this formation appears on a downtrend, it could act as a reversal candle in a similar fashion to a hammer.

On the other hand, in a sideways or range bound market, the dragonfly doji simply represents indecision. As always with candlesticks, location is everything.

In Figure 14.10, we see a dragonfly doji (arrow) on the daily chart of Sirius XM Holdings (SIRI) that occurred on August 22, 2014. On that day, $3.58 was the stock's opening price, high of the day, and closing price.

The Gravestone Doji

A gravestone doji has similar opening and closing prices that occur at the lower end of the candle's range. It also has a long upper shadow or wick, indicating that a push higher by the bulls was rejected.

As with the dragonfly doji, location is everything. In an uptrend, the effect of the gravestone doji could be similar to that of a shooting star pattern, as it is indicative

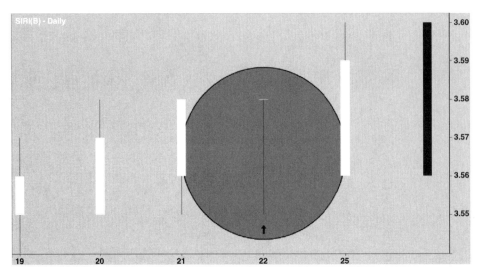

FIGURE 14.10   A Dragonfly Doji (arrow) Forms on the Daily Chart of Sirius XM Holdings (SIRI)

of a bullish thrust that met with rejection. In a sideways or range bound market, the gravestone doji candlestick merely represents indecision.

In Figure 14.11, a gravestone doji is visible on the 30-minute chart of Sprint Corporation (S). The opening, low, and closing price of the candle is $4.16.

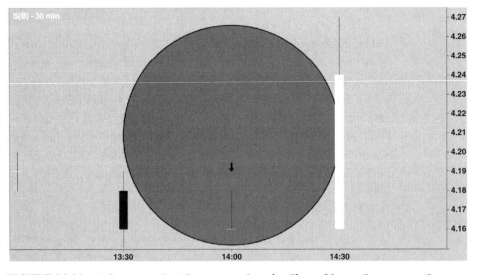

FIGURE 14.11   A Gravestone Doji Forms on an Intraday Chart of Sprint Corporation (S)

The Spinning Top

The spinning top candle is similar to a doji in that it represents indecision; however, this candle's opening and closing prices are not the same.

Instead of representing both the open and close with a thin horizontal line, the spinning top candle possesses a small real body. The color shading of the real body is irrelevant.

This candle has upper and lower shadows or wicks. These wicks indicate that a battle between bulls and bears had no *decisive* victor. Like the doji candle, the spinning top represents indecision.

In Figure 14.12, three consecutive spinning tops are visible on the daily chart of Wal-Mart Stores (WMT) in September of 2015.

High Wave Candle

The high wave candle is similar to a spinning top candle, in that it has a small real body. The difference lies in the high wave candle's longer wicks, which are an indication of high volatility. In a high wave candle, both the bulls and bears were able to move the price substantially, but neither side could maintain control.

In Figure 14.13, we see a high wave candle on the daily chart of Wal-Mart Stores (WMT) in September of 2015.

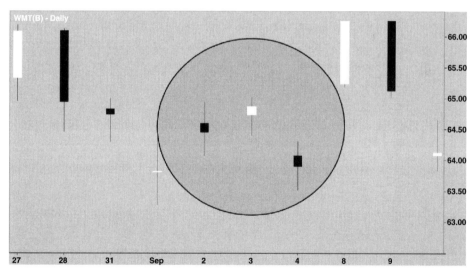

FIGURE 14.12   Three Consecutive Spinning Tops Appear on the Daily Chart of Wal-Mart Stores (WMT)

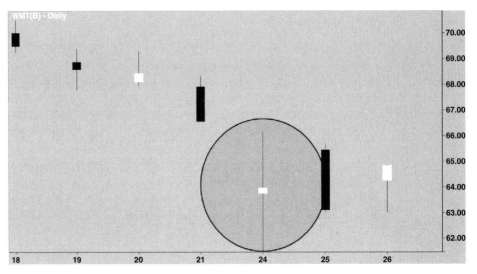

FIGURE 14.13   A High Wave Candle Appears on the Daily Chart of Wal-Mart Stores (WMT)

■ Final Thoughts on Candlesticks

Not every candlestick on a chart contains meaning. If you find yourself examining and analyzing each and every candlestick on the chart, you run the risk of assigning meaning to a candle that simply isn't significant. This leads to a condition technicians refer to as "paralysis by analysis."

Instead of overanalyzing each candlestick, examine the charts with an open mind and wait for a pattern to present itself to you. Major reversal patterns aren't invisible; in fact, they often scream to be noticed. Obvious candlestick patterns tend to work well, as noted in the section on hammers. This is also true for most of the other patterns mentioned herein.

PART V

FIBONACCI

CHAPTER 15

Fibonacci Trading Techniques

How does an idea gain traction? How does a concept spread from one place to another?

In ancient Rome, a numeric system was developed using letters from the Latin alphabet. The Roman numeral for representing "thirty-eight" was written "XXXVIII." Eventually this was supplanted by the Hindu-Arabic version, "38."

How did we get from XXXVIII to 38? The Hindu-Arabic system is obviously more efficient, but in order to reach new adherents, that concept had to travel across the Mediterranean Sea.

An early appearance of the Hindu-Arabic system in Europe occurred when it appeared in the *Codex Vigilanus*, a collection of historic documents that was compiled in the year 976 A.D. Since the invention of the printing press was still centuries away, the system failed to gain widespread traction.

■ Leonardo Bonacci and *Liber Abaci*

About 200 years later, a young man named Leonardo Bonacci traveled with his wealthy merchant father from Italy to ports around the Mediterranean. Somewhere along the way, possibly in Algeria, young Mr. Bonacci, who also was known by the names Leonardo di Pisa and Leonardo Fibonacci, learned of the Hindu-Arabic system.

In 1202, Bonacci wrote *Liber Abaci*, which roughly translates to *The Book of Calculations*. In it, Bonacci detailed the efficient numeric system he'd learned of during his travels. The Hindu-Arabic system could be used to perform calculations without the aid of an abacus.

This was a revolutionary shift. Consider for a moment the tremendous advantage such a system would provide the user in transactions and negotiations during this era. Bonacci would publish a second version of *Liber Abaci* in 1227.

The influence of *Liber Abaci* helped convince Europe to adopt the Hindu-Arabic numeric system, which was featured in the first part of the book. That accomplishment alone makes Leonardo Bonacci a significant figure in the field of Western mathematics.

However, there was more to *Liber Abaci*. During his travels, Bonacci discovered something even more incredible.

The Fibonacci Numeric Sequence

In another section of *Liber Abaci*, Bonacci described a numeric string, or sequence. This sequence is believed by some to have its origins in Indian mathematics. There is considerable disagreement as to the timing and origin of the sequence.

It may have started with the work of an Indian author named Pingala over 2,000 years ago, although some claim its origins are rooted even deeper in the past. Some believe the concept can ultimately be traced to ancient Greece and that civilization's use of a similar concept known as "phi."

How is the sequence created? Take the numbers zero and one and add them $(0 + 1 = 1)$. To get the next number in the sequence, add the two most recent numbers in the sequence $(1 + 1 = 2)$. Continue adding the two most recent numbers in the sequence $(1 + 2 = 3)$ to get to the next number. Keep repeating this process $(2 + 3 = 5; 3 + 5 = 8; 5 + 8 = 13)$.

The result is a string of numbers that is now popularly known as the Fibonacci sequence:

$$0, 1, 1, 2, 3, 5, 8, 13, 21, 34, 55, 89, 144, 233, 377, 610\ldots$$

Next, working from left to right, divide each number into the preceding number. For example, $0/1 = 0, 1/2 = 0.5, 2/3 = 0.66, 3/5 = 0.6, 5/8 = 0.625, 8/13 = 0.615, 13/21 = 0.619, 21/34 = 0.617, 34/55 = 0.618$, and so on.

Now review the outcome of the preceding calculations. Notice how the results swing like a pendulum, above and below a particular number. Eventually, the results center on that number:

$$0.5, 0.66, 0.6, 0.625, 0.615, 0.619, 0.617, 0.618, 0.618, 0.618, 0.618\ldots$$

■ The Golden Ratio and Fibonacci Rabbits

That number, 0.618, lies at the heart of the Fibonacci concept. A different method of calculation involves adding the number 1 to the result. This is how we arrive at 1.618, which is popularly known in mathematics as the Golden Ratio.

The Golden Ratio is considered significant because of its frequent appearance in nature. In *Liber Abaci*, Fibonacci demonstrated this concept via a hypothetical math problem: How does one anticipate the growth rate of a population of rabbits? Here is the outline of the problem:

> Start with one pair of newborn rabbits in a field. By the age of two months, the rabbits will be able to reproduce. Every month, starting with the second month, the two original rabbits will produce a pair of rabbits—one male and one female. The newborn female rabbits will also reproduce at the same rate, and with the same male/female balance, once they reach the age of two months. Assume that none of the rabbits die. How many pairs of rabbits will be in the field in one year?

Here is the answer to the problem: After both the first and second month, there will be just one pair of rabbits. By the end of the third month, there will be two pairs. By the end of the fourth month there will be three pairs, and at the end of the fifth month there will be five pairs. By now you may have noticed that the results match the Fibonacci sequence:

$$1, 1, 2, 3, 5, 8, 13, 21, 34, 55, 89, 144$$

If we continue to follow the sequence, the result by the end of month twelve will be 144 pairs of rabbits. The number 0 is not included in the sequence because at least one pair of rabbits is required in order for the animals to reproduce.

If we wish to split hares (pun intended), there are many potential issues with Fibonacci's brainteaser. For example, difficulties may arise due to rabbits reproducing with their siblings.

Over the centuries, more refined versions of the rabbit conundrum have appeared. British writer Henry Dudeney created a version that used cattle instead of rabbits, focusing only on the number of female calves born.

Keep in mind that this is just an exercise that is designed to explain a mathematical theory. Don't allow minutia to distract from the important concepts presented by Fibonacci's rabbit puzzle.

Fibonacci in Nature

The concept detailed in Fibonacci's rabbit problem applies to other aspects of nature as well. For example, most flowers have 3, 5, 8, 13, or 21 petals. These numeric relationships can be found in the growth patterns of leaves on a tree and in the reproductive rates of honeybees. There is evidence that Fibonacci relationships even occur at a molecular level, within strands of DNA.

Despite their prevalence in nature, these are not magical numbers. Some mathematicians believe the Fibonacci patterns merely represent the most efficient means for nature to achieve its ends.

Fibonacci Spirals

Within nature, there are many examples of objects that grow in the shape of a spiral. Fibonacci ratios can also be expressed in the form of a spiral. This occurs when an object grows by an amount equal to the golden ratio (1.618%) per every quarter turn of growth.

Fibonacci spirals can be found in objects as massive as a galaxy, as powerful as a hurricane, or as fragile as a mollusk's shell. A sunflower's seeds form their patterns in a series of spirals, often totaling 34, 55, or 89 spirals of seeds.

Fibonacci in Architecture

The ancient Greeks had a concept similar to the Golden Ratio, and described it with the term "phi." The concept of phi is expressed in the use of ratios in Greek architecture.

For example, a rectangle can be designed using Fibonacci ratios. The sides of such a rectangle might measure 5 × 8, or 13 × 21, or perhaps 8 × 13—in other words, the sides would express a Fibonacci relationship.

In each of the previous cases, the rectangle's sides would utilize the Golden Ratio. The long sides of the rectangle would be approximately 1.618 longer than the short sides. A rectangle that uses these proportions is referred to as a Golden Rectangle.

The Parthenon

The Acropolis is a series of buildings and structures that was constructed high on a hillside in Athens approximately 2,500 years ago. The most famous of these buildings is the Parthenon, a temple dedicated to the Greek goddess Athena.

The Parthenon's exterior dimensions roughly conform to the Golden Rectangle. The height, width, and structure of its beams also conform roughly to the Golden Ratio, or phi. Some architects believe these numeric relationships are what make the Parthenon pleasing to the eye.

This raises the question: Were Fibonacci relationships discovered in Europe before they appeared in the East? There is really no way to tell. Because Fibonacci relationships appear throughout nature and in all parts of the world, it's entirely possible that two or more civilizations became aware of these numeric relationships independently.

Fibonacci in Art

Fibonacci relationships are prominent in many famous works of art. Many of the works of Leonardo da Vinci, most notably *The Last Supper* and *The Annunciation*, make extensive use of the Golden Ratio. The works of artists such as Michelangelo, Botticelli, Salvador Dali, Georges-Pierre Seurat, and Edward Burne-Jones also contain these numeric relationships.

■ Significance in Trading

By this point we should all have a pretty good grasp on the concept of Fibonacci numeric relationships. The question is, what on earth does any of this have to do with trading?

Since Fibonacci relationships are within us and all around us, some believe that they influence everything—including financial markets. Others are more skeptical and believe that Fibonacci has no relationship to financial trading whatsoever. While these two views are at odds, they are not entirely incompatible. How can this be?

Consider this: What if Fibonacci relationships have no *direct* impact on the financial markets, but some traders are influenced by the *belief* that they do?

If enough traders believe that the price will rise (or fall) when it reaches point X, and if they act on that belief, then their actions can make it so. This is what is known as a "self-fulfilling belief," and there are logical reasons why such beliefs can work in the financial markets. What follows is a hypothetical example of a self-fulfilling belief in action.

The Power of a Self-Fulfilling Belief

Suppose that a large number of traders, including some major financial institutions, believe that stock XYZ will bounce when it falls to $20 per share. It doesn't matter *why* they think it will bounce, only that they believe it.

What is the logical course of action for these traders? If they truly believe XYZ will rise when it reaches $20, they should place orders to buy the stock at or near that price. As time passes, a large number of buy orders may accumulate at $20 due to this belief.

Eventually, stock XYZ declines to $20 per share, triggering the buy orders. As the buy orders are executed, the resulting buying pressure pushes XYZ sharply higher from the $20 level.

Why did the price rise from $20? Ultimately, it is buying and selling pressure that moves the markets. The reasons attributed to this buying and selling are secondary to this fact.

What is the role of time in this example? It's logical to assume that a longer gestation period would allow a greater number of orders to accumulate. Because of this, any tactic that has a self-fulfilling nature is probably going to be more effective on a weekly or daily chart than it would be on an intraday chart.

Fibonacci and Trading Culture

Another factor to consider is what I'd refer to as the "culture" of a particular trading vehicle. For example, when I started my first trading assignment on an equities desk, Fibonacci was scorned by many of my colleagues. Later, when I got involved with currencies, I noticed a much greater level of acceptance.

Fibonacci levels are sometimes found in the forex research reports of major banks, but are rarely seen in stock research reports. You could say that the use of Fibonacci is more closely associated with the culture of currency trading than it is with the culture of stock trading.

Application of Fibonacci to Technical Analysis

The key number for trading purposes is .618, which can be obtained by dividing any number in the sequence (beyond the first half-dozen or so) into the number that follows it; for example, $89/144 = .618$, which can be expressed as 61.8%.

Another important number is .382, which is the inverse of 0.618 ($1 - 0.618 = 0.382$). That number can also be obtained by dividing a number in the sequence by the number two spaces to the right; for example, $55/144 = .382$. This can also be expressed as 38.2%.

The halfway point between .618 and .382 is 0.5. This can also be expressed as 50%.

In addition, we can divide a number in the sequence by the number three spaces to the right; for example, $34/144 = .236$, or 23.6%. If we subtract .236 from 1, the result is its inverse number of .764, or 76.4% ($1 - .236 = .764$). These figures can be expressed as 23.6% and 76.4%.

▪ Fibonacci Retracement Levels

We have learned how to obtain the following Fibonacci retracement levels: 23.6%, 38.2%, 50.0%, 61.8%, and 76.4%. In addition, you may see other numbers used in Fibonacci calculations. The number .786 (78.6%) is sometimes used because it is the square root of .618.

On a chart, we can use a Fibonacci drawing tool. These tools often have the aforementioned figures as their default settings. When we draw from a low point to a high point on a chart, the retracement levels should populate automatically.

Since we are attempting to draw from the lowest point in a movement to the highest point, it would be a good idea to use a chart type that includes the highs and lows for each individual time period, such as bars or candlesticks. I would avoid using line charts, since these are usually based on closing prices and therefore may not accurately reflect the high and low of each individual time period.

Figure 15.1 demonstrates the use of Fibonacci retracements on a chart. In March of 2015, shares of Halozyme Therapy Inc. (HALO) began a rally from the $13 area (point A) that ended in July after the stock reached an all-time intraday high of $25.25 (point B). From there, the stock began to retreat.

Traders who were searching for potential support levels for HALO were then able to draw Fibonacci retracement levels on the chart. First, a line is drawn from left to right, from a major low point (point A) to the major high (point B). Retracement levels then populate the chart automatically.

As the price retraced its rally, HALO fell by an amount equal to approximately 23.6% of the preceding rally before finding support (point C). The stock bounced several times from that level. Eventually, HALO broke through the 23.6% retracement level.

HALO then fell until it reached the 38.2% retracement level (point D), where it bounced again. When the price broke through the 38.2% level, HALO dropped to the 50% retracement level, which acted as support for about a week (point E).

FIGURE 15.1   Fibonacci Retracements on the Daily Chart of Halozyme Therapy Inc. (HALO)

When the price fell through the 50% level, HALO dropped straight through the 61.8% retracement level. The stock finally rallied when it reached the 76.4% retracement level (point F).

In this example, Fibonacci retracement levels were used in the same way that one might utilize horizontal support levels. Similarly, we can use Fibonacci retracements to locate potential resistance levels when a downtrend begins to reverse.

This is demonstrated in Figure 15.2, which shows the euro/U.S. dollar currency pair (EURUSD) in a steep downtrend starting in October of 2014 (point A). By March of 2015, the EURUSD exchange rate hit bottom and began to rise (point B). At that time, traders who wished to short EURUSD applied Fibonacci retracement lines to the chart in order to search for an entry point.

This was achieved by drawing from a major high point (A) to a major low point (B). EURUSD climbed to the 23.6% retracement level for the first time on March 18 and was rejected. Subsequently, EURUSD failed to break through the 23.6% barrier on five separate occasions between that date and April 6 (arrows).

In the previous section, we used the phrases "major high point" and "major low point." Why not simply draw from the lowest price on the chart to the highest price, or vice versa?

The answer: because the highest price and lowest price on the chart can vary, depending on how much of the chart you are viewing at any given moment. The farther we look back into the past, the more likely we are to find lower prices and higher prices.

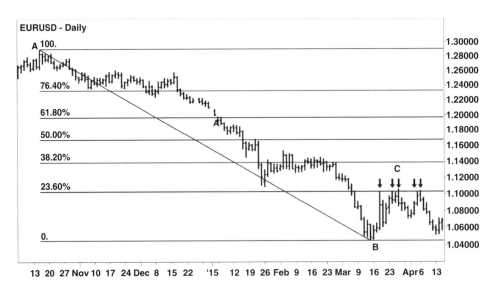

FIGURE 15.2 Fibonacci Retracements on the Daily Chart of EURUSD

Fibonacci Confluence

Just as with trend lines, we can draw more than one set of Fibonacci lines on the chart. In fact, many traders search for situations in which Fibonacci retracement levels overlap.

For example, they might search for a situation in which the 38.2% retracement of one set of Fibonacci lines lies directly on top of the 61.8% retracement of a separate set of lines. Such a situation is referred to as "confluence," and some Fibonacci traders will only accept trading opportunities that feature this phenomenon.

Figure 15.3 shows an example of bullish confluence in the Australian dollar/ U.S. dollar currency pair (AUDUSD). On the chart, two separate sets of Fibonacci retracement lines have been drawn: one from a major high in May of 2015 (point A), and another from a lower point in June of that same year (point B).

The low point for both sets of lines occurred in early September (point C). To prevent confusion from too many lines, I've removed all of the retracement levels except one from each set.

The remaining line from the first set is the 38.2% retracement, which is located just below .74000. The 50% retracement of the second set of lines is also visible, and is located in the same price area. In fact, the retracement lines are nearly on top of one another (circled).

Therefore, we could say that AUDUSD had a Fibonacci confluence located just below .74000. When AUDUSD attempted to breach the .74000 area in October, it failed (arrow), as the Fibonacci confluence acted as resistance.

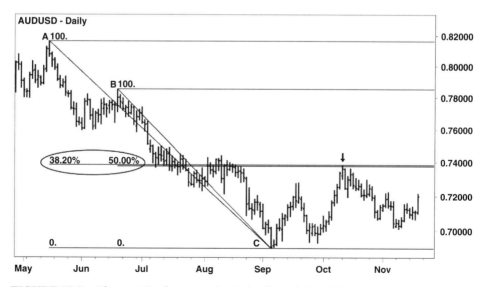

FIGURE 15.3   Fibonacci Confluence on the Daily Chart of AUDUSD

This example shows a confluence of two retracement levels. However, we can draw an unlimited number of sets of Fibonacci lines on a chart, so it is possible to have a confluence involving three or more retracement levels. In fact, there are traders who will only use a Fibonacci confluence that has three or more matching levels.

Figure 15.3 demonstrates a bearish confluence, because both sets of lines were created to measure a downtrend. A bullish confluence would consist of two or more matching retracements that are drawn to measure an uptrend. A bearish confluence creates resistance levels, and a bullish confluence creates support levels.

In order for confluence to work, is it necessary for the overlapping lines to match exactly?

Consider Figure 15.4. Two sets of Fibonacci lines are drawn on the British pound/Japanese yen currency pair (GBPJPY). The first set is drawn from October 2014 (point A), and the second begins in April of 2015 (point B). Both sets are drawn to the June high (point C).

The 38.2% retracement of the longer set of lines matches closely, but not exactly, to the 50% retracement of the shorter set, which is slightly higher. The price bounced sharply when coming into contact with both Fibonacci retracement levels (arrow).

Consider the possibility that some traders drew the first set of lines, and others drew the second set. If both groups of traders took action and placed orders based on the results of their Fibonacci lines, their respective orders would not be in the exact same location, but they would be in close proximity to one another. The effect would be the same as having two resistance levels located very close together.

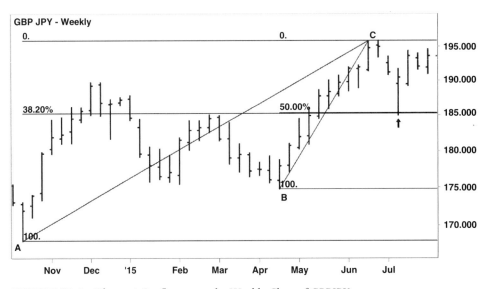

FIGURE 15.4 Fibonacci Confluence on the Weekly Chart of GBPJPY

Whether they are used in bullish or bearish situations, it's helpful to think of Fibonacci retracement lines as artificial support and/or resistance levels. Because the price levels are horizontal, the price associated with each level remains constant. This creates the potential for many orders to accumulate at a single price over time.

■ Fibonacci Extensions

If a price falls to a new low that has never been reached before, where is support located? By definition, when a price reaches a new all-time low, there can be no support based on previous price action. Similarly, when a price reaches a new all-time high, there can be no overhead resistance based on previous price action.

This section has covered Fibonacci retracements of various percentages, but it hasn't yet addressed retracements of greater than 100%. It also hasn't addressed the need to project price targets into previously uncharted territory. Fibonacci extensions allow traders to do both.

How do we create Fibonacci extensions? The key number for our purposes is 1.618, which can be obtained by dividing a number in the Fibonacci sequence into the number that precedes it. For example, $89/55 = 1.618$, or 161.8%. The square root of 1.618 is 1.272 (127.2%). That number also appears frequently in Fibonacci extensions.

Figure 15.5 demonstrates the use of Fibonacci extensions as targets. Shares of Facebook (FB) began to rally on September 29, 2015 (point A) and reached a new all-time high one month later, on October 29 (point B). At the time when the price reached point B, there was no overhead resistance.

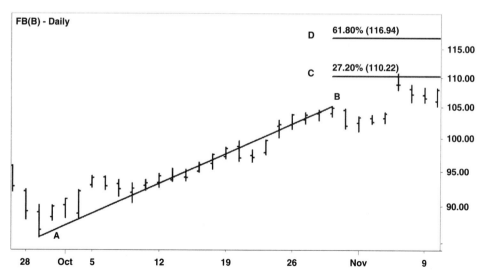

FIGURE 15.5   Fibonacci Extensions on the Daily Chart of Facebook (FB)

In order to create a target, a trader could draw a Fibonacci line from point A to point B. Point A represents 0% of the move, or the number 0, and point B represents 100% of the move, or the number 1. Instead of creating retracement lines on the chart, the Fibonacci tool is adjusted to create extensions.

Two Fibonacci extensions appear on the chart: one at 27.2% above point B, and another at 61.8% above point B. Since point B = 1, these extensions could also be expressed as 127.2% (point C) and 161.8% (point D).

The extension levels can be used as targets. Facebook reached point C, a potential target, in early November.

■ Fibonacci Retracements of Greater Than 100%

In Figure 15.5, extensions were used to create overhead targets beyond recent highs. However, we can also use Fibonacci retracements to create potential targets for shorts when prices retrace beyond 100%.

For example, in Figure 15.6, a bullish move occurred in the iShares MSCI Brazil Capped ETF (EWZ), originating from point A and concluding at point B. EWZ then reversed and found temporary support at the 61.8% and 76.4% retracement levels (points C and D) before collapsing.

The stock continued its slide, retracing more than 100% of the original move. Traders targeting the 127.20% retracement level (point E) or the 161.80% retracement level (point F) would have achieved their goals.

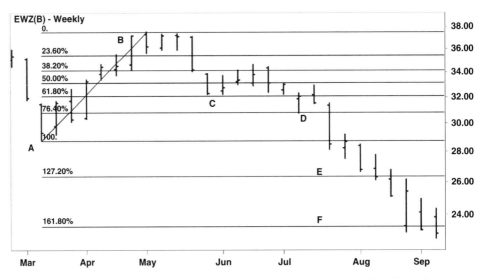

FIGURE 15.6 Fibonacci Retracements of Greater Than 100% on the Weekly Chart of EWZ

Fibonacci Time Applications

To this point, Fibonacci retracements and extensions have been expressed in terms of price. On a chart, those numerical relationships are usually represented by horizontal lines that relate to the price axis.

However, Fibonacci relationships can also be expressed in terms of time. The lines that are used to create Fibonacci time cycles are usually vertical and relate to the chart's time axis.

Fibonacci Cycles

Fibonacci cycles are not created by drawing from point A to point B; instead, just one point on the chart can be utilized. That point usually represents a major high or a major low point in terms of price.

The chart is then populated with vertical lines based on the Fibonacci sequence. If the chart is in the daily time frame, lines are placed 1, 2, 3, 5, 8, 13, 21 days apart, and so on. This is demonstrated in Figure 15.7, which shows a Fibonacci time cycle for the Dow Jones Industrial Average ($INDU).

On March 9, 2009, the Dow Jones Industrial Average closed at 6,547.05, its lowest closing point since 1997. Starting from that date (point A), a series of solid vertical lines populate the chart, representing the Fibonacci sequence.

The early numbers in the sequence (1, 2, 3, and 5) are bunched together, and because of this they are generally ignored. As the Fibonacci sequence spreads out over time, notice how major turning points tend to occur at the vertical lines.

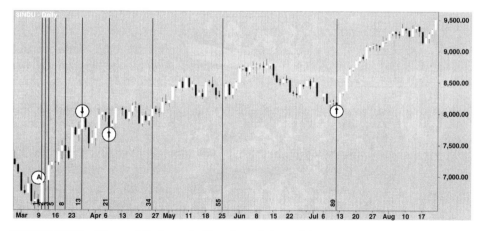

FIGURE 15.7   Fibonacci Cycle on the Dow Jones Industrial Average ($INDU)

This is particularly true of the lines marked 13, 21, and 89 (arrows). The chart tell us that turning points occurred 13, 21, and 89 trading days after the initial major low. This example uses trading days, but calendar days can also be used.

Fibonacci cycles can be created using various time frames. While Figure 15.7 demonstrates the use of a Fibonacci cycle on a daily chart, the same effect can be achieved on a monthly, weekly, or intraday chart.

Just as multiple Fibonacci retracements can be combined to search for price confluence, multiple Fibonacci cycles can be combined to search for time confluence. Since these lines project beyond the current date and into the future, they can be used to determine potential future turning points for a stock, an index, or a commodity.

■ Fibonacci Time Extension Lines

Like Fibonacci price retracements, Fibonacci time extension lines can be drawn from a high price to a low price, or from a low price to a high price. Unlike retracements, they can also be drawn from one high price to another high price, or from one low point to another low point.

The important factor here is that they are drawn from left to right, so that the lines project forward in time. After two points are chosen, the drawing tool is used to populate the chart with vertical lines based on the Fibonacci sequence.

In Figure 15.8, a line is drawn on the daily chart of the Crude Oil Continuous Contract (@CL) from a low on August 24, 2015 (point A) to a high on October 9, 2015 (point B). The chart is then populated with vertical lines that represent Fibonacci time retracements. The percentages are divided by the length of the time that it took for the price to travel from point A to point B.

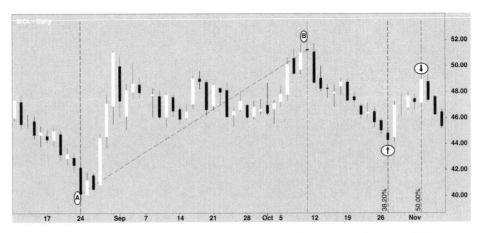

FIGURE 15.8 Fibonacci Time Extensions on the Crude Oil Continuous Contract (@CL)

Note how the price behaves when it reaches those vertical lines. When the 38.2% time extension is reached, the price of oil reverses course and moves higher (up arrow). The price then peaks at the 50% time extension line before turning sharply lower (down arrow).

Fibonacci time extension lines can be drawn to and from multiple levels in order to search for time confluences. They can be combined with Fibonacci price retracements and extensions in order to determine both the date and price of a likely reversal.

◼ Final Thoughts on Fibonacci

The way a trader chooses to approach Fibonacci techniques is often influenced by his or her belief system. If a person truly believes that Fibonacci numerical relationships are at the core of all things, and that they influence price movement and direction in the financial markets, then that trader is likely to assume that all Fibonacci techniques are equally valid.

On the other hand, there are traders who believe that Fibonacci relationships are tremendously important in nature, but are not necessarily the main driving force behind price action in the financial markets.

This group is more likely to consider Fibonacci somewhat self-fulfilling, and therefore will place greater emphasis on the most widely used techniques, such as Fibonacci retracements of 38.2% and 61.8%. This type of trader would also be less likely to assign importance to the more esoteric uses of these numeric relationships.

Ultimately, any technical analysis technique that has a self-fulfilling nature will benefit from longer time frames. A Fibonacci retracement that appears on the daily chart gives all market players an opportunity to participate, because there is time for word to spread among them about a key retracement level.

Additional time pulls in more players, reinforcing the self-fulfilling pattern. Meanwhile, a Fibonacci retracement on a five-minute chart could quickly appear and then disappear before traders have the opportunity to recognize and utilize it.

PART VI

TECHNICAL INDICATORS

CHAPTER 16

Moving Averages

Moving averages are one of the most widely used groups of technical indicators. They present a smoothed version of the price action of a stock, commodity, or currency, so investors can more easily see the general price trend.

Moving averages are usually constructed from closing prices, but this is not always the case. They are normally created from prices that are spaced at equal time intervals.

It's easy to create an average price; in this case, we will create a three-period average price. If we take three consecutive closing prices, we can create an average of those prices:

Closing price #1 = 23: This is the most recently ended time period.
Closing price #2 = 22: This is the second most recently ended time period.
Closing price #3 = 24: This is the third most recently ended time period.
Closing prices 23 + 22 + 24 = 69; 69/3 = 23

The average price for these three time periods is 23. That explains the concept of an average price, but how do we arrive at a "moving average" of those prices?

Let's assume that a fourth time period passes. Now we need to obtain the average price for the three most recent time periods:

New closing price (now closing price #1) = 21
Former closing price #1 (now #2) = 23
Former closing price #2 (now #3) = 22
Former closing price #3 (now #4) = 24. *This price is no longer part of the equation.* Since we are attempting to create only a three-period moving average, the fourth time period is no longer relevant.
Closing prices 21 + 23 + 22 = 66; 66/3 = 22

Another time period passes. Again, we need to obtain the average price for the three most recent time periods:

New closing price (now closing price #1) = 19
Former closing price #1 (now #2) = 21
Former closing price #2 (now #3) = 23
Closing prices 19 + 21 + 23 = 63; 63/3 = 21

We now have three consecutive average prices, each representing the three most recent time periods at that time. The data points are 23, 22, and 21. These average prices can be plotted on a chart. If they were, that chart would show a line sloping downward from 23 to 22 to 21.

This line is referred to as a "simple" moving average, or SMA. The downward slope indicates that the average price is falling, despite any ups and downs that may have occurred along the way. The SMA gives investors a clear picture of the price's general direction. Any short-term bullish or bearish moves have now been smoothed over.

Notice that I never specified the length of the time periods that were used. If the closing prices used in the previous calculation were obtained from a daily chart, the result would be called a three-day SMA. If they were obtained from a weekly chart, this would result in a three-week SMA. If the prices were obtained from an hourly chart, the result would be a three-hour SMA, and so on.

What if the prices were derived from a five-minute chart? In that case, we'd refer to it as a three-period SMA. This would hold true for any intraday time frame, such as the 30-minute chart or the four-hour chart. The term "period" is a catchall; it can refer to literally any time period, including daily, weekly, and hourly charts.

In reality, a three-period moving average would be of little use, because it would track the price very closely. Shorter moving averages (those consisting of fewer time periods) tend to be more sensitive to changes in the price, while longer moving averages (those consisting of a high number of time periods) adapt to changes in price more slowly. When more time periods are included in the calculation, the moving average gives a broader picture of the price action.

Figure 16.1 depicts the use of a 20-day SMA on the daily chart of Taser International (TASR). Notice how the ups and downs of the stock are smoothed over by the moving average, allowing the investor to observe the price in two separate ways. The individual bars consist of high, low, open, and closing prices, while the 20-day SMA presents a smooth, more general image of closing prices.

Which moving averages should a trader use? While there are no correct or incorrect moving averages, the most commonly used ones are the 10-, 20-, 50-, 150-, and 200-day SMAs. Some investment strategies involve selling stocks as they break below a key moving average, such as the 50-day or 200-day SMAs. Likewise, some investors consider a break above these moving averages to be a buy signal.

FIGURE 16.1 A 20-Day Simple Moving Average on the Daily Chart of Taser International (TASR)

◼ Order of Moving Averages

The location of moving averages in relation to one another can also be considered a signal. For example, some traders seek out situations where a stock's 10-period SMA is above its 20-period SMA. In turn, the 20-period SMA should be higher than the 50-period SMA, and the 50-period SMA should be located above the 200-period SMA. Taken together, the moving averages would align in the following order:

$$10 > 20 > 50 > 200$$

For example, in Figure 16.2, shares of the Nasdaq PowerShares QQQ Trust (QQQ) are shown in a steep uptrend in 2013. This was confirmed by the stock's moving averages, which were aligned in the proper formation (10 > 20 > 50 > 200) for an uptrend. The point at which the moving averages fanned out into the proper formation is circled.

Because Figure 16.2 is a weekly chart, it depicts the 10-week, 20-week, 50-week, and 200-week SMAs of the QQQ. It informs us that on its weekly chart, QQQ was in a strong uptrend throughout 2013 and into 2014. This same concept can be applied to any time frame.

In the case of a downtrend, the concept remains the same but the order of the moving averages would be reversed. The following is considered the correct order of moving averages for a downtrend:

$$200 > 50 > 20 > 10$$

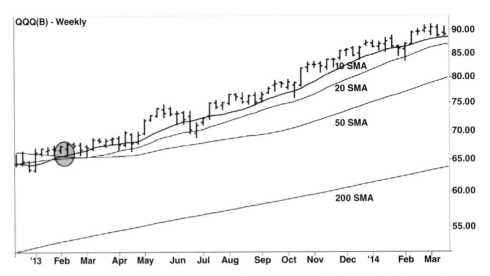

FIGURE 16.2 Moving Averages in Proper Order for an Uptrend on the Nasdaq PowerShares QQQ Trust (QQQ)

This order is demonstrated in Figure 16.3. In 2015, the S&P Select Energy SPDR (XLE) entered a steep downtrend, causing its SMAs to fan out as described earlier. The point at which the moving averages fanned out into the proper formation is circled.

Because Figure 16.3 is a daily chart, it depicts the 200-day, 50-day, 20-day, and 10-day SMAs of the XLE. It informs us that on its daily chart, XLE was in a strong downtrend in the summer of 2015.

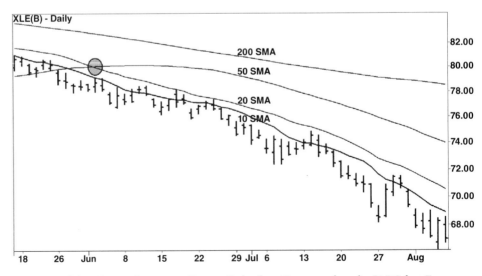

FIGURE 16.3 Moving Averages in Proper Order for a Downtrend on the S&P Select Energy SPDR (XLE)

Note that it is possible for the price to be in an uptrend or a downtrend without conforming to this guideline. However, when the proper order of moving averages is visible, then there can be no doubt as to the validity of the trend.

There are endless combinations of moving averages that can be used to create trading signals, but none of them are perfect. Some traders run "backtests" to see which combinations have worked the best in a specific time frame, asset class, or trading environment.

■ Moving Average Support and Resistance

Moving averages are useful tools in trending markets. They sometimes act as support or resistance within a trend; in this sense, they are similar to trend lines.

However, there is one important distinction: Moving averages are created by a computer program that, one would assume, is completely objective. The program isn't seeking to place a trade and doesn't have a biased opinion about a particular investment.

Trend lines, on the other hand, are usually drawn by the human hand, and therefore can be subjective when compared to moving averages. If you ask ten people to draw a trend line on a chart, you just might get ten slightly different trend lines. However, if you ask ten people to place a 50-day SMA on a chart, all ten should arrive at the same result.

Figure 16.4 provides an example of an SMA acting as resistance in the euro/U.S. dollar currency pair (EURUSD). On May 9, 2014, EURUSD fell beneath its 50-day SMA (point A).

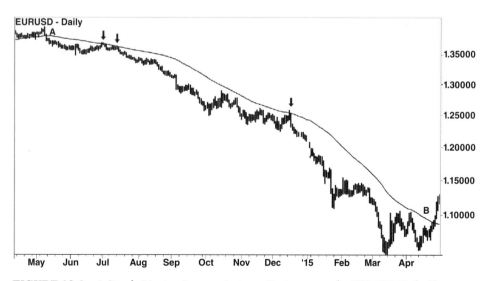

FIGURE 16.4 A Simple Moving Average Acting as Resistance on the EURUSD Daily Chart

On at least three occasions, the exchange rate climbed to the 50-day SMA, only to be rejected each time (arrows). Nearly a year later, on April 28, 2015, EURUSD finally closed above its 50-day SMA (point B).

■ Moving Average Trading Signals—Single Crossover System

Traders also use moving average crossovers to create buy and sell signals. One such example would be a 50-day SMA crossing above a 200-day SMA on a daily chart.

When the 50-day SMA crosses above the 200-day SMA, the crossover is popularly known as a "golden cross" and is considered bullish. When the 50-day SMA cuts below the 200-day SMA, it is referred to as a "death cross" and is considered bearish.

Some technical analysts insist that both moving averages should be rising for the golden cross to be considered legitimate, and that both moving averages should be falling in order to create a genuine death cross. Others define these terms in a less rigid manner.

An example of a golden cross is presented in Figure 16.5. On January 31, 2012, the S&P 500's 50-day SMA crossed above its 200-day SMA. That buy signal (circled) occurred as the index was trading just above 1,300. Nearly three years later, the 50-day SMA remained above the 200-day SMA, and the index had climbed above 2,000.

Figure 16.6 depicts a potent example of a death cross. In December of 2007, the S&P 500's 50-day SMA crossed beneath its 200-day SMA (circled). This crossover

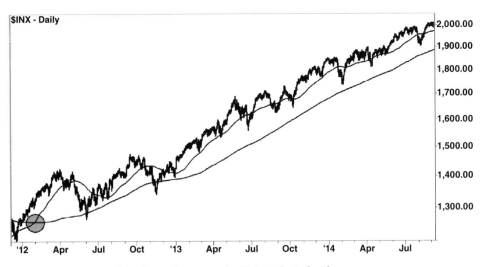

FIGURE 16.5 A Golden Cross Occurs on the S&P 500's Daily Chart

FIGURE 16.6   A Death Cross Occurs on the S&P 500's Daily Chart

occurred just below the 1,500 mark and proved to be an early warning signal for the coming stock collapse of 2008. By early 2009, the index was trading below 700, after suffering a loss of over 50%.

■ Average Returns of the Golden Cross and Death Cross

The golden cross and the death cross occasionally catch big moves, as indicated in the previous charts. However, they are not always accurate predictors of a coming move.

In 2015, a study by Bank of America Merrill Lynch analysts Stephen Suttmeier and Jue Xiong found that the death cross could actually be used as a buy signal. Between the years 1929 and 2015, the analysts found 45 occasions in which the S&P 500's 50-day moving average crossed beneath its 200-day moving average.

On those occasions, they determined that three months after the occurrence of a death cross, the average return of the S&P 500 was +2.57 percent. This was actually higher than the overall average three-month return of the index, which they found to be 1.82%. On average, the index traded higher by 3.53% six months after a death cross and 3.44% twelve months after an occurrence of the supposedly bearish signal.

The same study found that returns for the S&P 500 after a golden cross were superior to average market returns. In the three months after a golden cross, the index climbed an average 3.6% vs. the overall average of 1.82%. Six months after a golden cross, the S&P 500 rose by an average 5.12% vs. the overall return of 3.66%. In the twelve-month period after a golden cross, the average return for the S&P 500 was 9.52% vs. the overall average return of 7.6%.

Is the Death Cross Misunderstood?

Many market participants seem to believe that the market is supposed to crash every time the death cross signal occurs. However, the fact that some of the market's biggest crashes have been preceded by a death cross doesn't necessarily mean that every death cross signal will be followed by a crash.

Think of a smoke alarm in a house. Does the house catch fire every time its smoke alarm sounds? No, but that doesn't mean that the smoke alarm is broken.

Should we expect to see a market crash every time a death cross appears? No, but if a crash does occur, it could very well be preceded by a death cross. Like an alarm, the death cross is sending a warning signal—and there have been occasions when smoke has led to fire.

Playing the Odds

Why does the death cross fail to precede a crash more often than not? The answer is simple, yet important. It's the same reason why its opposite signal, the golden cross, tends to be a more successful indicator of directional change in the market.

Look at a very long-term chart of the major indices and you'll notice that over time, stocks tend to go up more than they go down. This means that in general, bullish signals should outperform bearish signals.

Figure 16.7 shows a 90-year segment of the price history of the Dow Jones Industrial Average ($INDU) from 1925 to 2015. Obviously, in the long run, a bullish stance would have paid hefty dividends. It's highly likely that, in general, buy signals were more effective than sell signals over this time.

Consider this: In the years 1975 through 2014, the S&P 500 had 31 "up" years and only 9 "down" years. This means that over that period of time, the bulls have been on the right side of the market over three-quarters of the time. In other words, it literally pays to be bullish.

It's hard to imagine any contest, inside a casino or otherwise, where the odds are this skewed in favor of one side. Yet the bulls aren't penalized in any way for standing with the winning team.

Some traders and analysts are criticized for being "perma-bulls," meaning that they consistently take a bullish stance regardless of market conditions. Is this stance due to their sunny dispositions? Perhaps, but it is more likely that they are simply playing the odds.

In horse racing, the return for betting on a heavy favorite is diminished, because the favored horse tends to offer the lowest payout. Being a bull in the U.S. stock market is the equivalent of betting on a Triple Crown champion to win a horse race, without the downside of a meager payout.

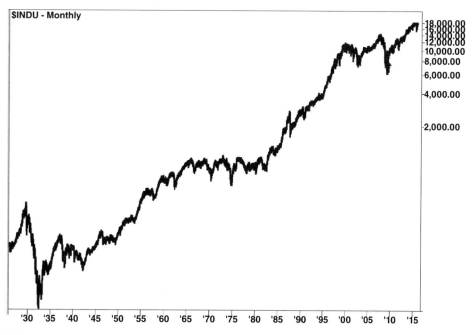

FIGURE 16.7 Rise of the Dow Jones Industrial Average ($INDU) from 1925 to 2015

Moving Average Trading Signals—Multiple Crossover Systems

One problem with the golden cross and the death cross is that they produce infrequent signals. To counteract this, traders use a variety of combinations involving shorter moving averages to create more frequent signals.

One variation on this theme has investors using the 4-period, 9-period, and 18-period moving averages to create buy and sell signals. The buy signal occurs when these moving averages are aligned in the following manner:

$$4 > 9 > 18$$

Figure 16.8 demonstrates both a buy and a sell signal using the 4/9/18 system. On January 23, 2015, Apple's 4-day SMA crossed above both its 9-day and 18-day SMAs, creating a preliminary buy signal (point A). This signal was confirmed when Apple's 9-day SMA crossed above its 18-day SMA on January 26 (point B), completing the alignment.

After a one-month rally, Apple's 4-day SMA crossed beneath its 9-day SMA on March 2, 2015 (point C). A preliminary sell signal occurred when Apple's 4-day

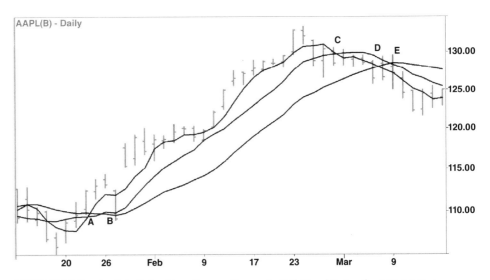

FIGURE 16.8   Apple's Daily Chart Shows a Buy and a Sell Signal Using the 4/9/18 System

SMA crossed below its 18-day SMA on March 6 (point D). This sell signal is confirmed when Apple's 9-day SMA crossed beneath its 18-day SMA on March 9 (point E).

■ Other Types of Moving Averages

There are other types of moving averages beyond the SMAs. The other types include linear weighted moving averages and exponential moving averages, which are discussed next.

Linear Weighted Moving Average

Up to this point, we've used SMAs in all of our examples. Now I'd like to introduce another type of moving average known as a "linear weighted" moving average (LWMA).

When we constructed our three-period SMA at the start of this chapter, we gave an equal weighting to all three time periods used in the calculation. However, it is possible to give a greater weighting to some time periods and a lesser weighting to others.

The LWMA places greater emphasis on the most recent time periods and less emphasis on older time periods. The greatest weight is placed on the most recent time period, and each successive period has a lesser weighting; in other words, the weighting of each time period is reduced in a *linear* fashion.

In the case of a weighted three-period moving average, the newest time period would have a weighting of three; the second newest would have a weighting of two, and the oldest time period would have a weighting of one. The reasoning behind this is that since the older time periods will soon fall out of the equation, they are treated as less significant than the more recent time periods.

Why would one do this? This emphasis on more recent time periods causes the weighted moving average to react more quickly to changes in price than its SMA counterpart. Note that this doesn't necessarily mean that the weighted moving average is superior to the SMA.

Figure 16.9 compares the 10-day LWMA (black) to the 10-day SMA (gray) of the euro/U.S. dollar currency pair (EURUSD) during the first half of 2015.

On the left side of the chart, the EURUSD exchange rate is falling sharply (down arrow). This causes the 10-day LWMA to fall beneath the 10-day SMA.

The LWMA falls more quickly because its newest periods are more heavily weighted to the current price. Meanwhile, the simple average's periods are equally weighted.

On the right side of the chart, the situation is reversed (up arrow). As the EURUSD exchange rate rises, the 10-day LWMA climbs back above the 10-day SMA.

On the far right edge of the chart, the exchange rate dives, and the 10-day LWMA drops below the 10-day SMA once again. Figure 16.9 clearly demonstrates that the 10-day LWMA reacts more quickly and follows the price more closely than the 10-day SMA.

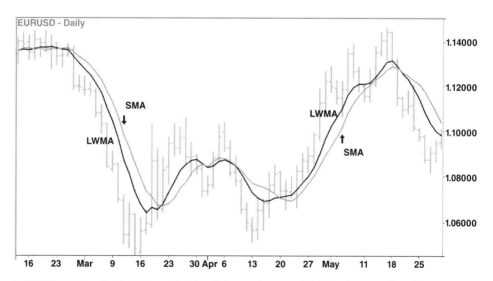

FIGURE 16.9   10-Day Linear Weighted Moving Average (LWMA) Compared to the 10-Day Simple Moving Average (SMA)

Exponential Moving Averages

An exponential moving average (EMA) is a type of weighted moving average, since it places greater emphasis on recent prices than it does on past prices. However, it differs from a LWMA in an important way. While the older prices fall out of the calculation of an LWMA, they are still part of the equation of an EMA.

The EMA calculates all of the historic ranges from a specific starting point. It takes new prices and combines them into the previous average. Because of this, older prices remain part of the equation.

This difference makes the EMA a smoother, slower version of an LWMA. The net effect is that an EMA tends to react more quickly to price than an SMA, but less quickly than an LWMA.

This is demonstrated in Figure 16.10. In late 2014/early 2015, shares of supermarket chain Kroger Co. (KR) were trending higher, as shown on the stock's weekly chart.

Kroger's 10-week LWMA climbed the fastest as it reacted most closely to the price. This was followed by the 10-week EMA (gray) and finally the 10-week SMA, which was the slowest of the three to react to Kroger's rally.

EMAs and LWMAs can be used in the same manner as SMAs. They can act as support and/or resistance, can be incorporated into crossover strategies, or simply provide the trader with a general idea of price direction.

In addition, other variants of moving averages can be applied to a chart. Here are just a few:

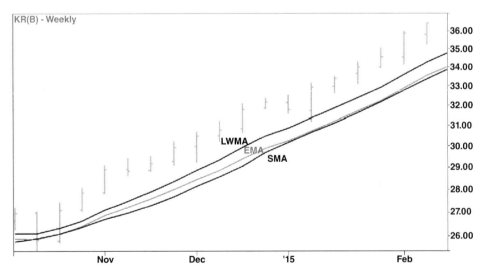

FIGURE 16.10 Comparison of a 10-Week Linear Weighted Moving Average (LWMA), Exponential Moving Average (EMA), and Simple Moving Average (SMA)

Wilder Moving Average: Created by J. Welles Wilder, this is similar to an EMA but uses different weightings. Wilder created a number of popular indicators, including the average true range indicator (ATR), and the relative strength index (RSI), both of which will be covered in later chapters.

Displaced Moving Average: Unlike LWMAs and EMAs, which have a shorter lag time when compared to a simple moving average, a displaced moving average can be used to create additional lag time.

When used in this manner, a displaced moving average is slower to react to the price than a similar-length SMA. This reduces noise and volatility, creating a smoother, slower version of the SMA.

Adaptive Moving Average: This version of the indicator adjusts its sensitivity to match the volatility of the instrument being analyzed.

A dull trading market causes the adaptive moving average to be less responsive; therefore, it creates fewer trading signals in a quiet market. However, if that market suddenly becomes active, the adaptive moving average quickly adjusts to the increased volatility and becomes more responsive to the price.

■ Final Thoughts on Moving Averages

A moving average can be applied to almost any set of numbers. An individual could create a moving average of their net worth or of the time spent each week performing a task, such as gardening.

In trading, moving averages are useful in trending markets. They present a smoothed version of the price, eliminating extreme high and low points.

CHAPTER 17

Moving Average Envelopes and Bollinger Bands

Moving averages can be used in the construction of other technical indicators, such as moving average envelopes and Bollinger bands. While they can be found in a variety of indicators, such as the MACD oscillator, moving averages literally constitute the centerpiece of these two indicators.

■ Reversion to the Mean

Because a moving average represents the general price of a trading instrument, it also serves as an "arithmetic mean." Many trading strategies place special emphasis on a concept called "reversion to the mean." This simply means that over time, the price is expected to return to a central point or area.

Moving averages are sometimes used as part of such mean reversion strategies. When the price moves sharply above or below a moving average, a reversion to the mean strategy assumes that the price will return to that moving average at some point.

This type of strategy can be easily visualized through the use of a "moving average envelope."

■ Moving Average Envelopes

This indicator is constructed with a moving average at its core, around which an envelope is created. The envelope consists of two lines, one above and one below the moving average.

The placement of these lines is usually based on a percentage of the price. The envelope's borders are commonly located 2%, 3%, or 5% above and below the moving average, depending on the volatility of the instrument being analyzed.

Figure 17.1 shows a moving average envelope (black lines) constructed around the 10-day SMA (gray line) of the Schwab U.S. Dividend Equity ETF (SCHD).

In this case, the upper border is fixed 2% above the moving average, while the lower border is fixed 2% below. The 10-day moving average (center line, gray) acts like a magnet, attracting the price from both above and below. Notice how the price continually reverts to the mean.

When the price extends more than 2% below the moving average, and therefore moves outside of the envelope (up arrows), a trader using a mean reversion strategy might use this as a signal to go long. If the price extends more than 2% above the moving average (down arrow), a mean reversion strategy would suggest a short position.

In either case, traders should take the current trend into account, and if one exists, reject trades that go against that trend. The target would be the center of the envelope, which is the location of the moving average itself.

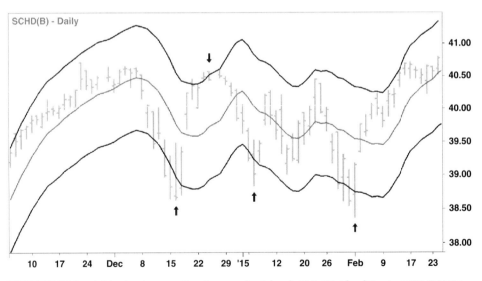

FIGURE 17.1   A Moving Average Envelope on the Schwab U.S. Dividend Equity ETF (SCHD) Daily Chart

Bollinger Bands

This indicator is the namesake of its creator, John Bollinger. Bollinger bands share a major similarity with moving average envelopes, in that both indicators are centered on a moving average.

Bollinger Bands consist of two dynamic bands that are normally centered by a 20-period moving average. The bands are sensitive to changes in volatility; they expand as volatility increases and contract as volatility ebbs. When the price nears the upper band, it is high relative to recent prices; when it nears the lower band, it is low relative to recent prices.

Standard Deviation

Unlike the moving average envelope, the width of the bands is not based on a percentage of the price. Instead, the bands maintain a distance of two standard deviations above and below the moving average. Standard deviation is a mathematical term that refers to the distribution of numbers or other data. For our purposes, we want to determine if a price move is within or beyond certain parameters.

With a setting of one standard deviation, the Bollinger bands would contain about 68% of all data points. When one uses this indicator with a one standard deviation setting, a great deal of the price action (about 32%) would occur outside of the bands, rendering that activity meaningless. If we were to use that information for trading signals, those signals would be frequent and noisy.

On the other hand, a setting of three standard deviations would keep approximately 99.7% of all price activity within the bands. This would make it exceedingly difficult for the price to move outside of the bands. Trading signals using three standard deviations might be potent, but would also be rare.

The most commonly used Bollinger band setting is two standard deviations, which would contain about 95% of all data points measured. Therefore, about 95% of all price activity, both above and below the moving average, would fall within the bands, and about 5% of the price action would occur outside of the bands. The Bollinger bands expand and contract in order to maintain this 95%-to-5% relationship. This makes the bands more dynamic than a moving average envelope.

Figure 17.2 shows Bollinger bands applied to the daily chart of Apple (AAPL). Notice how the price escapes the containment of the bands only about 5% of the time (circled). The 20-period SMA is visible in the center of the bands.

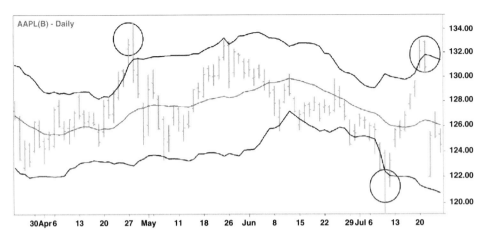

FIGURE 17.2 Bollinger Bands Using a Standard Deviation Setting of Two on Apple's Daily Chart

Bollinger Band Breakouts

Can Bollinger bands be used as part of a mean reversion strategy? They can be, and this type of tactic might work well in a range-bound market. However, a mean reversion strategy is just one way to use the bands.

When low-volatility conditions prevail, traders treat an excursion outside of the bands not as a mean reversion buy or sell signal, but as a breakout. Therefore, instead of fading a move that exceeds the upper or lower band, they assume that the price will continue to run.

The breakout could signal the start of a new trend, as the price awakens from a quiet slumber. In a low-volatility environment, traders playing a break outside of the bands assume the price will continue to run, pulling the centerpiece of the bands, the moving average, along behind it.

A low-volatility environment is marked by very tight Bollinger bands. An example of this is demonstrated in Figure 17.3; the iShares 20+year Treasury Bond ETF (TLT) broke above the upper Bollinger band in late November of 2014, kicking off a two-month rally (down arrow).

A trader could have used this Bollinger band breakout as a buy signal and initiated a long position. In this case, instead of using the moving average as a target, the trader could have used it to add additional shares to the position (up arrow).

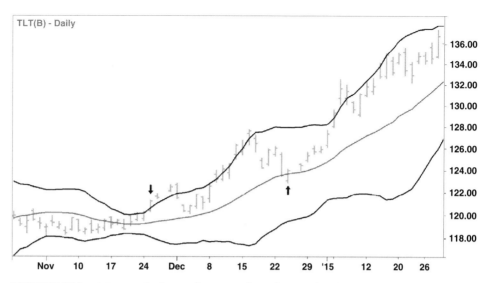

FIGURE 17.3 A Low-Volatility, Bollinger Band Breakout in the iShares 20+year Treasury Bond ETF (TLT)

◼ Cycle of Volatility

Take special note of the width of the bands just prior to the breakout and the subsequent rally depicted in Figure 17.3. The bands were extremely close together, which is an indication of unusually low volatility.

In a low-volatility environment, traders are either comfortable with the current price or are awaiting new information. That new information will inform traders of their next move, resulting in market movement.

When new information is released, the price breaks out and the bands split open, as that new information is digested by the market. As the price continues to run, the bands remain wide because volatility has increased. As long as the price is still moving, volatility will remain relatively high.

Eventually, that move will exhaust itself, and the bands will begin to narrow again. At some point, the new information will no longer be new; at this point the information is fully priced in to the market.

Traders once again become comfortable with the price. They await further new information, which is always on the way. This pause in the action causes the bands to tighten once again.

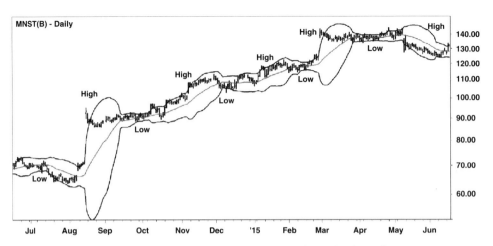

FIGURE 17.4 The Cycle of Volatility Is Demonstrated on the Daily Chart of Monster Beverage (MNST)

In Figure 17.4, shares of Monster Beverage Corp. (MNST) demonstrate this cycle of volatility. Notice how the Bollinger bands repeatedly contract prior to a big move (low, as in low volatility), and then split open as volatility returns (high, again referring to volatility rather than price).

The cycle of volatility is extremely important to options traders. Options tend to be cheap when volatility is low and tend to rise in value as volatility expands. This is because volatility is a key component in options pricing formulas.

■ Bollinger Bandwidth

The width of a pair of Bollinger bands can also be expressed via a separate indicator, called "Bollinger bandwidth." Bollinger bandwidth consists of a central line (the Bollinger bandwidth line) that rises and falls along with volatility. It represents the space between two Bollinger bands.

That line is bounded by the "squeeze line" on the lower side and the "bulge line" on the upper side. The squeeze line displays the lowest bandwidth value reached over a specific period of time, and the bulge line shows the highest bandwidth value reached over a specific period of time.

When the Bollinger bandwidth line sinks beneath the squeeze line, a breakout is considered imminent; when the bandwidth line rises above the bulge line, volatility is high and is therefore likely to contract. For traders who are concerned only with volatility, Bollinger bandwidth provides the same information that actual Bollinger bands provide, but in a different form.

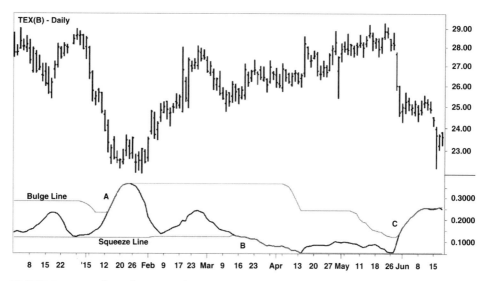

FIGURE 17.5   The Bollinger Bandwidth Indicator Is Applied to the Daily Chart of Terex (TEX)

Figure 17.5 depicts the use of Bollinger bandwidth on the daily chart of Terex Corp. (TEX). In January of 2015, the bandwidth indicator broke above the bulge line, indicating a highly volatile market (point A). By mid-March, volatility contracted, forcing the bandwidth line below the squeeze line (point B).

Volatility continued to fall until mid-April. Then in late May, a major breakdown occurred as Terex plunged (point C). The increase in volatility caused the bandwidth line to climb above the bulge line once again.

■ Final Thoughts on Moving Average Envelopes and Bollinger Bands

Moving averages literally constitute the centerpiece of these two indicators. While moving average envelopes are based on fixed percentages, Bollinger bands are more dynamic and incorporate the concept of standard deviation. Moving average envelopes are frequently used in conjunction with strategies that focus on mean reversion, while Bollinger bands are frequently used in the identification of breakouts.

CHAPTER 18

Oscillators

Imagine a seesaw. One end rises, and then falls, then rises again, and then falls. Imagine a pendulum. First it swings in one direction. Before long, the pendulum is swinging back the other way.

These are simple examples of oscillation. In technical analysis, an oscillator is an indicator that swings back and forth, giving overbought and oversold readings that can be used as trading signals.

■ Types of Oscillators

Oscillators can be divided into two main categories. A "centered" oscillator swings above and below a central point or line and creates a signal when it crosses that central point. When the oscillator swings above the central point, a bullish signal is given, and when it swings below that central point, a bearish signal occurs.

A "banded" oscillator exists on a numeric scale, for example from 0 to 100. This type of oscillator gives buy signals when it reaches extreme low points and generates sell signals when it reaches extreme high points on that scale.

■ Centered Oscillators

MACD—The Moving Average Convergence-Divergence Indicator

Perhaps the best-known centered oscillator is MACD, which stands for "moving average convergence-divergence." This indicator was created by Gerald Appel in the late 1970s and appeared in his book *Technical Analysis: Power Tools for Active Investors*. As its name implies, MACD is created from various combinations of moving averages.

MACD can be used in any time frame. The heart of this indicator consists of two lines. The faster of the two lines, known as the "MACD line," is actually created from two moving averages, the 12-period exponential moving average and the 26-period exponential moving average. The MACD line itself represents the difference between these two moving averages, which are calculated from closing prices.

A second line, known as the "signal line," is actually a nine-period exponential moving average of the MACD line. Because the signal line is a moving average of the MACD line, it is the slower of the two lines.

It is from this combination of moving averages that the MACD indicator derives its default setting of 12, 26, and 9. Other values can be substituted for these, depending on the desired frequency of signals. The use of shorter values results in more (but not necessarily better) signals, while the use of longer values results in fewer signals.

Figure 18.1 demonstrates the use of these two lines on the Cisco Systems (CSCO) daily chart in early 2015. When the MACD line (black) cuts downward through the signal line (gray), a sell signal is generated (point A). When the MACD line cuts upward through the signal line, a buy signal is generated (point B).

The MACD Histogram

In addition to the MACD line and the signal line, a series of vertical lines are visible with a single horizontal line, known as a "zero line," cutting through the center of the vertical lines. This section of the MACD indicator is called the "MACD histogram."

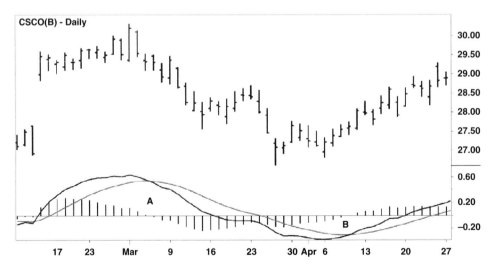

FIGURE 18.1 MACD Gives a Sell Signal and a Buy Signal on the Daily Chart of Cisco Systems (CSCO)

While this indicator may appear visually complex, it really isn't. The histogram simply reflects the information conveyed by the MACD/signal line crossovers. Notice that when the MACD line crosses the signal line, the vertical lines of the histogram cross the zero line at the same time.

Within the histogram, a cross from above the zero line to below indicates a sell signal (point A), and a cross from below the zero line to above indicates a buy signal (point B).

Because the histogram crossovers are synched with the MACD/signal line crossovers, traders need only focus on one or the other.

MACD Trading Signals Using Multiple Time Frames

MACD trading signals can be used in any time frame. Their usage is also popular in multiple time frame strategies. Figure 18.2 shows shares of FireEye Inc. (FEYE) in a steep downtrend on its daily chart in the second half of 2015. How might a trader capitalize on this trend using the MACD indicator?

Because FEYE is in a downtrend on its daily chart, trend traders would opt to sell short in order to place trades in the same direction as that trend. To do so, a trader with a shorter time horizon can seek out an MACD sell signal on a shorter time frame.

Figure 18.3 shows an MACD sell signal on FireEye's 60-minute chart in September of 2015 (point A). A trader might hold that short position until a MACD buy signal occurs (point B). When used in this manner, the MACD indicator allows a trader to capitalize on a downtrend by selling short.

FIGURE 18.2   Shares of FireEye Inc. (FEYE) Were in a Steep Downtrend in the Second Half of 2015

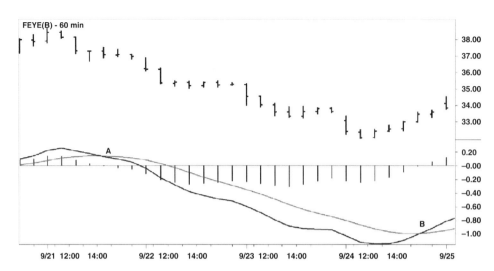

FIGURE 18.3   An MACD Sell Signal on FireEye's 60-Minute Chart (A), Followed by a Buy Signal (B)

In order to guard against a large loss, a protective stop could be placed above a prior high. That way, if the price breaks to a new short-term high, the trader would automatically exit the trade with a controlled loss.

In order to take profit, a limit order could be placed near a support area. The trader could also target a round number, knowing that orders have a tendency to accumulate at those points, and place a target just above it. Or, the trader could use an automatic trailing stop, which tracks the price until it is executed. These are just a few of the possibilities.

MACD Divergence

In addition to giving buy and sell signals, oscillators are commonly used to indicate a "divergence" between the price and the oscillator. Divergence simply means that the price and the oscillator are moving in different directions.

The MACD indicator is frequently used to locate such divergences, which are believed to foreshadow a change in the price's direction. When considering divergence, the analyst is working under the assumption that the price will follow the direction of the indicator.

Figure 18.4 provides an example of MACD divergence. In the early part of 2015, the U.S. Dollar Index ($DXY) was in an uptrend (section A).

Then in March and April, the index went through a period of sideways trading as it consolidated its gains (section B). During this time, the MACD indicator was trending downward, diverging from the price and foreshadowing a move lower. Note that a double top pattern formed during that same time.

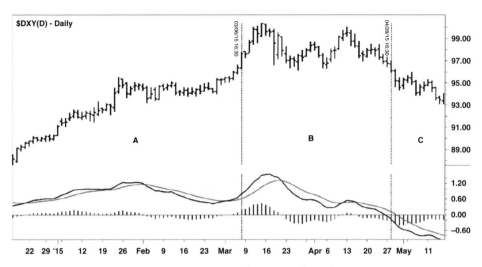

FIGURE 18.4 Negative MACD Divergence in the U.S. Dollar Index ($DXY)

In late April, the U.S. Dollar Index finally broke down and proceeded to follow the MACD indicator lower (section C). Because MACD was foreshadowing a negative move in the dollar index, this is referred to as "negative divergence."

At the same time that this was occurring, the euro was experiencing a "positive MACD divergence," which is depicted in Figure 18.5. In early 2015, the euro/U.S. dollar currency pair (EURUSD) was caught in a steep downtrend (section A).

Then in March and April, EURUSD consolidated its losses; while this was happening, the MACD indicator began trending sharply higher, an indication of

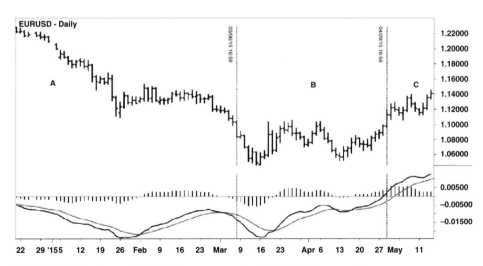

FIGURE 18.5 Positive MACD Divergence in the EURUSD Currency Pair

positive divergence (section B). Note that a double bottom pattern also formed in EURUSD at the same time.

Finally, in late April of 2015, EURUSD broke through resistance and began following the MACD indicator higher (section C).

The relationship between the EURUSD currency pair and the U.S. Dollar Index depicted in Figures 18.4 and 18.5 is an example of "negative correlation." This simply means that two instruments have shown a strong tendency to move in opposite directions.

Conversely, when two instruments have shown a strong tendency to move in the same direction at the same time, it is a sign of "positive correlation." The use of negative and positive correlation occurs frequently in cross-market analysis.

For example, certain commodities, such as crude oil, tend to correlate to certain currencies, such as the Russian ruble or the Mexican peso. This happens because those countries are major producers and exporters of oil.

While divergence gives clues about the next directional price move, it doesn't tell us when that move will occur. A divergence between the price and an oscillator can continue indefinitely, so the divergence itself doesn't necessarily create a buy or sell signal. That signal commonly occurs on a break of support or resistance. The divergence itself could be considered an early warning sign.

Momentum and Rate of Change

The momentum indicator is also a centered oscillator, and it is considerably less complex than MACD. It consists of a single line that oscillates above and below a central zero line.

The momentum oscillator measures the rate at which a price is rising or falling. When the oscillator crosses above the zero line, it generates a buy signal, and when it crosses below the zero line, it creates a sell signal.

It is also commonly used to determine if a trend is gaining or losing strength. This is accomplished by measuring not just price movement itself, but the speed of that movement. When the price is rising, the indicator is above zero and rising; however, if the price's ascent begins to slow, the indicator dips lower but remains above zero.

Conversely, when the price is falling, the indicator is below zero and falling. If the pace of the price's descent begins to slow, the indicator climbs but remains below zero.

In either case, when the momentum indicator begins to flatten, it's an indication that the trend is decelerating. The deceleration of a trend could be used as a warning that a trend is losing power.

Figure 18.6 shows the momentum indicator in action on the daily chart of Twitter Inc. (TWTR). In May of 2015, Twitter's momentum indicator crossed

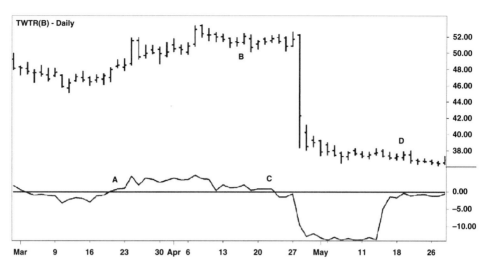

FIGURE 18.6 Buy and Sell Signals Using the Momentum Indicator on the Twitter (TWTR) Daily Chart

above the zero line, generating a buy signal (point A). After a brief rally from the high 40s to the low 50s, the price flattened out (point B), causing the momentum indicator to move close to the zero line.

Then a sell signal was generated on April 23 (point C) when the momentum indicator crossed below the zero line. This sell signal occurred just before Twitter's quarterly earnings report, which ignited a sharp sell-off three sessions later. The stock then drifted sideways for over a month, causing the momentum indicator to gravitate back toward the zero line (point D).

When the price is flat, the indicator moves to zero. If the momentum indicator rests at zero for an extended period of time, it's an indication of low volatility. The presence of a low-volatility environment could be confirmed by using a volatility indicator such as Bollinger bandwidth.

Rate of Change Oscillator

The rate of change (ROC) indicator is similar to the momentum oscillator with one key difference. The momentum indicator delivers that information in the form of a price differential, while the ROC indicator expresses that same information in terms of a percentage. Some traders prefer to analyze this information in percentage terms, so that it makes the information more adaptable to certain strategies.

The difference between these two oscillators is demonstrated in Figure 18.7, which shows the momentum indicator (top) and the ROC indicator (bottom) for semiconductor company Ambarella Inc. (AMBA). Both indicators are set to 14 periods on the daily chart.

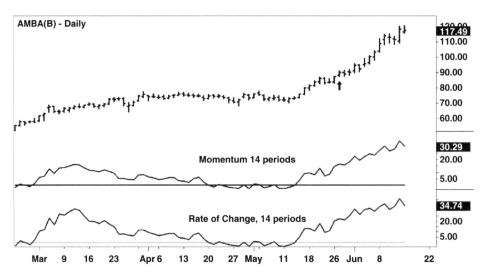

FIGURE 18.7 Comparison of the Momentum and Rate of Change Indicators on the Daily Chart of Ambarella Inc. (AMBA)

Ambarella's momentum indicator informs us that the stock has climbed $30.29 since its closing price from 14 periods earlier. That same move is expressed as a percentage gain of 34.74% by the ROC indicator. Both results are based on the closing price of the session 14 periods prior to the calculation (arrow), which was $89.88 on May 27, 2015.

What do the figures on the right axis represent? The closing price of AMBA on June 15, 2015 was $117.49.

Here is the calculation for momentum: $117.49 (closing price of AMBA on June 15) minus $87.20 (AMBA's closing price 14 periods earlier, on May 26, 2015) = $30.29, which mirrors the figure given on the right axis next to the momentum indicator.

The calculation for ROC is as follows: $117.49 \div 87.20 = 1.3473623$. That figure is rounded to 1.3474 and represents a gain of 34.74% over that same time period. Note the figure 34.74 on the right axis next to the indicator.

These calculations were done on a daily chart. Keep in mind that these calculations occurred after the market closed, as momentum and ROC are both calculated from closing prices.

■ Banded Oscillators

Relative Strength Index

The relative strength index (RSI) oscillator measures current prices against recent prices. The goal is to determine if the current price is overbought or oversold.

Like other oscillators, it is also used to generate buy and sell signals and to identify positive and negative divergence.

RSI consists of a single line that exists on a band or scale of 0 to 100 and uses a normal default setting of 14 time periods. Traders who wish to receive a larger quantity of signals can use a smaller number of periods; nine periods is a popular setting for traders who wish to receive many signals. A longer setting would generate fewer signals.

Within RSI's 0 to 100 band are two horizontal lines: one at 30, and another at 70. When RSI falls below 30, the instrument is oversold, and when it rises above 70, the instrument is overbought. It's important to understand that a stock, currency, or commodity that is overbought can always become more overbought, and one that is oversold can always become more oversold.

The terms "overbought" and "oversold" are *conditions*; in other words, they are not signals in and of themselves. A stock or currency can rise to an overbought level, and then just continue rising for a very long time. If you are selling short simply based on an overbought reading, you could find yourself on the wrong side of a very strong trend!

Figure 18.8 demonstrates the dangers inherent in using an overbought condition as a sell signal. Shares of Netflix Inc. (NFLX) shot higher on April 16, 2015, causing the stock's RSI to rise above 70 on the daily chart (point A). The stock opened for trading that day at $530.

The overbought condition didn't prevent Netflix from making a spectacular run to close above $633 on June 5 (point B). The stock remained overbought for eight straight weeks, and shares climbed by over $100 before Netflix's RSI dipped

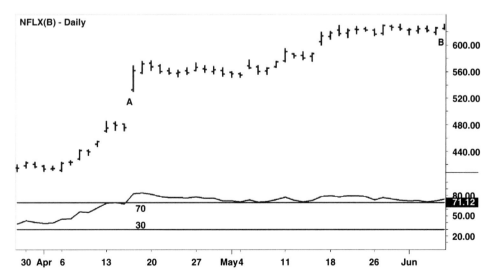

FIGURE 18.8 Netflix (NFLX) Rallies for Months Despite an Overbought Condition

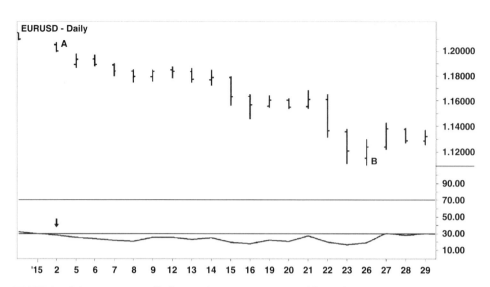

FIGURE 18.9   EURUSD Falls for Weeks Despite an Oversold Condition

back below 70. A trader who shorted NFLX on the overbought condition at $530 would've been crushed.

Just as an overbought condition doesn't equate to a sell signal, an oversold condition doesn't equate to a buy signal. A stark example of this occurred in the currency market and is illustrated in Figure 18.9.

The euro/U.S. dollar currency pair (EURUSD) entered an oversold condition on January 2, 2015 (point A) when its daily RSI reading closed below 30 (arrow). That day, EURUSD closed for trading at about 1.20, the point at which one euro is equal to $1.20 when measured in U.S. dollars.

EURUSD's oversold condition persisted for most of January as the euro continued its decline against the dollar. The currency pair was still oversold when it reached an intraday low near 1.11 on January 26 (point B).

That nine-cent move may not sound like much, but in the highly leveraged world of currency trading, it equates to 900 pips. Traders caught on the wrong side of this move could have suffered a catastrophic loss.

If an oversold reading doesn't constitute a buy signal, then what does? A buy signal occurs when the RSI indicator rises *from below 30 to above 30* after falling into oversold territory. Conversely, a sell signal occurs when RSI falls *from above 70 to below* 70 after giving an overbought reading. The move back into the neutral area between 30 and 70 indicates that the trading vehicle's momentum is starting to turn.

Figure 18.10 demonstrates an RSI sell signal on shares of healthcare provider Aetna Inc. (AET). Aetna's RSI closed above 70 on Sept. 9, 2014, and then closed beneath 70 the following day (point A). At the time, the stock traded at just under $85.

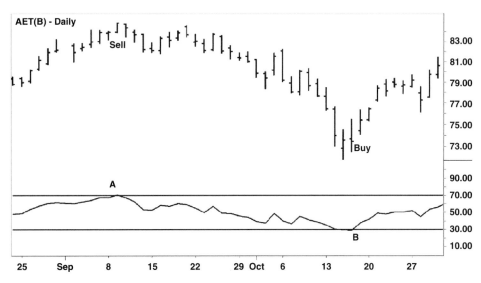

FIGURE 18.10 An RSI Sell Signal and Subsequent Buy Signal on Aetna Inc.'s (AET) Daily Chart

One month later, Aetna's RSI dipped below 30 and remained there for several days before closing back above 30 on October 17 (point B). This created an RSI buy signal at about $75.

RSI and Multiple Time Frames

Instead of taking buy or sell signals from a long-term chart, many traders use RSI on short-term charts as part of a "multiple time frame" strategy. Traders use a longer time frame to determine the direction of the trend, and then fine-tune the entry, stop, and targets on a shorter time frame by using RSI.

Here's an example of an RSI multiple time frame setup. Figure 18.11 shows the S&P Biotech SPDR (XBI) in a strong uptrend in early May 2015.

A trader who wished to go long XBI could employ a shorter time frame, such as a 15-minute chart, to locate a long entry opportunity. An example of this can be seen in Figure 18.12.

On May 14, 2015, an entry opportunity occurred when XBI dropped sharply at the open, creating an oversold condition on its 15-minute chart (circled). The RSI indicator quickly climbed back above 30, creating a buy signal with XBI trading at about $220 (arrow). XBI would climb to $230 within a few days.

Notice on the left side of Figure 18.12 that a buy signal nearly occurred at the open on May 12. However, XBI's RSI indicator failed to close beneath 30, so an overbought condition didn't exist at that time. Would a signal have occurred if the RSI were set to 9 periods instead of 14?

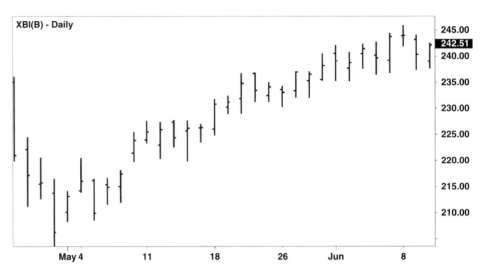

FIGURE 18.11   The S&P Biotech SPDR (XBI) Is Shown in a Strong Uptrend in May of 2015

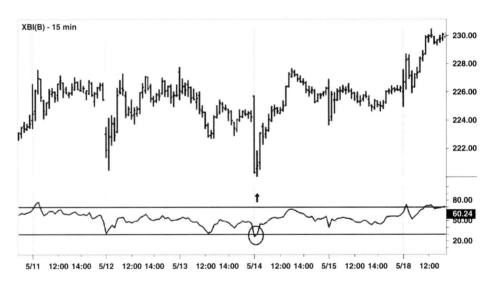

FIGURE 18.12   An RSI Buy Signal on XBI's 15-Minute Chart, Using a 14-Period Setting

As we can see in Figure 18.13, the answer is yes. In fact, there were two additional buy signals: one on May 12 (point A) and another on May 13 (point B). Does this mean that the 9-period RSI setting is superior to the 14-period RSI setting?

Not necessarily. Note that the May 13 setup (B) would have resulted in a break-even trade at best, and possibly a losing trade if the position were still open at the start on trading on the May 14. More signals will result in more trading opportunities, but not every trading opportunity results in a profitable trade.

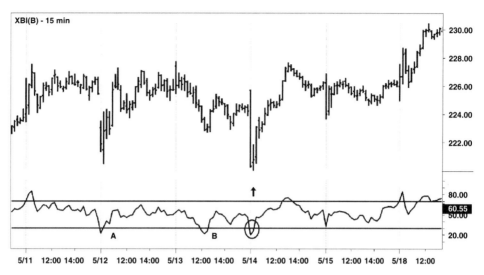

FIGURE 18.13   Several RSI Buy Signals on XBI's 15-Minute Chart, Using a 14-Period Setting

RSI Divergence

Like the MACD oscillator, RSI is frequently used to locate both positive and negative divergence. An example of negative divergence using RSI is demonstrated in Figure 18.14.

On the left side of the chart, shares of L Brands Inc. (LB) are making a series of higher lows and higher highs. At the same time, LB's RSI indicator formed a series

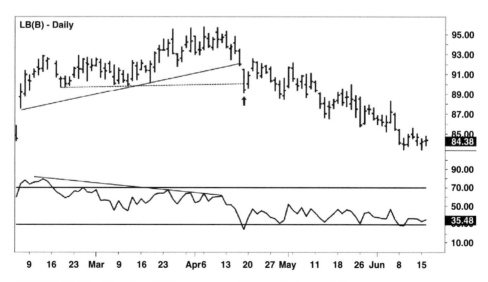

FIGURE 18.14   Negative RSI Divergence on Shares of L Brands (LB)

of lower highs. This divergence of LB's price and RSI foreshadows a coming drop in price.

The negative divergence in Figure 18.14 is not a sell signal; that occurs when the price breaks through support (arrow). A dotted line is drawn across a series of lows; that line is located approximately at the $90 level. The price broke through that line on April 17, 2015.

That break of support would be considered an opportunity to sell short. After an initial bounce, LB's trend changed from bullish to bearish.

Commodity Channel Index

The commodity channel index, or CCI, is another banded oscillator similar to RSI. The two indicators have much in common, but there are some important differences. For example, the default setting for RSI is usually 14, while a setting of 20 is generally used for CCI.

CCI's creator, Donald Lambert, introduced the indicator in a 1980 edition of *Commodities* magazine. As its name implies, it was designed as a timing tool for trading cyclical or seasonal commodities contracts. CCI compares a trading instrument's current price to a moving average of prices to determine if the current price is overbought or oversold.

While RSI exists on a scale from 0 to 100, the CCI scale runs from -300 at the low end of its range to $+300$ at its upper end. The indicator features two horizontal lines, located at -100 and $+100$. According to Lambert, 70% to 80% of random price fluctuations should fall between the -100 and $+100$ lines.

Perhaps the most critical difference lies in CCI's usage. Instead of using readings that fall outside of those two lines as overbought and oversold signals, they are used as buy and sell signals.

When CCI rises above $+100$, it generates a signal to enter a long position; if CCI subsequently falls back below $+100$, the trader should close that long position.

Figure 18.15 demonstrates a long trading signal using CCI on shares of Palo Alto Networks Inc. (PANW). On May 18, 2015, PANW's CCI reading closed above $+100$ (point A).

Since there is no way of knowing if the CCI will close above $+100$ until the time period (in this case, day) ends, a long entry would most likely occur at the open of the following bar at $158.50.

PANW's CCI remained above $+100$ for several weeks before closing below that level on June 4, 2015 (point B). This was the signal to close the long position. On that day, PANW closed at $168.75.

Figure 18.16 provides an example of a short trade using the CCI indicator. On April 24, 2015, the CCI reading for the U.S. Dollar Index ($DXY) fell below -100, a signal to sell short (point A). The opening price for the index on the following trading day was 96.94.

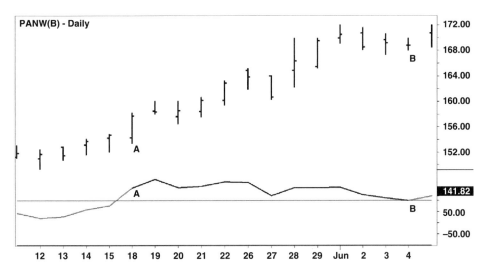

FIGURE 18.15 A CCI Buy Signal (A) in Palo Alto Networks (PANW), Followed by a Sell Signal (B)

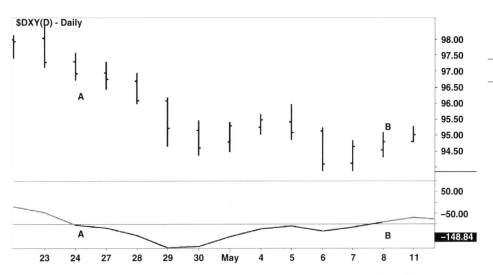

FIGURE 18.16 A CCI Sell Signal (A) in the U.S. Dollar Index ($DXY), Followed by a Buy Signal (B)

For two weeks, CCI remained below the −100 level. On May 8, 2015, the CCI reading climbed back above −100, signaling that the short position should be covered. The opening price of the following session was 94.80.

Although daily charts were used in these examples, this type of trade can be created using any time frame. An intraday chart, such as a five-minute chart, could have been used just as easily.

The traditional method of using this indicator calls for the trader to wait for the bar or candle to close before considering the CCI level. During the course of one bar or candle, the CCI reading could rise above and/or fall below the +100 and/or −100 levels on numerous occasions. Using the reading at the close provides a standardized method for dealing with these fluctuations.

Although its most commonly used default setting contains more time periods than RSI, the nature of CCI's construction makes it a more sensitive indicator. Because of this, it is relatively easy to generate buy and sell signals when using CCI's default setting of 20.

Is it necessary to understand the formula behind CCI in order to use the indicator effectively? While learning how to construct an indicator from the ground up can be a fascinating exercise, it is not an essential skill for becoming a trader. Consider this: You may not know how to build a car from scratch, but that shouldn't affect your ability to drive one. The same holds true for indicators.

■ The Stochastic Indicator

This oscillator was developed in the 1950s by a Chicago grain futures trader named George Lane. Lane was quoted as describing the stochastic oscillator in the following way:

> If you visualize a rocket going up in the air—before it can turn down, it must slow down. Momentum always changes direction before price.

That change in momentum is what the stochastic indicator attempts to identify. It focuses on the closing price relative to the range of a bar or candle. Stochastic answers the following question: Did the instrument close near the high, middle, or low end of the time period's range?

Why ask that question in the first place? Lane observed that in a strong uptrend, the price keeps closing near its highs as the instrument continues to rise. Later, although the instrument is still rising, the price begins to close in the middle or lower end of the range. The price is no longer able to close near its highs. Lane believed that this was an early sign that a trend was about to reverse.

Stochastic is a banded oscillator that exists on a scale of zero to 100. When the indicator is in the area below 20, the trading instrument is consistently closing near the low end of its range; when stochastic is in the area above 80, the trading instrument is consistently closing at the high end of its range.

Stochastic consists of two lines, %K and %D. %K measures the closing price relative to the price range and is the faster of the two lines. Common settings for %K include 14 and 5.

%D is a moving average of %K; in its most commonly used form, it is a three-period moving average. This makes %D the slower of the two lines, as well as a signal line. This version of the stochastic oscillator is called "fast stochastic."

A more refined version of this oscillator replaces %K with %D and then uses a moving average of %D as the signal line. This additional refinement slows and smoothens the indicator and is referred to as "slow stochastic."

Perhaps because this oscillator predates many of its peers, different methods of using stochastic have proliferated. For example, some traders consider a buy signal to have occurred when %K or %D rises above 20 after falling beneath that level.

Others simply go long when %K crosses above %D. A third entry method combines the first two; the trader goes long when %K crosses above %D while both lines are under 20.

Figure 18.17 provides several examples of the third method using fast stochastic on the daily chart of the S&P Biotech SPDR ETF (XBI). On March 19, 2015, the fast %K line (black) crossed above and then fell below the %D line (gray) while both were above 80, generating a sell signal (point A).

After a sharp sell-off, XBI's %K and %D lines fell below 20. While beneath 20, %K turned upward and crossed through %D, creating a buy signal on March 26 (point B).

XBI then rallied, causing both %K and %D to climb above 80. At the far right edge of the chart, %K crossed beneath %D while both lines were above 80, creating another sell signal (point C).

In Figure 18.18, the same chart is used to compare the fast stochastic (top) and the slow stochastic (bottom) versions of the oscillator on XBI's daily chart.

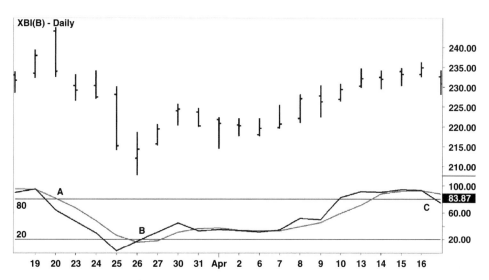

FIGURE 18.17 Buy and Sell Signals on XBI Using Fast Stochastic

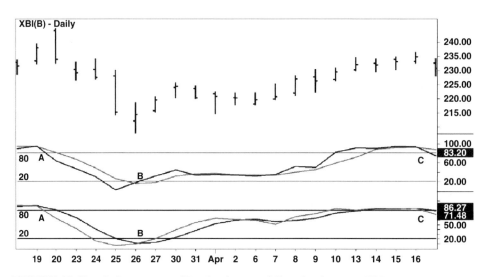

FIGURE 18.18 A Comparison of Fast Stochastic and Slow Stochastic on XBI

Note how the stochastic lines are less jagged when slow stochastic is applied. While a typical setting for fast stochastic would be 14, 3, and 3, the slow stochastic is created with the setting of 5, 3, and 3.

■ Final Thoughts on Oscillators

While we've covered most of the major oscillators here, we've only scratched the surface of this topic. There are countless variations of the more popular oscillators, and new ones are constantly being created.

You may have noticed that many oscillators are similar in form and use. Because of this, they can be redundant. There is usually no need to use more than one oscillator on the same chart at the same time.

This redundancy is demonstrated in Figure 18.19, which compares the RSI (top), slow stochastic (center), and MACD (bottom) oscillators on the daily chart of Dominion Resources Inc. (symbol D).

All three oscillators gave a buy signal within a short span of time. RSI climbed above 30 after falling below that level on June 16, 2015 (point A), creating a buy signal.

One day earlier, slow stochastic gave a buy signal when %K and %D crossed above 20 (point B). Several days before that, %K crossed above %D while both were beneath 20, which also could be interpreted as a buy signal.

Finally, the lagging MACD indicator gave a buy signal on June 18, 2015 (point C).

If you receive simultaneous buy signals from RSI, slow stochastic, and MACD, don't be surprised, as this is normal. Don't fall into the trap of believing that

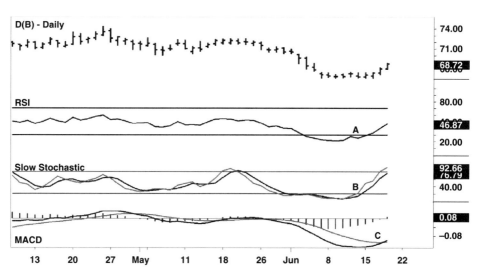

FIGURE 18.19 A Comparison of RSI, Slow Stochastic, and MACD on Dominion Resources Inc. (D)

you've discovered some amazing secret. Many oscillators give simultaneous or near-simultaneous signals.

Earlier, we referred to technical indicators as tools. To take that analogy a step further, if you were a construction worker on your way to a job site, would you pack six hammers into your toolbox?

I'm guessing that you wouldn't, because that would make your toolbox very heavy. You probably only need one or two good hammers anyway. Similarly, don't waste time working with too many oscillators when one or two will accomplish the task.

CHAPTER 19

Average True Range (ATR)

Imagine that you live by the ocean. This is a fortunate circumstance, because it just so happens that you also like to surf. Every morning you look out your window and check the conditions. Is the ocean flat, or is it rough? Are conditions optimal for a day spent riding the waves?

Occasionally, there are days or even weeks when the waves are very high and the surf is extraordinarily difficult to navigate. You notice that at these times, some of the other surfers choose to stay out of the water, while others shout, "Cowabunga!" as they charge into the sea. Some surfers shun a volatile ocean, while others embrace it.

■ The Market and the Sea

By now you've ascertained that this is an analogy for trading and the markets. I'm not going to lecture you to be mindful of the undertow, or admonish you to stay out of the ocean when the water is rough.

Not everyone thrives in the same type of trading environment. Who am I to tell people not to trade, just when the conditions suit their style? I can't tell you what type of environment you should shun or embrace, because that is for you to decide. You might be a trader who enjoys highly volatile markets.

Besides, you might not be given that choice; markets can become volatile after you are already fully invested.

I think we can all agree that a volatile market, like a rough ocean, presents greater danger than a placid market. Instead of spinning a cautionary tale, let's focus on a tool designed to help identify volatile and non-volatile trading conditions.

Before a surfer jumps into the water, one of the first things he or she is likely to do is determine the height and frequency of the waves. The surfer needs to know what to expect, and so does the trader. From the perspective of the technical analyst, one of the first things we should do before diving in is to measure volatility.

One indicator well suited to performing this task is average true range (ATR). ATR measures the price range, from high to low, of a stock, index, currency, or commodity.

It's important to note that opening gaps are included in the calculation of ATR. A range calculation that ignores gaps would provide very different results.

ATR provides the average price range over 14 time periods. Those time periods could be days, months, hours, or even five-minute blocks of time, depending on your chosen time frame.

A trader who plans and executes most of his or her trades in the daily time frame would measure 14 days when applying ATR. A trader who is focused on the hourly chart would measure 14 hours. The indicator measures volatility, which has no bearing on the direction of the price. ATR can be used in any time frame.

■ Creation and Development of ATR

ATR was developed by J. Welles Wilder, Jr., a prolific creator of indicators. In addition to ATR, Wilder has been credited with the development of many technical indicators, such as relative strength index (RSI), average directional index (ADX), and parabolic SAR (stop and reverse). The ATR indicator was featured in his book *New Concepts in Technical Trading Systems* in 1978.

A later book by Wilder, titled *The Delta Phenomenon*, claimed there was a hidden order in the markets that was strongly influenced by the orbital patterns of the earth, moon, and sun. The book expanded on Wilder's use of lunar cycles as a predictive mechanism.

This supposed link between lunar cycles and market activity may shed some light on Wilder's choice of 14 periods as a default setting for ATR and most of his other indicators. This is because 14 days is approximately the same length of time as one-half of a lunar cycle.

Personally, I'm skeptical about the existence of any link between the movement of heavenly bodies and trading markets. The former seems orderly, while the latter is prone to fits of randomness. However, I still find the ATR indicator, as well as other indicators created by Wilder, to be useful tools. The ability to measure

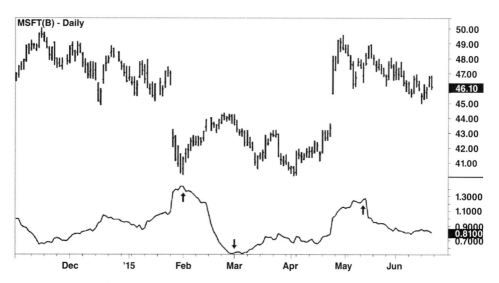

FIGURE 19.1 The ATR Indicator Applied to the Daily Chart of Microsoft (MSFT)

volatility using ATR has proven extremely helpful to traders, regardless of the rationale behind the indicator's construction.

Figure 19.1 shows the average true range indicator applied to the daily chart of Microsoft Corp. (MSFT). As of the close of June 19, 2015, Microsoft had an average true range of 81 cents per day, based on the previous 14 time periods. That figure appears on the far right bottom of the chart.

If you look to the left, you can see that that Microsoft's volatility was higher in February and May, when its daily ATR was in the 1.30/1.40 range (up arrows). The stock's volatility was considerably lower in early March, when Microsoft's ATR bottomed at about 50 cents per day (down arrow).

The Ten-Cent Trader

Imagine that a stock trader has decided to use a protective stop of ten cents on every trade. Is this a good idea? In a very basic way, we could say that it is, because that trader is at least attempting to use protection on every trade. It's also positive because the trader is focused on holding losses to a minimum.

However, the use of such a tight stop alone does not eliminate the possibility of a large loss. Since there is always the potential for a large price gap, the possibility for a large loss always exists.

Using a fixed price such as ten cents is an extremely basic method for placing a stop. Simply via observation, we can see that some stocks are extremely volatile, while others barely move. We may also observe that a trading instrument can go through wildly varying periods of volatility, both on an intraday basis and in the long run as well.

ATR and Risk Management

How can a trader deal with changes in volatility within one instrument, or across a variety of instruments? The trader could start by using ATR to measure that volatility.

Figure 19.2 applies the ATR indicator to the iShares 20+Year Treasury Bond Fund ETF (TLT) after the close on June 19, 2015. Over the prior 14 days, TLT had an average true range of $1.60 per day. Note that this almost exactly doubles the ATR shown in the Microsoft chart in Figure 19.1.

At this point in time, TLT's ATR was 2× that of MSFT. If TLT is twice as volatile as Microsoft, doesn't it stand to reason that a protective stop for TLT should be twice as wide as it would be for MSFT?

For example, a day trader might employ a strategy that requires that a protective stop would be equivalent to one-tenth of the daily ATR. One-tenth of Microsoft's ATR would be 8.1 cents, while one-tenth of TLT's ATR would equal 16 cents. ATR is frequently used in this manner.

Does this mean that the trader is risking twice the amount of money on the TLT trade compared to the MSFT trade? No, because the trader can compensate by making the TLT position half as large as the MSFT position.

This is absolutely critical to understand: A wider stop does not necessarily result in greater risk. A trader can control risk by adjusting the position size.

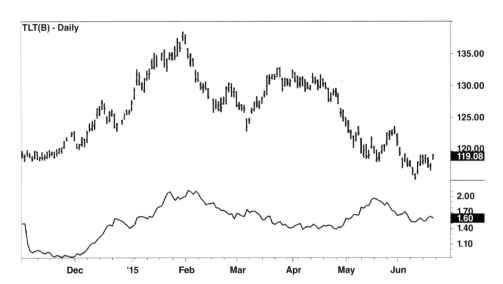

FIGURE 19.2   Application of the ATR Indicator to the iShares 20+Year Treasury Bond Fund ETF (TLT)

Let's assume that a day trader goes long 2,000 shares of MSFT with an eight-cent stop. The risk on the MSFT trade would be calculated as follows:

$$2,000 \times .08 = \$160$$

Now let's assume that the same trader enters a long position consisting of 1,000 shares of TLT with a 16-cent stop. The risk on the TLT trade would be calculated as follows:

$$1,000 \times .16 = \$160$$

The two positions have a similar level of risk, despite the difference in the volatility of the two trading vehicles.

Using ATR to Create Targets

We could also apply the same concept of volatility to the creation of a target. Since TLT's daily ATR is double that of Microsoft, we could say that TLT travels twice as far as MSFT on an average day. If that's the case, wouldn't it make sense that the profit target on TLT would be twice as far away as the target on MSFT?

For example, a day trader could choose to use three-tenths of the daily ATR to create a target. Three-tenths of Microsoft's daily ATR of .81 cents (as shown in Figure 19.1) would be approximately 24 cents, while three-tenths of TLT's ATR reading of $1.60 (as shown in Figure 19.2) would be equal to 48 cents.

Therefore, we could calculate the potential profit for the TLT trade as follows:

$$1,000 \text{ shares} \times .48 = \$480$$

The potential profit for the MSFT trade would be:

$$2,000 \text{ shares} \times .24 = \$480$$

This is just one of many potential methods one can use in determining a target price.

Keep in mind that volatility is in a constant state of flux. TLT's volatility was twice that of MSFT at the time of this writing, but volatility isn't static.

It would not be correct to assume that the 2:1 volatility relationship will remain intact. In fact, it would be safe to assume that the 2:1 volatility relationship will change in the future, perhaps drastically. Volatility levels are not constant, which is why we always measure volatility prior to considering the trade.

Changes in Volatility

Just as we can measure differences in volatility among several trading instruments, we can also measure changes in the volatility of a single instrument over time.

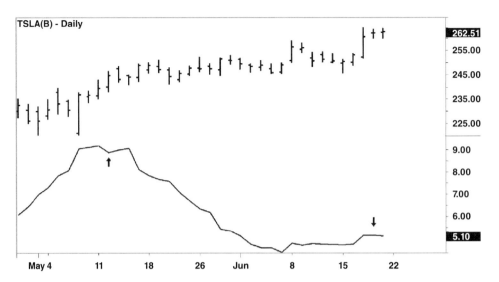

FIGURE 19.3 ATR Measures Changes in Volatility in Shares of Tesla Motors (TSLA)

Figure 19.3 provides an example of this by applying ATR to the daily chart of Tesla Motors (TSLA).

On the right side of the chart, Tesla displays an ATR of 5.10 ($5.10) per day, based on the prior 14 days, as of June 19, 2015 (down arrow). If a day trader were using one-tenth of the daily ATR to determine the distance of the stop, that protective stop would be 51 cents from the entry point.

However, on the left side of the chart we can see that in early May 2015, Tesla's volatility was much higher (up arrow). If the same trader had used the same method of stop placement at that time, the stop would have been placed 91 cents away from the entry point instead of 51 cents away.

Since the volatility of most trading instruments is in a constant state of flux, we can't assume that prior levels of volatility are applicable to the current market environment.

ATR and Other Markets

ATR readings are easy to understand when they are applied to individual stocks. As we saw in the previous examples, a reading of 0.81 equals 81 cents, and an ATR reading of 1.60 equals $1.60.

What happens when we apply ATR to a trading instrument in which movement isn't measured in dollars and cents? In Figure 19.4, we see the ATR indicator applied to the Dow Jones Industrial Average ($INDU). As a result, the indicator is now measuring points instead of dollars and cents.

At the time, the index had an average true range of 162.15 points based on the previous 14 trading sessions. We can also see that the reading is showing volatility at an approximate mid-range between its highs in January/February and the lows of early March.

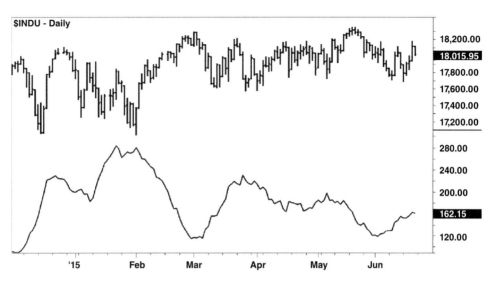

FIGURE 19.4   The ATR Indicator Applied to the Dow Jones Industrial Average ($INDU)

ATR can be used to analyze a variety of trading vehicles, but its application to the currency markets occasionally results in confusion, due to the pricing dynamics of that market. Because currency pairs are priced in fractions of pennies called "pips" instead of in dollars or points, the readings can be confusing to traders who are less experienced with this trading vehicle.

Figure 19.5 demonstrates the use of ATR on a currency chart. In the upper portion of the euro/U.S. dollar (EURUSD) chart, we see the exchange rate of 1.1348. This means that at the time this chart was created, one euro was worth 1.1348 U.S. dollars.

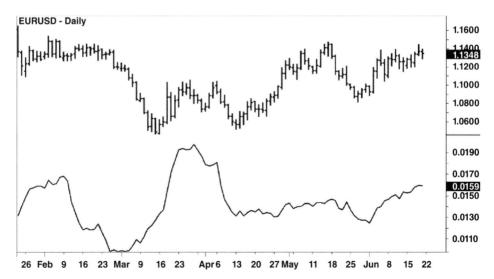

FIGURE 19.5   The ATR Indicator Applied to the Euro/U.S. Dollar Currency Pair (EURUSD)

In the lower portion of Figure 19.5, the ATR reading of 0.0159 is visible. This equates to an average true range of 159 pips per day, based on the prior 14 trading sessions. Note that we are only counting four decimal spaces; if a fifth decimal space were visible, the result would remain 159 pips.

In Figure 19.6, this same concept is applied to the U.S. dollar/Japanese yen (USDJPY) currency pair. In the upper portion of the chart, the exchange rate of 122.67 is visible. This means that at the time, one U.S. dollar was worth 122.67 Japanese yen. Note that the exchange rate decimal is two spaces farther to the right in Figure 19.6 than it was in Figure 19.5.

To compensate for this, we must mentally move the decimal in the ATR reading of Figure 19.6 two spaces to the right. Instead of using the visible ATR reading of 1.0894, move the decimal two spaces to the right, and the result is 108.94.

We have just determined that at the time this chart was created, based on the prior 14 trading sessions, the U.S. dollar/Japanese yen currency pair moved an average of about 108 pips per day. We would round this figure up to 109 pips per day, based on the .94 of one pip visible in the last two decimal spaces.

ATR readings on the yen currency pairs are substantially different from most other pairs because the value of one yen is so small compared to other currencies. In

AVERAGE TRUE RANGE (ATR)

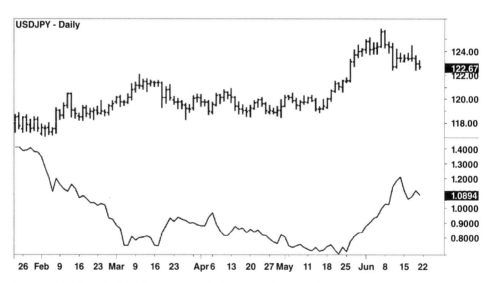

FIGURE 19.6 The ATR Indicator Applied to the U.S. Dollar/Japanese Yen Currency Pair (USDJPY)

other words, if one dollar is worth over 122 yen, but worth only 100 pennies, then it's safe to say that one Japanese yen is worth less than one U.S. penny.

■ Final Thoughts on ATR

ATR is frequently used as a risk management tool. When using ATR in this manner, it helps to have a predetermined maximum allowable risk for each trade. For example, a trader who has $100,000 in an account might decide to risk no more than 1% of that account, or $1,000, on any one individual trade.

Once the maximum risk has been decided, and the current volatility of the instrument being traded has been determined using ATR, these two factors are used together to determine the proper position size.

This is just one of many ways to manage risk when trading volatile instruments. With so much emphasis on entries and exits, position sizing is an extremely important, yet often overlooked aspect of risk management.

CHAPTER 20

Complex Indicators

The following two indicators were created by the prolific J. Welles Wilder, Jr. Some analysts might consider these more than mere indicators, because each provides enough information to create a cohesive trading strategy.

◼ Average Directional Index

The average directional index (ADX) was created by Wilder and introduced in his 1978 book *New Concepts in Trading Systems*. This indicator is used to determine the strength of a trend. ADX is a fairly complex indicator, as it is constructed from several sub-indicators.

Directional Movement Index

The ADX indicator is constructed from a separate indicator called the directional movement index (DMI), which itself can be divided into two indicators: plus directional movement index (+DI) and minus directional movement index (−DI). As with most of Mr. Wilder's indicators, the default setting for both ADX and DMI is 14 periods.

When prices are rising, the +DI line (black) is rising and the −DI line (grey) is falling. The opposite is true when prices are falling. This is demonstrated on the daily chart of Cisco Systems (CSCO) in Figure 20.1.

On Cisco's chart, we can see the +DI rise and fall along with the price, while the −DI line moves in the opposite direction of the price.

The directional movement index is calculated by comparing a current bar's high to the previous bar's high, and by comparing the previous bar's low to the current bar's low.

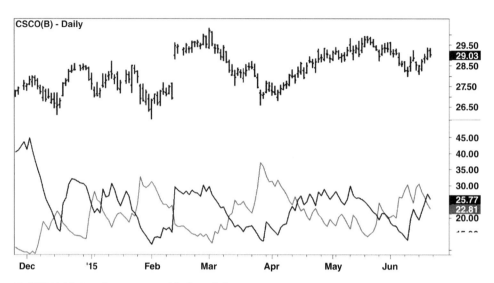

FIGURE 20.1 The +DI Line (black) and the −DI Line (gray) Move in Opposite Directions on the Cisco Systems Daily Chart

Whichever is greater—the distance between the two highs or the distance between the two lows—determines the reaction of the directional movement index. For example:

Current bar or candle's high of $35.00 − previous high of $34.00 = $1.00
Previous bar or candle's low of $33.50 − current low of $33.25 = $0.25

Since the difference between the two highs ($1.00) is greater than the difference between the two lows ($0.25), the directional movement is positive. This positive activity causes the +DI line to rise, and forces the −DI line to fall. If the difference between the two lows had been greater than the difference between the two highs, −DI would have risen and +DI would have fallen.

Some traders use crossovers of the +DI and −DI lines as trading signals, going long when the +DI line crosses above the −DI line and selling short when the opposite occurs. Using this signal alone without any confirmation is inadvisable, since +DI and −DI can cross frequently in a range bound market. For example, the chart in Figure 20.1 shows many +DI/−DI crossovers, but the price has no real direction.

The ADX Line

If a trend exists, it should be identified by the +DI and −DI lines. Add to this the ADX line, a separate, third line that measures the strength of a trend. ADX exists on a scale from 0 to 100.

An ADX value below 25 indicates a trendless market, or one with a weak trend, while an ADX value above 25 indicates a trending market: the higher the number, the stronger the trend. Although it has been known to happen, the indicator rarely gives readings above 60.

ADX is frequently used as a precondition in nondiscretionary trend trading strategies. There are many nondiscretionary trading strategies that begin with the condition "If ADX is above 25 and rising," and this simply means that the strategy requires a strong trend.

When +DI is above −DI, and the ADX line is above 25 and rising, the instrument being analyzed is considered to be in a strong uptrend. When −DI is above +DI and the ADX line is above 25 and rising, the instrument is considered to be in a strong downtrend.

Traders can employ greater selectivity and locate stronger trends by rejecting opportunities that have a rising ADX reading of below 30. Conversely, they can employ less selectivity by accepting trades with a rising ADX of 20 or above.

When interpreting ADX, it's not the level of the indicator but its direction that is of the greatest importance. The fact that ADX is above 25 doesn't mean the trend is accelerating; this is determined by whether the ADX line is rising or falling. If the ADX line is falling, this means that a trend is decelerating. This is true regardless of the ADX level.

Figure 20.2 demonstrates the ADX line on the daily chart of Palo Alto Networks Inc. (PANW). Palo Alto began to trend higher in May 2015, and by the latter part

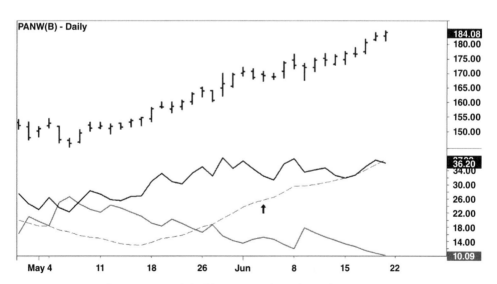

FIGURE 20.2 The ADX Line (dashed line) Is Visible on the Daily Chart of Palo Alto Networks Inc. (PANW)

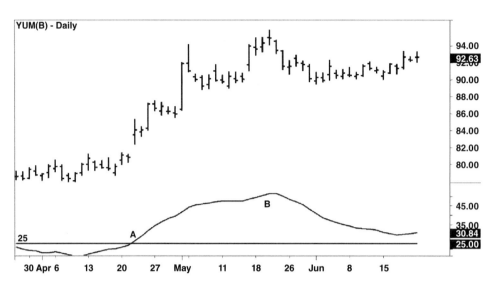

FIGURE 20.3 A Stand-Alone ADX Line on the Daily Chart of Yum Brands (YUM)

of that month the ADX line (dashed line) started to climb. The solid black line represents +DI, while the solid grey line represents −DI.

On June 3, 2015, Palo Alto's ADX line finally crossed above 25, indicating that it was in a strong uptrend (arrow). In the two weeks after June 3, shares of Palo Alto climbed from $169 to $184.

By the June 19 close, Palo Alto's ADX had climbed above 37 and was still rising. This was indicative of a very strong trend.

While it is often viewed as a component of ADX/DMI, the ADX line itself can be viewed as a stand-alone indicator. This is demonstrated on the daily chart of Yum Brands (YUM) in Figure 20.3.

YUM gapped higher and closed above the ADX 25 level (black horizontal line) on April 22, 2015 (point A). This was followed by a fierce rally from the $83 area. After peaking near $95 on May 20, the ADX line began to decline (point B).

YUM proceeded to drift sideways for a month. Notice that the ADX line began to decline after YUM peaked, but remained above the 25 level. The fact that the ADX line was no longer rising indicated that the stock was no longer trending. This was true despite the fact that the ADX reading was above 25.

■ Parabolic Stop and Reverse

Parabolic stop and reverse (SAR) is another complex indicator designed by Wilder. Parabolic SAR is more than an indicator; it is a complete trading system that includes entries and dynamic trailing stops. No exit point is provided, as the price will eventually come into contact with the trailing stop by design.

This is an "always-in" strategy, meaning that a trader using this technique will always be either long or short. It also requires that the user adhere to one of the basic principles of risk management. Parabolic SAR requires that the user *always tighten, and never loosen* a protective stop. What does that mean?

■ Always Tighten, Never Loosen

The theme of this book isn't risk management, but that topic must be considered a key component of successful trading, one that is just as important as technical analysis. The two disciplines mesh in the use of the parabolic SAR indicator.

When a trader is in a long position, the protective stop, if one is used, is located beneath the price. It is acceptable to raise the stop, but not to lower it.

Raising the protective stop of a long position is encouraged because it results in a reduction of risk, while lowering that stop would be unacceptable because it would result in a higher level of risk.

When we raise the stop on a long position, it is said that the stop has been "tightened"; in other words, the stop has been moved closer, or tighter, to the price.

In the event of a short positon, the protective stop would be located above the price. It is acceptable to lower the stop, but not to raise it.

Lowering the stop on a short position is another form of tightening, because it results in a reduction of risk. If we were to raise or "loosen" the stop on a short position, this would be unacceptable because it would result in a greater level of risk.

This is a valuable risk management concept, one that should be retained regardless of whether the trader is using the Parabolic SAR indicator.

Figure 20.4 provides an example of the use of Parabolic SAR on a 30-minute chart of Sonic Corp. (SONC). On the far left edge of the chart, SONC's bar rises and comes into contact with a black dot located above the price (point A). This black dot represents the location of a protective stop.

The fact that the dot is above the price indicates that the trader is short SONC. Then the stop is hit.

Once the stop has been hit, the strategy assumes that the trader will flip from a short positon to a long position in SONC. We see that the black dot representing the protective stop is now located beneath the price (point B). As each new bar forms, the dot moves one space to the right.

As the price of SONC moves sideways, the stop slowly inches closer to the price. As each 30-minute bar passes, the dot is elevated slightly higher. This indicates that the level of risk present in this trade is being reduced over time (point C). In other words, the stop is being tightened.

At the June 18 open, SONC suddenly begins to accelerate to the upside (point D). Note that the dots are now spaced farther apart. The indicator has accelerated the

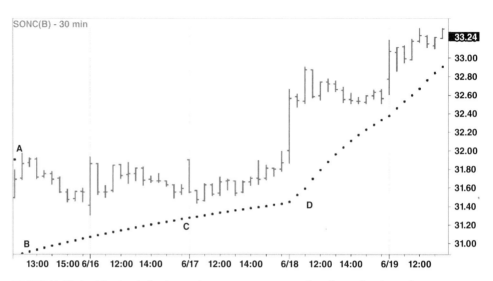

FIGURE 20.4 The Parabolic SAR Indicator Is Demonstrated on the Daily Chart of Sonic Inc. (SONC)

pace at which it is raising the stop in an effort to keep up with SONC's rapidly rising price.

There is no price target involved with parabolic SAR, because eventually, the price will fall back and hit the trailing stop. When it does, the SONC position will be flipped from long to short, and the process will begin again.

This indicator deviates from Wilder's usual 14-period setting. Instead, the normal default settings are as follows: An acceleration factor that begins at 0.02 and a maximum acceleration factor or "speed limit" of 0.20. As its name implies, the maximum acceleration factor prevents the indicator from tightening too quickly, which might cause the stop to collide with the price prematurely.

Parabolic SAR is structured so that the SAR dot must be below the prior two periods' lows in an uptrend, and above the prior two periods' highs in a downtrend. This is also done to prevent a premature exit of the trade.

■ Final Thoughts on Complex Indicators

Some indicators have multiple moving parts and can perform numerous tasks. For example, the average directional index provides several methods for creating trade entries and exits. Some of these complex indicators, such as parabolic stop and reverse, can act as strategies unto themselves.

PART VII

OSCILLATORS

CHAPTER 21

Point and Figure Charting

L ong before computer technology was widely available, investors and traders used various charting techniques. One of those techniques, known as "point and figure" charting, is still popular today. Point and figure provides a no-frills method for creating entries, exits, and stops, and many modern traders find its simplicity refreshing.

■ Point and Figure Basics

In nearly every chart we've viewed up to this point, price and time have been given equal weighting. Prices were analyzed on the Y-axis, where they move vertically between low and high points. Meanwhile, time was calculated in equal measurements on the horizontal X-axis.

What if we were to decide that price is more important than time? What if we decided that only major price events are worth analyzing? What if we completely ignored the length of time involved in the creation of those price movements? What if we set a minimum standard for price movement and disregarded any price changes that failed to meet that standard?

These concepts are not far-fetched. After all, there are periods of time on nearly every chart where little noteworthy activity occurs. How could we narrow our focus to strictly meaningful activity?

We would begin by determining which events would constitute noteworthy activity. We could choose to focus only on new major highs or lows, large directional moves, price reversals, and breakouts. This separation of the mundane from the meaningful is what point and figure (P&F) charting is all about.

In theory, if we remove all meaningless price activity from the chart, then meaningful activity is all that will remain. P&F charts make it easier to spot breakouts and reversals by filtering out the noise of the market.

A Highlight Film

Using a P&F chart is like looking at the highlights of a sporting event as opposed to watching the entire game. P&F charts get right to the point and take us to where the action is, while ignoring those periods of time where little of consequence occurred.

In P&F charting, the Y-axis represents the price, as it does on most charts. However, instead of focusing on time, the X-axis is focused on changes in the *direction* of the price.

This is demonstrated in Figure 21.1, which shows a P&F chart of AT&T Inc. (T). Note how time on the X-axis is unevenly distributed. This is because periods of inconsequential price activity are missing from the chart.

As you can see, a P&F chart looks like a game of tic-tac-toe gone haywire. In P&F charting, X's and O's populate spaces called "boxes."

Columns of X's denote bullish periods when the price was rising, while columns of O's represent bearish periods when the price was falling. The price must move by a specified minimum amount in one direction to create a new X or an O; if it fails to do so, then no changes are made to the chart, regardless of the amount of time involved.

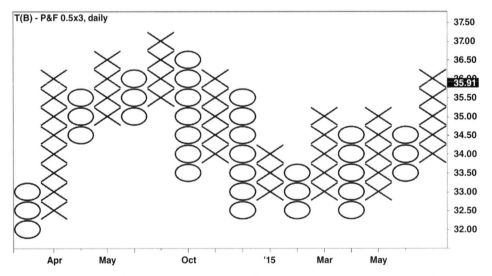

FIGURE 21.1 On This Point and Figure Chart of AT&T Inc. (T), Time on the X-Axis Is Unevenly Distributed

A column of X's or O's remains open for as long as the price movement persists in that direction. When prices change direction by a specified amount, the column is closed, and a new column is opened in the opposite direction, one space to the right.

This technique is a throwback to the days when charts were drawn by hand, as P&F charts are easy to create manually. One can imagine traders and investors scribbling X's and O's on a sheet of graph paper while obtaining the closing stock market prices from a newspaper or during a lull in the action on a trading floor.

There are no gaps on a P&F chart. If the price actually does gap higher or lower, the intervening spaces are normally filled with X's or O's.

■ Increment or Box Size

When using a P&F chart, we must determine what increment of price movement should be considered significant. The answer can vary, depending on the price and volatility of a trading instrument.

For example, there are some stocks that move $1 in one day on a regular basis, and other stocks for which a $1 move would be almost unheard of. In the case of the former, a price move of $1 would be considered insignificant, while for the latter, a $1 move in price could be considered very meaningful.

We refer to the size of the incremental moves that are required to create a new X or O as the P&F chart's "increment" or "box size." Each X or O occupies one box on the chart and represents the minimum price movement required by the chartist. Any price movement that is less than the box size is ignored.

In the AT&T (T) daily chart depicted in Figure 21.1, the box size is 0.5 or 50 cents. Using that setting, the price must move by an increment of at least 50 cents in order to create a new X or O. Since the column on the far right of the chart consists of X's, the stock would have to climb by at least 50 cents to create a new X.

Reversal Amount

Once we have determined the box size, we must now define the parameters for a reversal. The "reversal amount" is the minimum amount of movement required for the creation of a new column. That minimum movement is normally defined in terms of a number of boxes. When a reversal of a specified size occurs, a new column is started in the opposite direction.

If the current column consists of X's, meaning that the price is rising, how great of a price move in the opposite direction would have to occur before a new column of O's is created? The answer depends on the price and volatility of the instrument being analyzed.

One-Box Reversal

If we wish to define a reversal as a movement that is equivalent to one box, this is known as a "one-box reversal." Because the conditions for a one-box reversal are usually easy to meet, an investor who uses them can expect to see many reversals appear on the chart.

A one-box reversal is the only P&F chart in which both X's and O's can exist in the same column. If you notice an X and an O in the same column, the odds are you're looking at a one-box reversal chart.

The trouble with a one-box reversal is that it may place too much emphasis on moves that are insignificant. Remember, the object of using P&F is to eliminate meaningless activity. The use of a one-box reversal sets a very low bar for a reversal to occur. Because of this, many traders consider a one-box reversal to be overly sensitive.

Two-Box Reversal

To reduce sensitivity, a "two-box reversal" can be utilized. As the name implies, this reversal occurs when the price moves the equivalent of two boxes in the opposite direction of the current column. Two-box reversals filter out much of the extraneous price activity that occurs in one-box reversals.

In Figure 21.2, we see a side-by-side comparison of two P&F daily charts of General Electric (GE). Both charts cover about six years' worth of activity, from early 2009 through mid-2015. Both charts have a box size of one.

The main difference between the two charts is that the one on the left is a one-box reversal chart, as noted by the "1 X 1" legend in the upper left corner, while the one on the right is a two-box reversal chart, as we can see by the "1 X 2" inscription

POINT AND FIGURE CHARTING

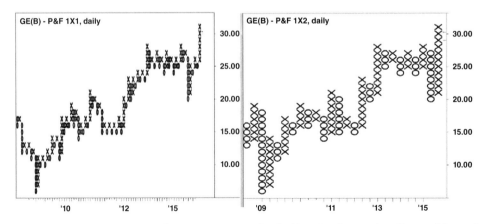

FIGURE 21.2 Comparison of a One-Box Reversal and a Two-Box Reversal on Shares of General Electric (GE)

next to the stock symbol. Note that the one-box reversal chart involves many more X's, O's, and columns than the two-box reversal chart.

Despite these differences, both charts depict the exact same price activity. Figure 21.2 demonstrates that the larger the reversal amount used, the less complex and muddled the charts will appear.

Three-Box Reversal

On many P&F charts, the minimum movement required to create a new column is three boxes. When this is the case, the reversal amount is referred to as a "three-box reversal." The three-box reversal is frequently used as a default setting on point and figure charts. When compared to a one- or two-box reversal, fewer changes in direction will be recorded, and therefore fewer new columns will be created.

Figure 21.3 shows a three-box reversal on the daily P&F chart of McDonald's Corp. (MCD). The representation "1 × 3" in the upper left corner near the stock symbol tells us that the box size for this chart is $1, and the reversal size is three boxes, or $3.

Note that the most recently formed column is composed of O's. This tells us that the price of McDonald's stock had been falling.

There are very few possibilities as to what might happen next. The next marking on the chart might be another O in the current column, which would be created if McDonald's stock price were to fall by another $1. Or, a new column will be created starting with three X's. A new column of three X's would appear if McDonald's stock were to rise by at least $3, creating a three-box reversal.

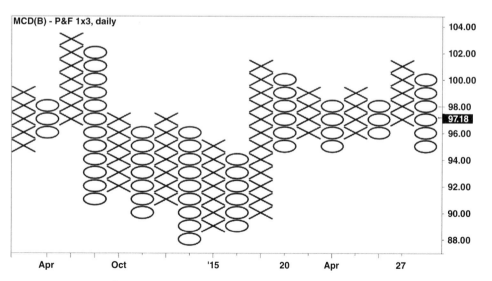

FIGURE 21.3 A Three-Box Reversal on the Daily P&F Chart of McDonald's Corp. (MCD)

Another possibility is that shares of McDonald's might fall by more than $1; if the stock falls by at least $2, then two new O's will be created in the current column; if it falls by at least $3, then three new O's will be created, and so on. If McDonald's gaps lower by $3, three O's will appear on the chart, and no gap will be evident.

If the price falls by less than $1 or rises by less than $3, the move would be considered insignificant, and there would be no need for any new notations to be made on the chart.

Notice also that there are no columns on this chart that have fewer than three consecutive X's or three consecutive O's. This is because every time a new column is started, the chartist must draw at least three X's or three O's to accurately represent the three-box reversal. If this chart had been set up as a two-box reversal, then each column would consist of a minimum of two X's and two O's.

■ Point and Figure Index Charts

While a $1 box size might be considered appropriate for a stock, a one-point move in an index would be considered insignificant in most cases. For example, in Figure 21.4, which shows the daily chart of the S&P 500 Index ($INX), a box size of 10 was applied. This means that the S&P 500 index would have to move higher by at least 10 points in order to create a new X, since the most recent column consists of X's.

The chart is set up as a three-box reversal, meaning that the index would have to fall by at least 30 points in order to force the creation of a new column. If the S&P 500 were to fall by 30 or more points, a new column of at least three O's would be created in Figure 21.4.

It wouldn't matter if the move occurred over the course of a minute, an hour, a week, or a year. When using P&F charts, time is not a consideration; the only thing that matters is that the movement occurred.

Day Trading with Point and Figure Charts

How can P&F charting be applied to intraday trading? For this more active style of trading, a smaller box size would be appropriate. In Figure 21.5, we see a five-minute P&F chart of Apple (AAPL). The box size on this chart is 25 cents, and the reversal amount is three boxes. This is indicated by the 0.25 × 3 legend that appears in the chart's upper left corner.

Since time is of little concern in P&F charting, volume also loses its significance. If we are going to disregard price movement during select periods of time, it would also make sense to disregard the volume that occurred during those time periods.

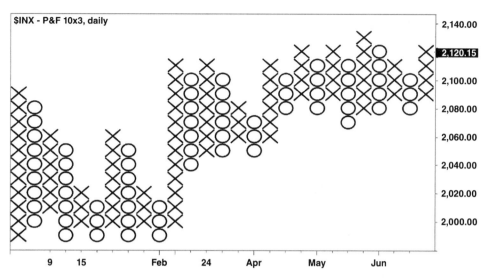

FIGURE 21.4 This Daily Chart of the S&P 500 Index ($INX) Shows a Box Size of 10

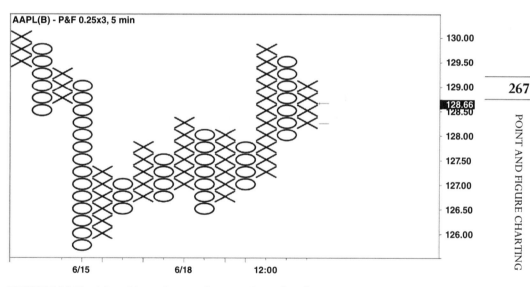

FIGURE 21.5 A Five-Minute Point and Figure Chart of Apple (AAPL)

For this reason, it makes little sense to apply volume analysis to a P&F chart. Many of the indicators that work well with traditional charts lose their effectiveness with P&F.

P&F is more than just a charting technique; it also can be used to create entries, stops, and targets. To understand how entries are created using P&F, we must first understand P&F chart patterns.

■ Point and Figure Patterns

Just as with other types of charts, there are significant price patterns that appear on P&F charts. In some cases, the name of a P&F pattern may be similar to that of a traditional technical formation, but the meaning may be different.

For example, there are double tops and double bottoms in P&F charting. However, a breakout from a double top is considered bullish, and a breakdown from a double bottom is considered bearish.

Point and Figure Double Top

In traditional technical analysis, a double top is a bearish pattern that often leads to a breakdown. However, in P&F analysis, it represents a potential break above resistance. The pattern consists of two columns of X's that have reached a similar price level.

Figure 21.6 provides three examples of double top breakouts on the daily chart of Apple (AAPL). On this chart, each X and O has a value of $3, and a reversal of three boxes is required to begin a new column. This is indicated in the upper left corner of the chart by the notation "3 × 3."

At point A, Apple formed a double top; then a new X was created that was higher than the previous X. This resulted in a double top breakout, since the price had broken above an old high. A similar double top breakout occurred at point B and led to a big rally. Apple shares gained about 30 percent on this rally.

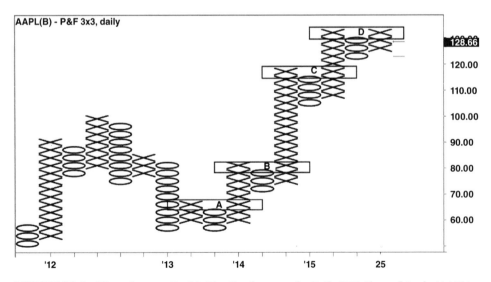

FIGURE 21.6   Three Separate Double Top Breakouts on the Daily P&F Chart of Apple (AAPL)

A third double top breakout at point C resulted in a modest gain. Point D depicts a double top, but the price failed to form a higher X, and therefore no breakout occurred.

On the P&F chart, there are only two things that can now happen. If Apple manages to climb by $3, a new X will be formed, and a fourth double top breakout will occur at point D.

Or, if Apple falls by at least $9, a three-box reversal will have occurred, and a new column of three O's will appear on the far right side of the chart. No new notations will be made on this chart until one of those two events occurs.

Note that in the cases of A, B, and C, the breakout involved the minimum possible number of columns for a double top, which is three. This is considered significant; a double top breakout that involves only three columns is considered superior to one that involves a greater number of columns.

Do point and figure chartists pay attention to trends? We can see from Figure 21.6 that Apple has formed a series of higher highs and higher lows and is therefore in an uptrend.

Trend traders will only enter a long position based on a double top breakout if it represents a continuation of the current trend. In this case, another X would create not only a double top breakout but also a new high and a continuation of the trend.

Point and Figure Triple Top

The same philosophy demonstrated in the double top applies to the triple top. The only difference is that a triple top consists of three peaks instead of two.

Figure 21.7 demonstrates a triple top breakout in shares of Tesla Motors (point A). Note that five columns are used to create the triple top pattern. This is the minimum number of columns that can be used in the creation of a triple top pattern. A triple top created from five columns is considered superior to one that utilizes a greater number of columns.

Farther to the right, a subsequent double top breakout is also visible (point B). Three columns were used in the creation of the double top, which is the minimum possible number of columns for that pattern.

Point and Figure Spread Triple Top

This is simply a triple top that forms over a larger number of columns than the minimum number of five.

Figure 21.8 demonstrates this concept using Google Inc. Class A shares (GOOGL). The stock peaks at point 1; at point 2, Google fails to break above that high. On the third attempt, the breakout finally succeeds.

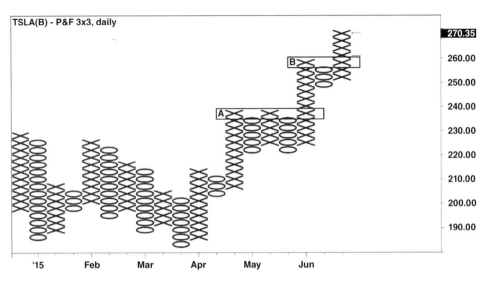

FIGURE 21.7 A Triple Top Breakout in Shares of Tesla Motors (TSLA)

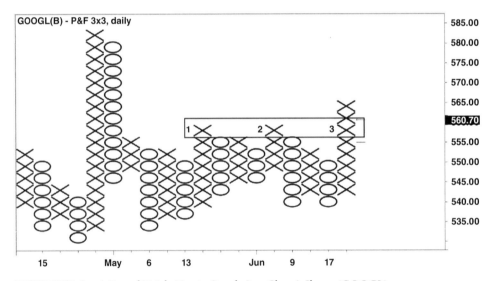

FIGURE 21.8 A Spread Triple Top in Google Inc. Class A Shares (GOOGL)

Note that in this case, the triple top was formed over a greater number of columns than the minimum. The minimum number of columns needed to form a triple top is five, but in this case, the triple top is composed of nine columns. A spread triple top is considered inferior to a five-column triple top.

All of the concepts that apply to the double top and triple top patterns would also apply to a quadruple top, a quintuple top, and so on, so there is no need to cover these individually.

Point and Figure Double Bottom

Just as with traditional technical patterns, bullish formations have bearish counterparts. This is true in P&F charting as well. The same concepts that apply to topping patterns also apply to bottoming patterns, which are essentially breaks of support.

Ideally, a double bottom consists of three columns. Figure 21.9 shows a series of five double bottom breakdowns in shares of mining company Vale S.A. (VALE).

While stocks in general were trending higher at this time, hard commodities like copper and iron ore were in steep downtrends, which pulled mining stocks lower. The fact that Vale was in a steep downtrend made it a good shorting candidate at the time.

Point and Figure Triple Bottom

This is similar in nature to a P&F double bottom, but consists of three columns of O's. Ideally, the pattern is formed using a minimum number of columns, which is five.

Figure 21.10 shows numerous sell signals during the downtrend in the Crude Oil Continuous Contract (@CL) in late 2014. The first signal occurred due to a triple bottom (point A), and was followed by several double bottom sell signals (points B, C, and D).

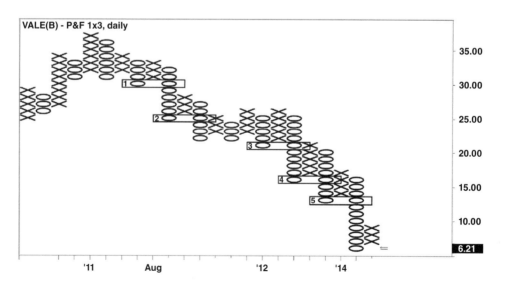

FIGURE 21.9   A Series of Five Double Bottom Breakdowns in Shares of Vale S.A. (VALE)

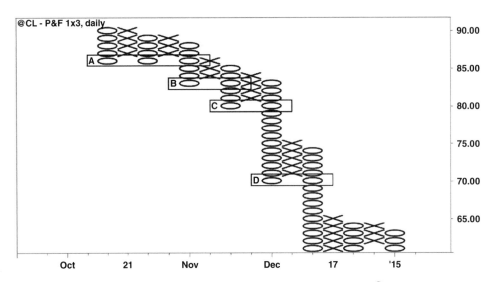

FIGURE 21.10 A Triple Bottom in the Crude Oil Continuous Contract (@CL) Is Followed by a Series of Double Bottoms

■ Point and Figure Catapult

When two P&F trading signals occur in the same direction and in the same general price area, one after the other, it is referred to as a catapult.

Bullish Catapult

An ideal bullish catapult consists of a triple top breakout, augmented by a double top breakout.

Figure 21.11 provides two examples of bullish catapults on the daily chart of Home Depot (HD). In the first bullish catapult (1), a triple top is formed over five columns, leading to a bullish breakout (point A). When the price retreated from the initial breakout, a double top pattern is formed (point B) using three columns. This catapult led to a successful breakout in late 2014.

As the rally from the ensuing breakout stalls, a new triple top forms over five columns (point C). A breakout from the triple top quickly fails, leading to the formation of a double top that consists of three columns (point D). This completes the catapult and leads to another successful breakout.

Bearish Catapult

An ideal bearish catapult consists of a triple bottom breakdown, augmented with a double bottom breakdown.

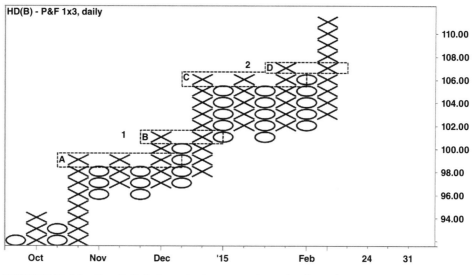

FIGURE 21.11 Two Bullish Catapults Appear on the Daily Chart of Home Depot (HD)

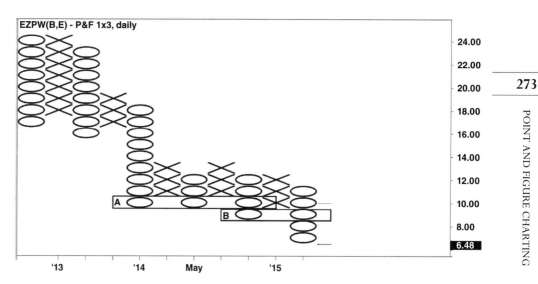

FIGURE 21.12 A Bearish Catapult Appears on the Daily Chart of EZCORP Inc. Class A Shares (EZPW)

Figure 21.12 is an example of a bearish catapult that appears on the daily chart of EZCORP Inc. Class A shares (EZPW). First, the stock broke to a new low from a bearish triple bottom pattern (point A). The price reversed, but a double bottom pattern formed immediately afterward (point B), leading to a new 52-week low for the consumer financial services company.

■ Point and Figure Triangles

Point and Figure Symmetrical Triangle

On a P&F chart, a symmetrical triangle occurs when a series of X columns forms lower highs, and a series of O columns forms higher lows. Just as with a normal symmetrical triangle, this represents a period of price action that is dominated by neither bulls nor bears. Both sides show an equal level of commitment as the price consolidates.

In Figure 21.13, we see a symmetrical triangle on the chart of Cisco Systems (CSCO) that formed from mid-2013 through mid-2014.

When trading symmetrical triangles, consider the price's direction prior to the formation of the triangle. If there is a clear trend or directional bias prior to the formation of the triangle, trend traders will favor a break in that direction and place less emphasis on a break in the opposite direction.

Another way to trade the symmetrical triangle would be to simply trade in the direction of the break. This tactic leaves the trader vulnerable to false breakouts, but it clearly would have worked in the case of Cisco Systems in Figure 21.13.

Figure 21.14 provides another example of a symmetrical triangle in shares of biotech firm Celgene Corp. (CELG). In July of 2015, an explosive breakout occurred as Celgene surged through the upper trend line of the triangle. After a long bullish run, Celgene formed a double top (upper right corner of Figure 21.14) and then broke to new highs again.

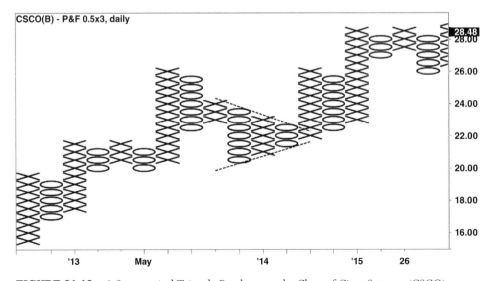

FIGURE 21.13   A Symmetrical Triangle Breakout on the Chart of Cisco Systems (CSCO)

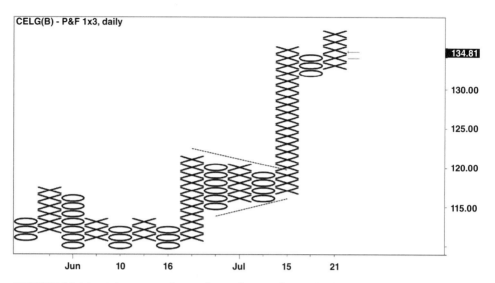

FIGURE 21.14   A Symmetrical Triangle Breakout in Shares of Celgene Corp. (CELG)

Point and Figure Ascending Triangle

Just as in other forms of charting, a P&F ascending triangle pattern demonstrates an imbalance in the level of commitment between buyers and sellers. Bulls create a series of higher lows, while bears simply try to maintain the status quo. Usually, the more committed or aggressive party is the victor.

In Figure 21.15, the daily chart of Barnes and Noble (BKS) depicts an ascending triangle. Note the rising trend line beneath the columns (diagonal line), which indicates that the bulls were aggressive buyers of BKS.

Meanwhile, the stock formed a flattish top, indicating that the bears were less committed than the bulls. The bulls were pushing higher while the bears were just hanging on. The buy signal occurred when an X was placed above the fifth column of the triple top (point A), causing a triple top breakout.

Figure 21.15 shows more than just an ascending triangle on the BKS daily chart. Keen observers will also note that this particular chart provides an example of a bullish catapult.

First, a triple top was formed over five columns, leading to a bullish breakout (point A). When the price retreated from the initial breakout, a double top pattern formed (point B), leading to a successful breakout.

Point and Figure Descending Triangle

The psychology behind the descending triangle is the same as the ascending triangle, with one important difference—in this case the bears have the upper hand.

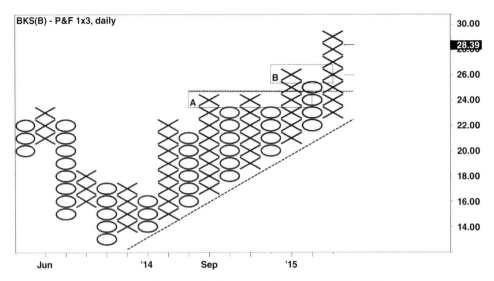

FIGURE 21.15   An Ascending Triangle Breakout in Barnes and Noble (BKS)

The descending triangle shows lower highs and flat lows, and represents a situation in which sellers threaten to overpower buyers.

The concept is depicted in Figure 21.16, which shows a descending triangle formation on the daily chart of Scana Corp. (SCG). Bears were selling at lower and lower prices (diagonal line) while bulls attempted to prop up the stock. A triple bottom is visible at the base of the triangle, presaging a sharp move lower.

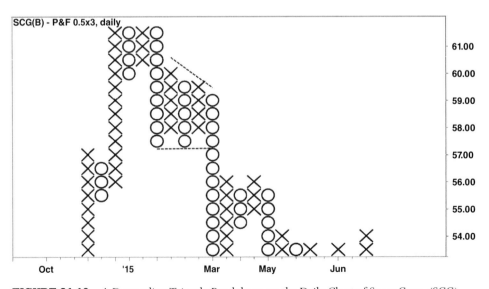

FIGURE 21.16   A Descending Triangle Breakdown on the Daily Chart of Scana Corp. (SCG)

The sell signal occurred when a new O was added to the fifth column of the triangle, just beneath the dotted line. In this sense, the entry would be no different from that of a triple bottom breakdown.

■ Point and Figure Price Targets

In addition to the entry signals demonstrated in the previous sections, P&F charting techniques can also be used to create targets. Since these targets are created on charts that have no time scale, it follows that these targets have no expiration date. P&F targets project price, but offer no time frame for the achievement of those targets.

Multiple Box Reversals

When using multiple-box reversals, there are two main ways to create targets using P&F charts: vertical counts and horizontal counts. A vertical count involves counting the number of X's or O's according to the height of a column; a horizontal count involves counting the number of columns.

Vertical Count

In a vertical count, the process of determining a target begins with the "count column." There are numerous ways to determine the count column, but using the first move off of a major top or a bottom is considered superior to the other techniques.

A major bottom occurs at the end of a downtrend, and a major top occurs at the end of an uptrend. It is impossible to know for certain that a market is in the process of making a major top or a major bottom; these things are only obvious in retrospect.

Fortunately, the fact that we can only determine a top or bottom in retrospect doesn't affect the process or negate the effectiveness of the count. The first directional price move after a major bottom will be a column consisting of X's, and the first directional price move after a major top will be a column consisting of O's.

Upside Vertical Count

Figure 21.17 shows an example of a major bottom on the daily chart of Yahoo Inc. (YHOO). This stock bottomed in early 2009, which is not surprising because the stock market as a whole bottomed at that time.

Notice how the column of O's that is circled coincides with Yahoo's lowest trading price in years. In retrospect, this is a major bottom (point A), as it represents a seven-year low. The column of X's that follows (also circled) is the first move off

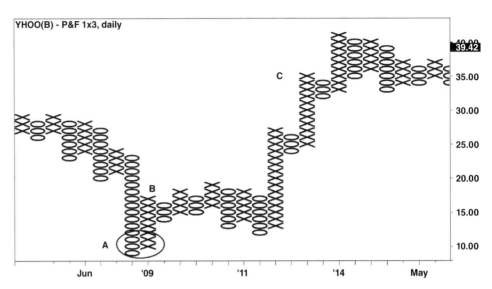

FIGURE 21.17 An Upside Vertical Count Results in a Target Price of $35 for Shares of Yahoo (YHOO)

of what is indisputably an important bottom. Therefore, the first rising column of X's after the important bottom is the count column.

In order for that column to be considered the count column, it must be closed. That means there must be a column of O's immediately to its right. This assures the technical analyst that no more X's can be added to that column, and therefore the count is correct. In this case, the column is closed, so we can proceed (point B).

Next, we count the number of X's in the count column. The closed count column consists of eight X's.

Now that we have determined the count column and counted the number of X's, how do we determine the target price? First, take note of the "1 × 3" inscription in the upper left corner of the chart; this indicates that the box size is one, and the reversal amount is three.

First, multiply the number of X's by the box size; in this case, the box size is one: 8 × 1 = 8.

Next, multiply the product (8) of the previous calculation by the reversal amount. In this case, the reversal amount is three. Therefore, 8 × 3 = 24.

Now, add the product (24) of the prior calculation to the lowest O of the major bottom. This is the column that preceded the count column. The lowest O of the major bottom is $9. Therefore, 9 + 24 = 35.

Based on this method of calculation, the target price for Yahoo was $35. That target was eventually reached (point C).

Downside Vertical Count

A similar method of calculation can be used to create bearish target prices. In this case, we'll identify a major top and measure the first move off of that top. On this occasion, we'll analyze an example that shows how these targets could be used on an open position.

Figure 21.18 depicts a major top in the iShares 20+ Year Treasury Bond ETF (TLT). The point and figure chart shows TLT reaching an all-time high (point A, circled). When the price falls away, it can be considered an important top in retrospect.

The column of O's adjacent to the all-time high can be considered the count column, as it represents the first major move away from the top (also circled). We can tell by the subsequent column of X's to the right that the count column is closed.

There are five O's in the count column (point B). Note that the inscription "3 × 3" appears at the top left corner of the chart; this tells us that the box size is three, and the reversal amount is also three.

First, multiply the number of O's (5) by the box size (3). The result is 15.

Next, multiply 15 by the reversal size of 3. The result is 45.

Next, determine the high point of the X column directly before the count column. The high point was 138.

To determine the target price, subtract 45 from 138. The result is 93 (point C). This is the target price. Therefore, a trader who sold short on the double bottom breakdown (rectangle, point D) could use $93 as a target.

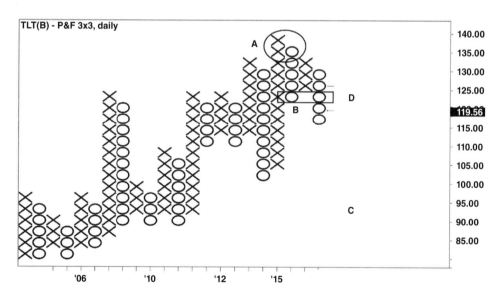

FIGURE 21.18 A Downside Vertical Count Results in a Target Price of $93 for the iShares 20+ Year Treasury Bond ETF (TLT)

Horizontal Counts

If vertical counts are measured by the number of X's and O's in a particular counting column, then how are horizontal counts created? They stem from the measurement of the number of columns in a sideways consolidation.

When using this technique, the target is determined by the width of the congestion area. One condition of this method is that the consolidation area should also serve as a top or bottom.

The other condition is that the consolidation area must be bordered by "walls" of X's and O's. An upside congestion pattern is bordered by a column of O's to its left and a column of X's to its right. A downside congestion pattern is bordered by a wall of X's on its left and a wall of O's on its right.

The number of columns in the congestion area is measured, and that measurement includes the walls. Once the count is obtained, it is multiplied by the box size and the reversal size; in this respect, the horizontal counting method is similar to the vertical counting method.

Once that figure is obtained, it is either:

a. Added to the lowest O of the congestion area, in the case of an upside measurement, or
b. Subtracted from the highest X of the congestion area, in the case of a downside measurement

Upside Horizontal Count

Figure 21.19 provides an example of how to create a price target using an upside horizontal count. In this example we'll use the P&F chart of AbbVie Inc. (ABBV). This chart has a box size of one and a reversal amount of three, as noted in the upper left corner of the chart.

Two walls encompass an area of consolidation that also serves as a bottom: a column of O's on the left (down arrow) and a column of X's on the right (up arrows). Next, we count the number of columns in the consolidation. Including the walls, there are six columns in the consolidation (point A).

In the next step, we multiply the six columns by the box size (1) and the reversal amount (3). So, $6 \times 1 \times 3 = 18$. Then we add 18 to the lowest O in the consolidation pattern; that O is located at 55 (point B).

Adding 55 to 18 results in a price target of 73. As of this writing, AbbVie was closing in on this target, but had not yet reached it. The stock had just broken out from a double top pattern (point C) and was trading less than $3 below the price target.

Downside Horizontal Count

Figure 21.20 provides an example of how to create a price target using a downside horizontal count, using a 1×3 P&F chart of Virgin America (VA). Two walls

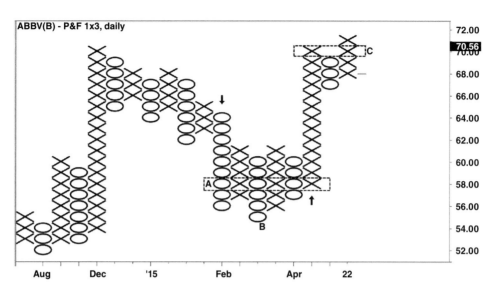

FIGURE 21.19 An Upside Horizontal Count Yields a Target Price of $73 for AbbVie Inc. (ABBV)

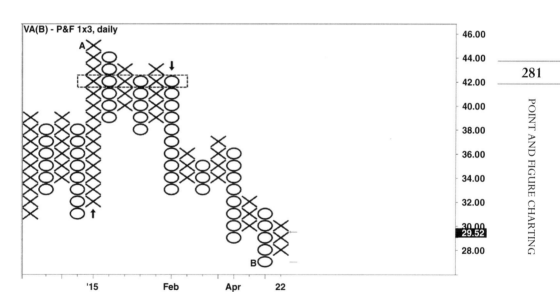

FIGURE 21.20 A Downside Horizontal Count Yields a Target Price of $27 for Virgin America (VA)

bracket the consolidation area on the chart: a column of X's on its left (up arrow) and a column of O's on its right (down arrow).

Next, the number of columns is measured, including the walls (rectangle). In this case, the number of columns is six. Six is then multiplied by the box size (1) and the reversal amount (3): $6 \times 1 \times 3 = 18$.

The number 18 is now subtracted from the highest X in the consolidation pattern (point A). The highest X occurred at 45. Therefore, the target is $27 (45 − 18 = 27). That target was successfully attained, if only by a small margin (point B).

■ One-Box Reversal Targets

Creating targets with a one-box reversal chart can be complicated.

In this book I've bypassed one-box reversals, as I believe multiple-box reversals eliminate a greater degree of market noise. However, I will share with you a simple technique for finding a target on a one-box reversal chart. This technique employs a horizontal count only. It consists of four steps:

1. Locate an area of congestion. This could represent a top, a bottom, or merely a period of consolidation.
2. Count the columns in the row with the most filled boxes.
3. Multiply the number of columns counted by the box size.
4. Add and/or subtract the result from the value of the box on the row from which the count was taken.

Figure 21.21 provides an example of how to create a target using a one-box reversal on the P&F chart of Yahoo (YHOO). First, an area of consolidation is identified (point A). Next, the row of the consolidation with the most filled boxes is identified (rectangle). We'll refer to this row as the "counting row." On this chart, the counting row is located at $35.

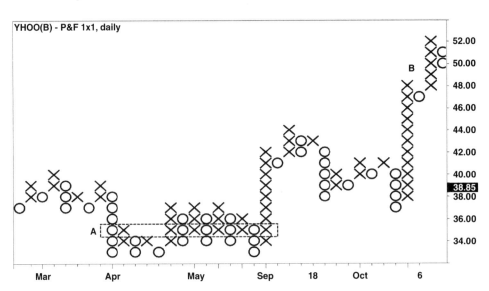

FIGURE 21.21 A One-Box Reversal on the Point and Figure Chart of Yahoo (YHOO)

If we count the number of columns within that rectangle, including boxes that have no X's or O's, the result is 14 columns. Multiply 14 by the box size, which is 1, and the result is 14.

Finally, we add and/or subtract 14 from the counting row. This would give us two potential targets: an upside target of 49 (35 + 14 = 49) and a downside target of 21 (35 − 14 = 21). In this case, the target of 49 was achieved (point B).

■ Final Thoughts on Point and Figure Charting

Hopefully, this chapter has provided a basic understanding of P&F. If you wish to gain a deeper and more detailed understanding, there are several excellent books on the subject. Jeremy du Plessis' book, titled *The Definitive Guide to Point and Figure,* provides considerable depth and detail on this topic.

PART VIII

ATR, ADX, AND PSAR

CHAPTER 22

Cycles and Tendencies

Investors attempt to predict future price movement based on past market behavior. The belief that past price activity can be used to determine future price activity is at the heart of technical analysis.

In addition to simply analyzing price and direction, market movements can be viewed in the context of recurring events. Investors analyze cycles of time and of price to search for patterns that coincide with past events, either natural or artificial. Cycles can also be used to gain insight into the timing of a potential directional move.

Cycles are based on recurring events that are believed to have a degree of predictability. Some of these events occur in nature, such as the change in seasons. Naturally, seasonal changes are closely associated with the agricultural cycle of planting and harvesting. Because of this, cycles are frequently used in the analysis of agricultural commodities, such as corn and soybeans.

Cycles can also revolve around manufactured recurring events. For example, every four years, on the Tuesday following the first Monday in November, the U.S. presidential election is held. Is it possible that U.S. stock market activity is influenced by this recurring event?

■ The Presidential Election Cycle

The U.S. presidential election cycle is perhaps the most compelling example of a cycle, because it involves a widely followed, regularly scheduled recurring event. This event has provided significant market timing advantages over an extended period of time.

Statistically, the year prior to the election is the best year in the cycle to own stocks. The reasons behind this are the topic of much speculation. Some believe increased government spending is responsible, as incumbent politicians have an incentive to spend in order to curry favor with the electorate. Think of this as the party before the election.

If the year prior to a presidential election features the best returns, then the year after the election produces the worst results. Think of this as the hangover after the party. Numerous bear markets and other negative events, including the infamous stock market crash of 1929, occurred during the year after a presidential election.

Again, the reasons behind this price activity are open to speculation, but there are plausible theories. For example, disappointing post-election market returns may be due to political expediency.

For example, a politician may prefer to enact unpopular or economically unfavorable legislation, such as a tax increase, shortly after an election. The politician hopes that with the passage of time, the legislation will be forgotten, and that by the following election, it is no longer a politically harmful issue.

The concepts behind the U.S. presidential election cycle seem to make sense, but are they backed by market performance?

From 1833 through 2012, the year prior to the election saw a net gain of 469.5%, and the year of the election netted a gain of 254.5%. Meanwhile, the year after the election has only netted a gain of 86.1% over that span. Midterm election years saw a net rise of 187%.

We could also say that the combined performance of the pre-election year and the election year far outstrips the combined performance of the post-election year and the midterm year. From 1833 through 2012, the Dow Jones Industrial Average (and the indices that preceded it) netted a gain of 724% during the combined pre-election and election year period. Meanwhile, markets netted just 273.1% during the combined post-election year and midterm year period.

Another interesting aspect of the presidential cycle is the tendency for markets to improve as the election draws near. While overall returns during election years tend to be strong, they are even better if we eliminate the first five months of the election year. From 1948 through 2012, the final seven-month period of a presidential election year has only coincided with market losses in two years, 2000 and 2008.

■ The Decennial Cycle

In 1939, the book *Tides and the Affairs of Men* was published by Edgar Lawrence Smith. Smith theorized that stocks operated on a ten-year cycle. Smith noted that both strong decades and weak decades showed a bias toward strength during the middle of the decade. Years that ended with the number "5" showed particular strength.

Not only was this true at the time, it has continued to be the case into the present. Measuring from 1895 to 2014, the average return of the Dow Jones Industrial Average in years ending in "5" is a gain of 28.93%. Years ending in "8" were the next best performers, at 14.44 percent. The year 2005 marked the only occasion during this span where the Dow Jones Industrial Average lost ground during a year ending in "5," when it slipped by a mere 0.61%.

■ The "Sell in May" Cycle

You may be familiar with the phrase "sell in May and go away." As market platitudes go, this ranks right up there with "buy low and sell high" as one of the most overused phrases in all of finance.

Is there some truth behind this saying? The answer is yes; this saying refers to an annual cycle in the Dow Jones Industrial Average.

When measured from 1950 through 2015, the six-month period starting in the beginning of November and ending at the start of May shows a robust net gain of 17,822.70 points. Meanwhile, the period starting at the beginning of May and ending at the start of November showed a net loss of 316.32 Dow points over that same 65-year span.

The Optimism Cycle?

The "sell in May" cycle is sometimes referred to as the "optimism cycle." Some folks hypothesize that investors become optimistic as they look forward to a new year. Hooray, it's November!

Optimism? Really? Like much of the nation's population, I live in the northeastern part of the United States. Starting in November, the weather begins to change. Everything that's green and growing turns brown and dies.

Long days become short; the sun sets before dinnertime. Tens of thousands of people become depressed due to Seasonal Affective Order (SAD). It's cold, it's dark, and everyone catches the flu.

Anyone expressing unbridled enthusiasm in such an environment is liable to get kicked hard in the shins. Let's just say I'm skeptical about any theory that states that mere optimism is the force behind this particular cycle.

Keep this in mind when considering cycles—coincidence isn't causality. The market may behave a certain way when Event X occurs, but that doesn't necessarily mean that Event X *caused* the market to behave that way. Markets are moved by a variety of known and unknown factors. It's possible that the movements we are analyzing are caused by an entirely different set of factors than the ones attributed to a cycle.

While it's fun and interesting to speculate about the forces that drive market performance, the reasoning behind any cycle isn't nearly as important as the returns generated during that cycle. For example, the "sell in May" cycle could simply be coincidental. Some analysts hypothesize that corporate earnings rise and fall on a similar cycle, which in turn drives market performance and creates the "sell in May" cycle, but there is no firm evidence of this.

Building an Ideal Scenario

An investor could combine several performance cycles to create an ideal scenario. The "sell in May" cycle could also be called the "buy in November" cycle, because it refers to a strategy that consists of holding stocks from November through April, and then exiting the market from May through October.

Ideally, an investor would buy stocks at the start of November of a midterm year in the presidential election cycle. That way, the investor could be long during November-December-January, which is on average the best consecutive three-month period to own stocks.

The investor would then hold the position into the best performing year of the election cycle, which is the pre-election year. Ideally, the pre-election year would end in the number "5."

Historically speaking, it would be better still if this were to occur while a Democratic president occupies the White House, and while Congress is controlled by the Republican Party.

The position would be held through the pre-election year and the election year. The investor would continue to hold the position until the beginning of May of the post-election year. Then, as the saying goes, the time would come to sell in May and go away.

Keep in mind that all of this is based on past performance. There is no guarantee that these particular cycles, or any cycle for that matter, will be effective in the future. While past performance is not indicative of future results, the performance of the "sell in May" cycle, when combined with the U.S. presidential election cycle, is quite impressive.

■ The Santa Claus Rally

Many investors believe that the term "Santa Claus rally" refers to general bullishness during December, which statistically tends to be a strong month. From 1950 through 2014, the average December return for the S&P 500 and the Dow Jones Industrial Average was a healthy 1.7%.

However, the term Santa Claus Rally actually refers to a narrow and specific time frame. This time frame spans the last five trading days of December and the first two trading days of January. The returns for that short stretch of time have been impressive, with the S&P 500 gaining an average of 1.5% from 1953 through 2014. That's an extremely potent return for such a narrow time frame.

The January Barometer

There is a maxim in the trading markets: As goes January, so goes the year. While a year that begins with a positive month clearly should have a statistical advantage over one that does not, the reliability of this indicator has been impressive. From 1950 through 2014, the annual market direction has tracked January's direction about 90% of the time.

First Five Days of January

Another version of the January barometer that uses a smaller sample size has also shown interesting results. The net return of the first five trading days of the year provides a reasonably accurate foreshadowing of the coming year, but only in bullish scenarios.

From 1950 through 2014, a bullish first five days has led to a bullish year for the S&P 500 nearly 85% of the time. However, a bearish first five days has no predictive power regarding the full year's returns.

The January Barometer Portfolio

If full-year market returns can be foreshadowed by a bullish January, can a more targeted approach be employed? According to Sam Stovall, the chief equity strategist at S&P Capital IQ, the answer is yes. He targets the three strongest sectors of the S&P 500 during the month of January.

According to Stovall, the three top performing sectors in January have outperformed the S&P 500 over the following 12 months about two-thirds of the time from 1990 through 2014. Mr. Stovall says that a variation of that strategy that focuses on the top ten subsectors of the market during January has achieved even better results.

The January Effect

The January barometer is often confused with the "January effect." To clarify, the January effect has nothing to do with the January barometer; it refers to the tendency for small cap stocks to outperform the overall market during the month of January.

According to Ibbotson Associates, in January, from the years 1926 through 2002, the smallest 10% of stocks in the market (as measured by market capitalization) outperformed the largest 10% of stocks by an annual pace of 9.35%. Ibbotson, which has since been acquired by Morningstar, also concluded that small cap stocks outperformed large caps in January during 70 of those 77 years, making it by far the best month for small caps during that span.

While those figures are statistically significant, the January effect has lost its effectiveness in recent years. Some have theorized that this is because investors are buying small cap stocks earlier in anticipation of a strong January. Others believe that the rise of trading in tax-sheltered retirement accounts has nullified this market tendency.

■ Seasonal Cycles

Seasonal cycles tend to appear in various agricultural products due to the patterns of planting and harvest. Seasonal cycles are predictable, and sometimes lead to recurring price patterns.

For example, the price of wheat shows a tendency toward weakness during the first half of the year and tends to strengthen during the second half of the year. This is demonstrated over twenty-year (top line) and thirty-year (bottom line) time horizons in Figure 22.1.

Seasonality is so prevalent that it is recognized by the bodies that produce our most closely followed economic indicators; the term "seasonally adjusted" refers to a statistic that has been modified to account for these patterns. While this practice acknowledges the importance of seasonality, it is sometimes controversial because some analysts would prefer to view the numbers in their raw form.

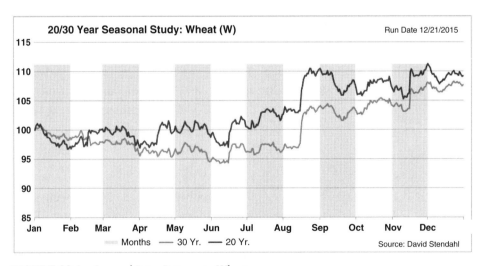

FIGURE 22.1 Seasonal Price Patterns in Wheat
Source: Signal Trading Group

While seasonal trends are most closely associated with soft commodities such as wheat and corn, hard commodities such as metals and oil also fall under their sway.

Crude Oil Seasonality Pattern

Crude oil prices have shown a long-term tendency to peak in September/October. Some have suggested this is partly due to the start of hurricane season in the Gulf of Mexico. That region accounted for 17% of U.S. crude oil production in 2015, according to the U.S. Energy Information Administration (EIA).

Oil isn't the only commodity affected by this phenomenon. In addition to oil production, area refineries are also affected by these giant storms. According to the EIA, 45% of total U.S. petroleum refining capacity is located along the Gulf coast, along with 51% of total U.S. natural gas processing plant capacity.

As the storm season progresses, crude oil prices tend to decline as the U.S., the world's number-one consumer of the product, moves into peak winter consumption. Crude oil prices tend to form a bottom in December, as demonstrated in Figure 22.2.

This brings up an interesting question: Shouldn't oil prices rise, not fall, as cold winter temperatures engulf the U.S.? This is a great example of an event being "priced in" to the market—not just on one occasion, but on an annual basis.

Because energy distributors assume that consumption will rise during the cold U.S. and European winter months, they stock up their inventories by purchasing oil before winter arrives in the northern hemisphere. This factor contributes to crude oil price strength in September and October.

Traders who wish to play this tendency might short oil via the February contract in mid-September and hold the position until mid-December. Using this technique

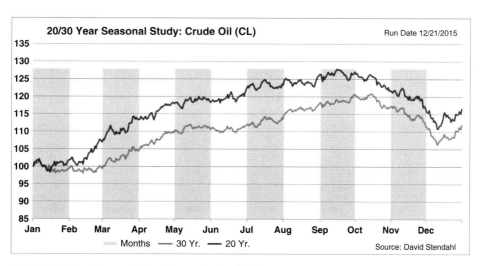

FIGURE 22.2   Seasonal Price Patterns in Crude Oil
Source: Signal Trading Group

has resulted in a winning trade approximately two-thirds of the time from 1983 through 2014, according to Jeffrey Hirsch, author of *The Traders' Almanac*.

Soybeans Seasonality Pattern

Soybean prices have demonstrated a long-term tendency to peak in July and bottom out in October. This has been the case over a variety of time horizons. Figure 22.3 reveals that when measured over twenty years (1995–2015) and thirty years (1985–2015), seasonal studies of soybeans contained a similar price pattern.

There are two major producers of soybeans, Brazil and the U.S. Because the two countries are located in separate hemispheres, their seasons run on an opposite schedule—summer in Brazil occurs when it is winter in the U.S., and vice versa. Because of this, the soybean crop has two major harvest seasons—November/December in the U.S., and May/June in Brazil.

As we can see from the chart, soybean prices have a tendency to rally in the early part of the year, and then peak just as the Brazilian crop comes to market. The price then begins to decline, usually reaching its zenith in early October. By this point, the majority of the Brazilian supply has been disseminated, and the price begins to rally through year-end.

Soybean prices also tend to dip early in the year, usually in January or February. This phenomenon is known as the "February break." Some traders try to take advantage of the February break by purchasing May or July futures contracts, while others purchase call options on those contracts.

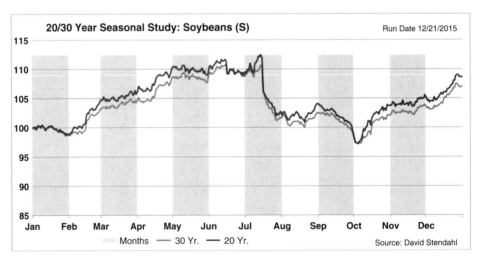

FIGURE 22.3   Seasonal Price Patterns in Soybeans

Source: Signal Trading Group

Corn Seasonal Pattern

Corn prices have a tendency to peak during the spring, which is a critical period in the growth cycle. At this point, there is usually considerable uncertainty regarding growing conditions, and the potential for a devastating drought still exists.

Any event that might damage or constrict the supply of corn would probably cause prices to rise, so a premium is added to the price in order to account for this uncertainty. Ideally, farmers would like to lock in a price for their crops when prices are high during the spring.

Within a few months, this premium has disappeared. If no disastrous floods or droughts have occurred by mid-summer, the price has likely already begun its descent. Even though the corn crop hasn't yet been harvested and disseminated, by now it's easy to estimate the size of the crop and the eventual availability of the product. The price of corn tends to bottom in August, as demonstrated in Figure 22.4.

One relatively new factor that could influence the price of and demand for corn is the use of ethanol in some types of fuel. Beginning in 2005, with the initial passage of the Renewable Fuels Standard, the U.S. required the addition of ethanol to gasoline, with the goal of reducing dependency on foreign oil. The program was expanded and extended by the Energy Independence and Security Act of 2007.

In subsequent years, U.S. crude oil production increased dramatically, causing many to question the continued need for the use of ethanol as a fuel additive. Because corn is used in the creation of some types of ethanol, its use is a bullish factor for corn, and farmers have lobbied the U.S. government for its continued use.

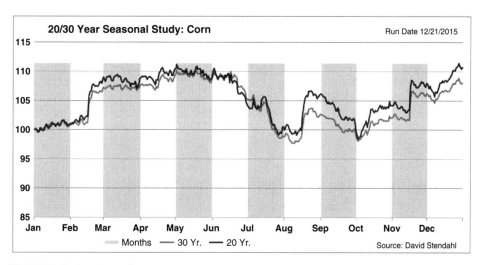

FIGURE 22.4 Seasonal Price Patterns in Corn

Source: Signal Trading Group

U.S. Treasuries Cycle

The concept of seasonal cycles in agricultural commodities can also be applied to non-agricultural trading vehicles. For example, there is some evidence of seasonal cyclicality in U.S. Treasuries.

Over the 20-year period starting at the beginning of 1995, and over the 30-year period beginning in 1985, the 10-year U.S. Treasury Note has shown a tendency to bottom in April and May, and then rally through the end of the year. These tendencies are demonstrated in Figure 22.5.

Please note that Figure 22.5 refers to the *price* of the 10-year Treasury, as opposed to the *yield.* When dealing with fixed-income instruments, yield has an inverted relationship to price. Therefore, we could also say that the 10-year Treasury's yield tends to peak in the April/May period, and then tends to decline for the balance of the year.

Other Notable Tendencies

In addition to the cycles detailed earlier, there are strong seasonal tendencies associated with other trading vehicles, such as:

Lean Hogs: The seasonal trend for lean hogs is one of the strongest and most reliable of the agricultural cycles. On nearly every measurable time frame, this commodity shows a similar pattern—dynamic strength beginning in March, followed by an equally dramatic downturn in July. This tendency is demonstrated in Figure 22.6.

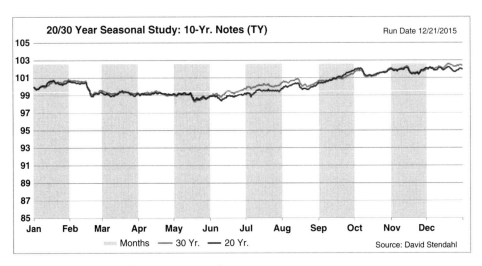

FIGURE 22.5   Seasonal Price Patterns in the U.S. 10-Year Treasury Note

Source: Signal Trading Group

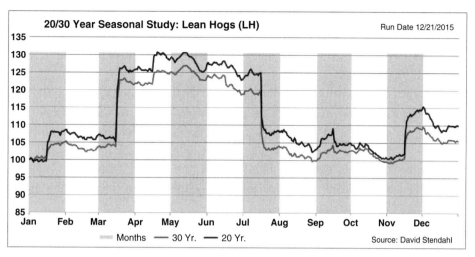

FIGURE 22.6   Seasonal Price Patterns in Lean Hogs

Source: Signal Trading Group

Copper: The price of the red metal tends to gain strength during the first half of the year. This held true over the 20-year period from 1995 through the start of 2015, as well as the 30-year period from 1985 through 2015, as shown in Figure 22.7.

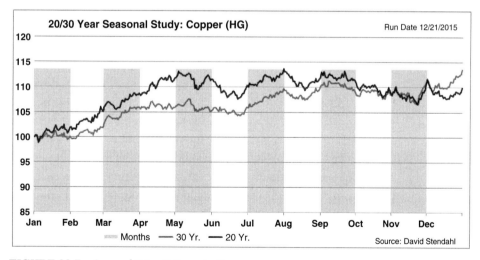

FIGURE 22.7   Seasonal Price Patterns in Copper

Source: Signal Trading Group

■ Currencies—A Special Situation

Currencies present a special problem because every currency exchange rate involves two separate currencies.

When we say the euro tends to be strong during a particular time of year, what does that really mean? Most references to the euro refer to its strength or weakness when measured against the U.S. dollar. However, in other cases the euro is measured against another currency, such as the British pound, or against a basket of currencies that might include the U.S. dollar, British pound, and the Japanese yen, among others. It's entirely possible for the euro to be strong against one currency and weak against another.

In fact, nearly all currencies share this conundrum. What is true for the euro in the previous example is also true for the U.S. dollar, the British pound, the Japanese yen, and other currencies.

Add to this the fact that many central banks attempt to artificially strengthen or weaken their currencies via direct intervention, and you can see why the study of seasonality in the currency markets can be problematic.

■ Longer-Term Cycles

298

CYCLES AND TENDENCIES

The 34-Year Cycle

There are some in the technical analysis community who believe that the Dow Jones Industrial Average (DJIA) runs on a 34-year cycle. The cycle is divided into two 17-year periods—one of which produces a long rally, and the other a range-bound period. Whether by coincidence or other factors, the 34-year cycle appeared to be legitimate for many years.

Figure 22.8 demonstrates this cycle. There was little net movement in the index from the beginning of 1932 through the end of 1948, a 17-year period (1932–1948).

This was followed by a rally that lasted from the start of 1949 through the end of 1965; during this 17-year stretch, the index climbed nearly fivefold (1949–1965).

Then the DJIA consolidated for almost 17 years before breaking out again in late 1982. The consolidation itself was volatile, resulting in many sharp price swings, but the end result was that the index made little progress during this time (1966–1982).

Continuing on Figure 22.9, the breakout in late 1982 ignited a rally that saw the index increase tenfold over the next 17 years.

Starting in 1999, the DJIA entered a long period of consolidation. This appears to have ended in early 2009—a period of only ten years. Then a huge rally began in early 2009, which saw the DJIA triple from then until early 2015.

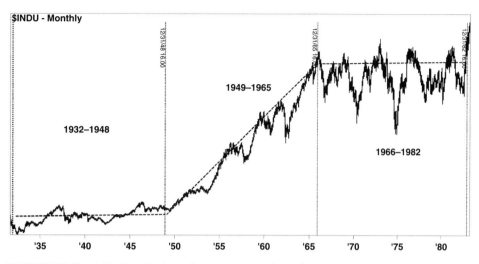

FIGURE 22.8   A 34-Year Cycle on the Dow Jones Industrial Average ($INDU)

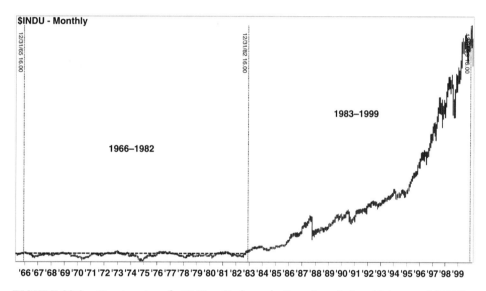

FIGURE 22.9   Continuation of a 34-Year Cycle on the Dow Jones Industrial Average ($INDU)

The 17-year period from the start of 2000 through the end of 2016 was incomplete as of this writing. It will only be possible to know how this period will be viewed in retrospect.

The massive rally that began in 2009 was ignited by an asset purchase program, instituted by the U.S. Central Bank. Between 2009 and 2014, trillions of dollars were poured into this series of programs, known as "quantitative easing."

The aim of these programs was to drive interest rates lower via the purchase of U.S. Treasuries and mortgage bonds. The program succeeded in driving interest rates to record lows. One side effect of this was that it made investing in stocks a relatively attractive proposition when compared to buying bonds or certificates of deposit.

Intentionally or not, the U.S. Federal Reserve's actions aided the U.S. stock market by creating an artificial environment in which it could rally. This brings up an interesting question—did this massive bond purchase program have an impact on the 34-year cycle?

There is no way to know the answer for certain, but it shouldn't matter. Many extraordinary events occurred during the course of this cycle—World War II, the collapse of the Soviet Union, and so on. Apparently, the cycle was robust enough to absorb those earlier events. If it is legitimate, it should be able to absorb quantitative easing as well.

■ The Kondratieff Wave

A Russian economist named Nicolas D. Kondratieff formed a theory of long-term economic cycles in the 1920s. Kondratieff's work initially focused on commodities prices, and then expanded to include general economics.

Kondratieff believed he had discovered cycles of greater than fifty years, with each cycle consisting of three phases—expansion, stagnation, and recession. In the 1930s, Kondratieff's work gained a following when it was endorsed by Harvard economics professor Joseph A. Schumpeter.

Kondratieff's long wave is sometimes referred to as the "K-wave" or "super cycle." While much has been written about Kondratieff's theories, they remain controversial. The extreme length of the waves makes this theoretical phenomenon difficult to observe.

■ Sector Rotation

Rather than simply focusing on market cycles, we can examine the way that a cycle unfolds.

Markets aren't always logical, and events don't always transpire as we believe they will. However, there is a logical progression involved in the way money flows from one group of stocks to another. In some situations, a trader might be able to anticipate this flow of capital from one sector to another, which is known as "sector rotation."

The theory of sector rotation began with a study by the National Bureau of Economic Research (NBER), a U.S. nonprofit economic research institute based in Cambridge, Massachusetts, and founded in 1920. This influential bureau performed research on economic cycles dating back to 1854, and used the information it gathered to create the theory of sector rotation.

In order to understand how sector rotation works, we first need to divide the overall market into groupings. Some of the key market groupings include technology, healthcare, housing, utilities, retail, energy, basic materials, consumer staples, and consumer discretionary products.

As an economic recovery or decline progresses, or more precisely, as market participants *perceive* it is progressing, funds are moved in and out of strategic areas.

For example, consider the early stages of an economic recovery. As the recovery takes hold, it is logical to assume that the central bank will raise interest rates. Which sectors will be most greatly affected by a rise in rates?

Utilities stocks are an obvious choice. This is because these stocks tend to have high-yielding dividends. If investors anticipate an interest rate increase in the near future, they'll sell these interest-rate sensitive stocks.

This is because in a rising rate environment, the high yield of a utility stock becomes less attractive, as there is less of a difference between the yield of a utility stock and that of a risk-free investment, such as a certificate of deposit.

Therefore, we would expect utilities stocks to fall in a rising interest rate scenario—not necessarily at the time that the central bank raises interest rates, but when market participants perceive that a rate hike is on the way. Conversely, utilities stocks would be expected to rise when interest rates are falling.

Figure 22.10 provides an example of a perceived rate hike on the utilities sector. On December 16, 2008, the U.S. central bank, the Federal Reserve, cut its key

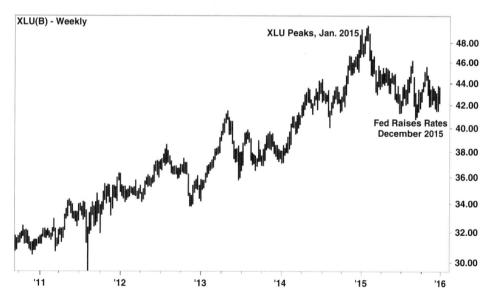

FIGURE 22.10 The S&P Select Utilities SPDR Fund (XLU) Reacts to Changing Perceptions of Interest Rates

interest rate, known as the Federal Funds Rate, to virtually zero. Technically, the Fed Funds Rate was reduced to a range of 0.00 percent to 0.25 percent.

The rate stayed there for seven years. During that time, the S&P Select Utilities SPDR Fund (XLU), which is an ETF that is composed of utilities stocks, enjoyed a massive rally, as depicted in Figure 22.10.

However, that rally terminated in early 2015, and XLU trended lower for most of that year. The rally ended long before the Fed actually raised rates. While Federal Reserve officials frequently discussed raising interest rates in 2015, they did not do so until December of 2015. In this case, the market was well ahead of the Fed, as investors moved away from utilities stocks in anticipation of a coming rate hike.

■ Early Stage of Economic Growth

When investment capital is pulled from utilities stocks and other interest-rate sensitive sectors, it is often reallocated into areas that stand to benefit from higher interest rates. The technology sector is often one of the beneficiaries.

Why technology? In many cases, interest rates are raised during periods of growth. This is done to prevent an economic expansion from occurring too quickly.

When economic growth is strong, investors take advantage of this by moving into areas that tend to grow at an above-average pace. Technology stocks are a good example of a sector that tends to outperform in a strong economic environment.

This is illustrated in Figure 22.11. Utilities stocks (black), represented here by XLU, peaked in late January of 2015 (arrow). As the XLU declined, the tech sector, represented here by the S&P Select Technology SPDR (XLK, gray), began to outperform the utilities sector. This signaled that capital was rotating from the utilities sector to the technology sector.

In the early stages of a recovery, financial stocks also tend to perform well. The assumption is that as rates rise, banks and other lenders will now have the ability to lend money at higher interest rates.

While this may be true, financials don't automatically benefit from higher rates. These companies perform well when they can borrow money at low interest rates and lend money at relatively high interest rates. To financial companies, the difference or spread between short-term interest rates and long-term interest rates is a major concern.

As the recovery continues to take hold, other areas should begin to rally. When employment is high and consumers have extra money in hand, the consumer discretionary sector tends to flourish. This sector consists of items that consumers may desire but don't really need to survive. Examples of consumer discretionary products include premium coffee, video games, and expensive vacations.

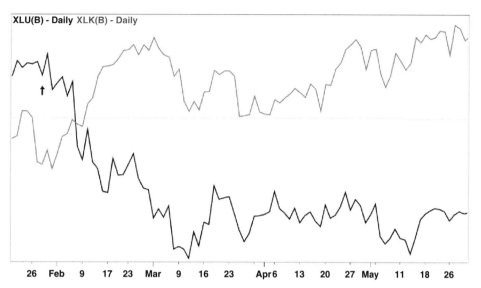

FIGURE 22.11   Funds Rotate from the Utilities Sector (XLU, black) to the Technology Sector (XLK, gray)

Middle Stage of Economic Growth

As confidence grows that the economy is strong and will remain that way, the basic materials sector begins to rise. This sector includes steel and chemical companies, which benefit from increased construction activity. Machinery companies also tend to perform well, as manufacturing companies reinvest their profits in new equipment.

Another area that performs well in the middle stages of an economic recovery is transportation. If more goods are being purchased, then it stands to reason that more goods are being shipped. Demand for shipping, trucking, and package delivery services tend to rise at this time, so investors gravitate toward companies that provide these services.

Industrial stocks also perform well at this time, as increased orders drive production. The tandem movement of the industrial and transport sectors is one of the hallmarks of Dow Theory.

Late Stage of Economic Growth

When investors perceive that the economy has peaked and that growth is slowing, they move away from high-growth areas and into so-called defensive stocks. The perception at this time is that interest rates have peaked; there is no need for further rate hikes as economic growth is now beginning to slow.

A good example of a defensive area is the consumer staples sector. These companies manufacture products that consumers will purchase regardless of the state of the economy, such as food and clothing. The reasoning is that as the demand for consumer discretionary products begins to slow, demand will remain constant for products like soap, toothpaste, and diapers.

Health care and pharmaceutical companies are also expected to do well in this environment. Health is an important concern regardless of the state of the economy, so these sectors should outperform those that are falling out of favor as the economy wanes.

Eventually, investors perceive that the economy has slowed enough that the central bank will likely begin to reduce interest rates. This causes interest rate sensitive stocks like utilities companies to rise, as their high yields become more attractive when compared to a risk-free investment like a certificate of deposit. This completes the sector rotation cycle.

Keep in mind that the theory of sector rotation is just that—a theory. Every economic boom or bust has its own unique circumstances, so we shouldn't expect events to unfold in the exact same sequence on every occasion.

■ Final Thoughts on Cycles

The phrase "past performance is not indicative of future results" certainly applies to this chapter. Since nobody can state with absolutely certainty all of the factors that go into the creation of any cycle, there is always a chance that any given cycle could lose its effectiveness over time.

While some of these tendencies may appear to generate easy money-making trades, keep in mind that experienced professionals on both sides of the market are well aware of these patterns. Seasonal changes in supply and demand are widely anticipated, and therefore are likely to be priced in by the market's discounting mechanism.

For example, traders anticipating a rally in soybeans after the February break may try to jump ahead of the crowd by going long in December or January. By the time prices begin to rise after the February break, these "early" traders may be already looking for an exit.

A trader who overpays for a contract because the result appears to be a "sure thing" is liable to meet with disappointment. This is true not only in the case of soybeans contracts, but for all of the commodities mentioned in this chapter.

There are always extenuating factors to consider, such as the effect of supply from new sources, potential changes in demand as a market becomes more developed, changes in weather patterns, and trade agreements between countries. There are many factors that could potentially change these cycles, either on a temporary or permanent basis.

PART IX

CYCLES

CHAPTER 23

Sentiment Indicators

Sentiment indicators can be used to capitalize on known patterns in human behavior. These behavioral patterns not only appear in trading markets, but in other areas as well. When money is made or lost, emotions come into play, and those emotions can sometimes lead to predictable reactions.

Consider the reaction of U.S. citizens to a sharp drop in housing prices in the 2000s. In 2006, over 69% of U.S. citizens owned homes. Then the real estate bubble burst, and housing prices collapsed as the country fell into a recession.

In response, the U.S. Federal Reserve cut its benchmark interest rate to nearly 0%. Mortgage rates responded by falling to record low levels. By 2012, the average interest rate on a 30-year fixed-rate mortgage fell to just 3.66%.

Logic would suggest that dramatically cheaper housing, combined with historically low interest rates, would generate buying interest. However, the reaction that occurred was more emotional than logical.

Instead of taking advantage of the opportunity at hand, fewer Americans aspired to become homeowners than prior to the price collapse. By the third quarter of 2014, the U.S. homeownership rate had steadily decreased to just 64.4%, as shown in Figure 23.1.

When homes were expensive, they were in great demand, but when the cost of acquiring a home fell dramatically, so did the desire to own one. Why did this happen?

For many, the fresh memory of the recent price collapse generated a level of fear and revulsion that outweighed the desire to purchase a home. Many Americans who had previously associated the concept of home ownership with pleasure now associated it with pain.

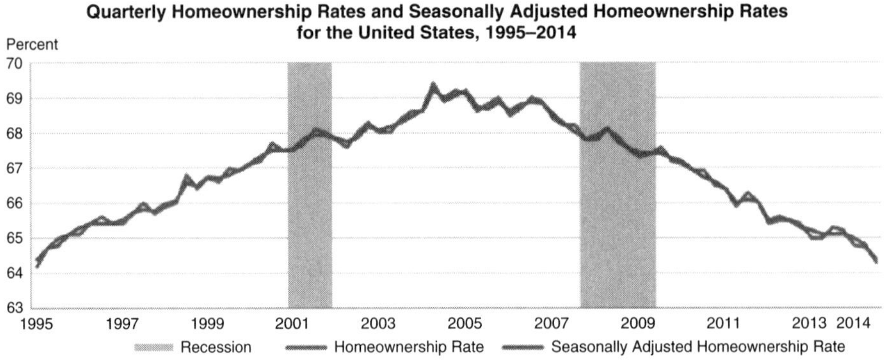

Quarterly Homeownership Rates and Seasonally Adjusted Homeownership Rates for the United States, 1995–2014

FIGURE 23.1   A Decline in U.S. Homeownership Rates

Source: U.S. Census Bureau

Human behavior is driven by the desire to gain pleasure and avoid pain, and the same type of behavior is evident in trading markets. Our reactions to situations, based on pleasure and pain, are somewhat predictable, and sentiment indicators seek to capitalize on this predictability.

■ A Bullish Bias

In general, the average level of bullishness measured by stock market sentiment indicators tends to be higher than the average level of bearishness. This is due to the fact that, despite its sometimes wild intermediate swings, the stock market has a long-term upward bias.

How can we demonstrate the market's long-term bullish bias? On February 16, 1885, its first day of trading, the Dow Jones Industrial Average closed at 62.76; one hundred years later, on February 15, 1985, it closed at 1,282.02. Thirty years after that, on February 17, 2015, the index closed at 18,047.58. This general upward bias is the most likely source of bullishness on the part of investors.

■ The AAII Sentiment Survey

The American Association of Individual Investors (AAII) conducts a weekly sentiment survey of its members, measuring the percentage of individuals who are bullish, bearish, or neutral on stocks for the coming six months. This widely followed survey is normally used as a contrarian indicator. In other words, when individuals are overwhelmingly bearish, it is time to buy, and when they are overwhelmingly bullish, it is time to sell.

One way for investors to determine if the stock market is in an overbought or oversold condition is by comparing current levels of sentiment to their long-term averages. For example, in the survey dated November 12, 2014, 57.9% of the investors surveyed were bullish, compared to the long-term average of 38.9%. This tells us that the level of bullishness is relatively high, which means the market is at risk for a reversal.

Why would a group of individual investors serve as a contrarian indicator? Are the respondents different from other people? In fact, the investors that make up the AAII survey tend to possess more education and greater wealth than the average U.S. citizen.

In this case, the contrarian element has nothing to do with the intelligence of those being surveyed. Instead, it is a logical response to the emotional behavior that most people exhibit when faced with rapidly changing prices and expectations.

Here's an example of the contrarian nature of the AAII Sentiment Survey at work. On the week of October 12, 2007, the S&P 500 reached an all-time weekly closing high of 1,561.80. That week's AAII survey indicated that 54.64% of respondents were bullish (a nine-month high) versus only 25.77% bearish.

Over the next 17 months, the S&P 500 would lose over half of its value, eventually falling to a weekly close of 683.38. As the market fell, investors became increasingly less bullish. By March 5, 2009, the level of bullishness had dropped to 18.92%, its lowest reading since July of 1993. With the markets crushed and with bullish sentiment at multi-decade lows, it was the perfect time to buy.

As shown in Figure 23.2, extreme positive sentiment marked the top of the bull market in 2007. Extreme negative sentiment marked the bottom of the bear market in 2009, and the beginning of a new bull market. That bull market was still going strong nearly seven years later.

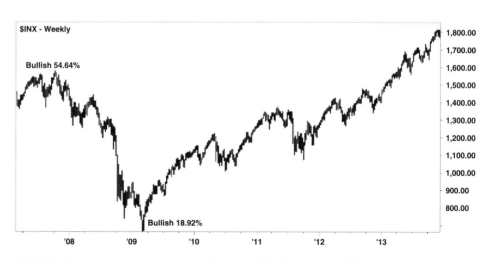

FIGURE 23.2   Extremes in Sentiment Mark the 2007 Top and the 2009 Bottom

Figure 23.2 demonstrates that an abundance of bullish sentiment is considered bearish. The same can be said for an absence of bearish sentiment. This is because many traders are not fixed in their outlook; instead, they shift between bull and bear modes. At any given moment, every trader is potentially a bull or a bear.

If there are very few current bears, then there is a greater percentage of traders who have the potential to become bears in the future. The same is true of bulls; when the percentage of bullish traders is extremely low, the number of potential future bulls increases.

Because of this, when levels of bearishness fall to extreme lows, the chance of a bearish reversal is on the rise. Likewise, when bullishness reaches a low point, the chance of a bullish reversal increases.

The Spread Between Bulls and Bears

Another way to view the AAII survey is to measure the difference, or "spread," between bulls and bears. For example, in the November 12, 2014 survey, bullish sentiment was measured at 57.9%, and bearish sentiment was measured at just 19.3%. We could say that the spread or difference between bulls and bears at that time was 38.6% (57.9% − 19.3%).

At the time, that figure represented the widest gulf between bulls and bears in nearly four years. The wider the spread between bulls and bears, the more likely a market reversal becomes.

If you're tempted to blindly buy or sell based on the AAII figures, be careful—you could find yourself shorting a bull market or buying into bear market. Instead, use the AAII survey as a confirming indicator.

For example, if both the market and the AAII survey have reached extreme levels, this is indicative, but not a guarantee, of a market reversal. Traders who are seeking evidence of a reversal may combine the AAII survey data with technical indicators.

Since the survey is generally used to spot reversals, it might make sense to use a reversal chart pattern or a reversal candlestick pattern to confirm the results of the survey. Doing so would provide evidence of both extreme investor sentiment and a price reversal.

There is always a chance that the reversal signal is false, and traders need to prepare for this in advance. In a scenario of overwhelmingly bearish sentiment, a trader could go long and place a protective stop beneath the low of a bullish candlestick reversal pattern, such as the wick of a hammer that appears in a downtrend. In a case of overwhelmingly bullish sentiment accompanied by a bearish candle pattern such as a shooting star, the trader could place the stop above the high of the wick of the shooting star.

The Put–Call Ratio

In the world of options trading, the buyer of a "call" contract takes a bullish position on a stock or index, and the purchaser of a "put" contract assumes a bearish position. These contracts can be used on a stand-alone basis, or they can be used as a "hedge," or protection for an existing position. They can also be traded in combinations called "spreads."

The put-call ratio is simply the ratio of bullish call volume versus bearish put volume. By comparing the volume of call contracts purchased versus the volume of put contracts purchased, stock traders can infer a general level of bullish or bearish sentiment in the market.

When traders are bearish, they purchase puts. This causes the put–call ratio to rise. Conversely, when traders are bullish, they purchase calls, which causes the put–call ratio to decline.

Traders use the put–call ratio as a contrarian indicator to identify levels of extreme bullish or bearish sentiment. A high put–call ratio is considered bullish, because the sentiment of traders is becoming overly bearish. A low put–call ratio is considered bearish, because trader sentiment is turning overly bullish.

When the put–call ratio closes above one, this means that the volume of puts purchased is greater than the volume of calls. This is considered unusual because call volume tends to be greater than put volume, due to the fact that both market indices and traders have a bullish bias. When the put–call ratio rises above one, sentiment has become overly bearish, and the market is due for a bullish reversal.

Figure 23.3 provides an example of the put–call ratio at work. The chart compares the weekly S&P 500 Continuous Contract (@SP, upper half of chart) with Put–Call

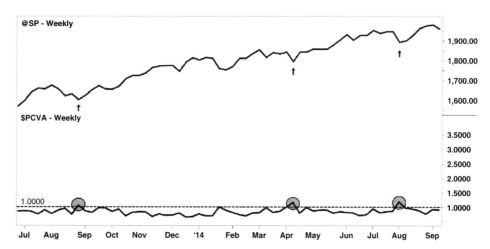

FIGURE 23.3 Comparison of the S&P 500 and the Weekly Put–Call Ratio

Volume Ratio for All Products ($PCVA, lower half of chart). The line chart is based on weekly closing prices.

Note that when put–call ratio closes above one for the week (circles), this frequently coincides with a major low point in the S&P 500 futures contract (arrows). This demonstrates why the put–call ratio is a popular mechanism for timing market bottoms.

■ The VIX

The Chicago Board Options Exchange (CBOE) Market Volatility Index, commonly known as the VIX, is similar to the put–call ratio in that it is an options-based market sentiment indicator. The VIX is constructed from a variety of S&P 500 options (both puts and calls) and moves in an inverse direction to that index.

The VIX is designed to project the anticipated movement of the S&P 500 over a 30-day period. What sets the VIX apart is that it measures implied volatility instead of price or volume. However, the VIX is valuable because it gives us clues about the sentiment of market participants.

A high reading on the VIX indicates a high degree of fear; in fact, some market participants refer to the VIX as the "fear index." However, a high VIX reading is also considered bullish. Market bottoms often coincide with high VIX readings. In this sense, it is a contrarian indicator.

There is no "magic number" or reading on the VIX that perfectly indicates when to buy or sell. Instead, current VIX levels are viewed within the context of recent VIX levels. The assumption behind its usage is that volatility will revert to its mean; in other words, markets will settle down after a period of high volatility, or perk up after a period of low volatility.

While the VIX is directly based on S&P 500 options, other major indices have their own variations of the index. The CBOE's volatility index for the Dow Jones Industrial Average is known as the VXD (symbol $VXD.X). The VXN (symbol $VXN.X) serves as the CBOE's options-based volatility index for the Nasdaq 100 index.

There are a variety of tradable instruments that are based on the VIX and its relatives. For example, the iPath S&P 500 VIX (VXX) can be used as a substitute for the VIX. Other instruments have been created that have an inverse relationship to the VIX, such as the ProShares Short VIX (SVXY).

Figure 23.4 demonstrates the inverse nature of the S&P 500 Index ($INX) and the VIX. In this example, the iPath S&P 500 VIX (VXX) is used as a proxy for the VIX. Notice how major lows in the S&P 500 (arrows) correlate to peaks in the VXX, and how the two instruments tend to move in opposite directions.

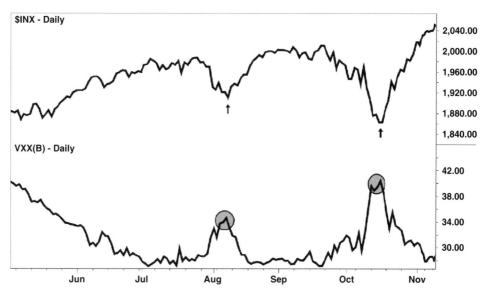

FIGURE 23.4 The Inverse Relationship of the S&P 500 Index ($INX) and the iPath S&P 500 VIX (VXX)

Commitments of Traders Report

The Commitment of Traders (COT) report gives investors a look at the inner workings of the U.S. commodities and futures markets. It provides valuable information on the positioning of traders, telling investors if speculators have taken a long, short, or neutral stance on a wide variety of trading vehicles.

Like the AAII index, the put–call ratio, and the CBOE Volatility Index, the COT report is frequently used as a sentiment indicator. An extreme level of bullishness or bearishness is considered a sign of an impending reversal.

The COT's predecessor was an annual report, published by the U.S. Department of Agriculture's Grain Futures Administration starting in 1924. The COT report itself was originally issued by the Commodity Futures Trading Commission (CFTC) on a monthly basis starting in 1962. Beginning in 1992, the report was released every two weeks; it became a weekly report in the year 2000.

At the time of this writing, the COT report is released on Friday afternoons in the United States, and the data that is compiled in the report is accurate as of the prior Tuesday. The delay period of three business days is quite a long lag time for such a report in the twenty-first century, but there appears to be no current plan to accelerate this process. The current COT report, as well as a library of previous COT reports, is available to the public at CFTC.gov.

How to Read a COT Report

Figure 23.5 shows a portion of a typical COT report, which provides information for instruments traded on the Chicago Mercantile Exchange. This particular COT report is of special interest to currency traders, since reports for the euro, British pound, Australian dollar, and Japanese yen can be found here.

Figure 23.5 displays a portion of a COT report for the British pound. The report's "as of" date is July 14, 2015, which was a Tuesday. This report was released three business days later, on Friday, July 17.

On the right side of Figure 23.5, the term "open interest" is visible. The CFTC defines open interest as follows:

> "The total of all futures and/or options contracts entered into and not yet offset by a transaction, by delivery, by exercise, etc. The aggregate of all long open interest is equal to the aggregate of all short open interest."

Open interest is somewhat similar to volume, in that an increase in open interest might display a greater level of commitment on the part of some traders. If the open interest of a futures contract is rising along with the price of the underlying commodity, this is considered bullish. This is because a rise in open interest represents new participants entering into the market.

On the other hand, if the price of the underlying commodity is rising while the open interest is dwindling, this could signal that the upward move is being caused by a short-covering rally. This could be an early indication that the trend is about to reverse, as a short-covering rally represents participants exiting the market.

Likewise, if the price of the underlying commodity is falling as open interest in the futures contract is rising, this is an indication that the downward trend should continue. If both the commodity's price and open interest are falling, this could be an indication that the downtrend is about to reverse.

```
BRITISH POUND STERLING - CHICAGO MERCANTILE EXCHANGE          Code-096742
FUTURES ONLY POSITIONS AS OF 07/14/15                        |
----------------------------------------------------------- | NONREPORTABLE
       NON-COMMERCIAL       |    COMMERCIAL    |    TOTAL     |   POSITIONS
----------------------------|------------------|--------------|-----------------
 LONG  | SHORT  |SPREADS |  LONG  | SHORT  |  LONG  | SHORT  |  LONG  | SHORT
-----------------------------------------------------------------------------
(CONTRACTS OF GBP 62,500)                        OPEN INTEREST:      157,073
COMMITMENTS
  32,162   56,361    1,322  100,879   77,666  134,363  135,349   22,710   21,724
```

FIGURE 23.5 COT Report for the British Pound

Source: Commodity Futures Trading Commission (CFTC.gov)

To summarize:

$$\text{Rising price} + \text{rising open interest} = \text{bullish}$$
$$\text{Rising price} + \text{falling open interest} = \text{bearish}$$
$$\text{Falling price} + \text{rising open interest} = \text{bearish}$$
$$\text{Falling price} + \text{falling open interest} = \text{bullish}$$

There are three main categories in Figure 23.5; the first two of these categories are deemed "reportable."

Non-Commercial: This category consists of large speculators. These speculators are solely involved in the purchase and sale of futures contracts with the intention of generating a trading profit. We describe them as "large" speculators because in order to qualify for this reportable category, their position size must exceed minimum levels set by the CFTC. These minimum reporting levels vary, based on the CFTC regulations for that particular commodity.

Commercial: This category refers to people and companies that deal with the underlying commodity on a regular basis for business purposes. This group isn't necessarily trying to make money by trading futures. In most cases, they are using futures as a hedge to protect their business interests. Examples of entities that fall into this category include farming companies, mining companies, and businesses that rely on imported or exported goods.

Non-Reportable Positions: This category consists of positions that fall beneath the CFTC's minimum reporting requirements. This group is often thought of as consisting of small, individual traders.

Notice also in Figure 23.5 that the contracts for each category are divided into long and short. For example, in the non-commercial category, just under the word "commitments," there are 32,162 open long contracts and 56,361 open short contracts. In the commercial category, there are 100,879 open long contracts and 77,666 open short contracts.

Notice how the totals for these two categories nearly balance out. The total number of reportable open long contacts is 134,363, and the total number of reportable short contracts is 135,349. The non-reportable category shows a total of 22,710 long contracts and 21,724 short contracts.

Based on this information, we could say that large speculators are leaning to the short side, because they hold 56,361 short contracts versus 32,162 long contracts. Commercials are leaning to the long side with 100,879 versus 77,666 short. Small traders appear to be evenly balanced between long and short.

Interpretation of the COT Report

One way that traders use this information is by searching for large imbalances between longs and shorts in the non-commercial category. When large imbalances occur, the odds of a reversal rise significantly.

Let's examine the psychology behind this concept. Since the members of this category are attempting to trade for a profit, we expect every trade to be closed at some point. Therefore, every long position will eventually result in a sale, and every short position will eventually result in a purchase in order to offset the position.

Because this is true, it stands to reason that a very large short position (when compared to its opposing long position) in the non-commercial category could eventually lead to a short-covering rally. It might help to think of the non-commercial shorts as "future buyers."

Conversely, if large speculators are leaning heavily to the long side, they will eventually sell, either to take profit or limit a loss. Think of the non-commercial longs as "future sellers."

Figure 23.6 demonstrates this concept, using the euro futures contract from the COT report of May 4, 2010. At that time, non-commercial shorts heavily outnumbered longs by a margin of 140,077 to 36,675 (highlighted).

Note the changes from the previous week, located directly beneath the long/short figures. This shows the long position growing by 2,213 contracts, and the short position increasing by 16,602 contracts. These figures show that open interest is rising, particularly among the non-commercial shorts.

Figure 23.7 shows the daily chart of the euro/U.S. dollar (EURUSD) currency pair at the time that the large short position existed. We can clearly see that the euro was in a steep downtrend against the U.S. dollar at that time, having fallen from 1.50 to 1.30 in less than six months. Point A on the bottom right of the chart is located at May 4, 2010, which is the "as of" date of the COT report shown in Figure 23.6.

Based on both the chart and the COT report, we would expect the trend to continue. This is because the open interest in the euro trade is rising as the euro is falling.

Now let's move a little further ahead in time. Figure 23.8 shows the COT report for the euro as of June 1, 2010, approximately one month later. There is still a

```
EURO FX - CHICAGO MERCANTILE EXCHANGE                          Code-09974
FUTURES ONLY POSITIONS AS OF 05/04/10                     |
---------------------------------------------------------| NONREPORTABLE
     NON-COMMERCIAL     |   COMMERCIAL    |    TOTAL      |   POSITIONS
--------------------------------------------------------------------------
 LONG  | SHORT  |SPREADS |  LONG  | SHORT  |  LONG  | SHORT  |  LONG  | SHORT
--------------------------------------------------------------------------
(CONTRACTS OF EUR 125,000)                     OPEN INTEREST:     261,070
COMMITMENTS
 36,675  140,077   2,898  175,841  62,928  215,414  205,903   45,662   55,17

CHANGES FROM 04/27/10 (CHANGE IN OPEN INTEREST:     22,778)
  2,213   16,602   -1,398   20,450   4,883   21,265   20,087    1,513    2,69
```

FIGURE 23.6 COT Report for the Euro

Source: Commodity Futures Trading Commission (CFTC.gov)

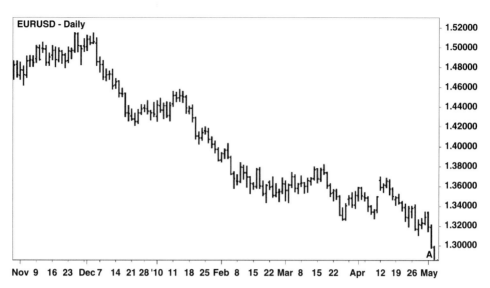

FIGURE 23.7 EURUSD Currency Pair Trends Lower as Short Position Increases

```
EURO FX - CHICAGO MERCANTILE EXCHANGE                        Code-099741
FUTURES ONLY POSITIONS AS OF 06/01/10                     |
- - - - - - - - - - - - - - - - - - - - - - - - - - - - - - - - - - - -| NONREPORTABLE
     NON-COMMERCIAL     |    COMMERCIAL    |    TOTAL      | POSITIONS
- - - - - - - - - - - - - - |- - - - - - - - - - - -|- - - - - - - - - -|- - - - - - - - - - - -
  LONG  |  SHORT  |SPREADS |  LONG  | SHORT  |  LONG  | SHORT  |  LONG  | SHORT
- - - - - - - - - - - - - - - - - - - - - - - - - - - - - - - - - - - - - - - - -
(CONTRACTS OF EUR 125,000)                           OPEN INTEREST:      275,266
COMMITMENTS
 45,006  138,331     3,249  176,197   79,109  224,452  220,689   50,814   54,577

CHANGES FROM 05/25/10 (CHANGE IN OPEN INTEREST:     -6,700)
   -624  -14,035     1,136  -14,010    6,155  -13,498   -6,744    6,798       44
```

FIGURE 23.8 COT Report Shows a Decline in Open Interest in the Euro.

Source: Commodity Futures Trading Commission (CFTC.gov)

large imbalance among the non-commercials, with 138,331 contracts short versus 45,006 long (highlighted).

However, if you look just beneath those figures, you'll see that the non-commercials, particularly the shorts, are exiting their positions. Short contracts numbering 14,035 were covered by non-commercial traders over a one-week period, and the overall change in open interest—which includes commercial traders— fell by 6,700. As mentioned earlier, a falling price combined with declining open interest is bullish.

Figure 23.9 updates the EURUSD chart and shows that as of June 1, 2010, the euro had fallen to 1.20 versus the U.S. dollar (point B). The euro was in crisis mode because of concerns about the ability of several of the European Union member states, particularly Greece, to repay their debts.

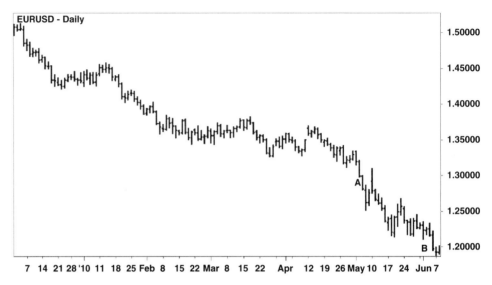

FIGURE 23.9   EURUSD Downtrend Continues as Open Interest Begins to Contract

At this point, many top analysts were predicting that the euro and the U.S. dollar would reach an exchange rate of 1.00, also known as "parity." However, traders who were mindful of the COT report knew that many of biggest speculators had already started to cover their euro shorts.

June of 2010 proved to be a major bottom for the euro, and what occurred next took many analysts and traders by surprise. A massive short-covering rally was about to take place, as shown in Figure 23.10.

FIGURE 23.10   A Short-Covering Rally in EURUSD

By November 4, just six months later, the euro/U.S. dollar currency pair had climbed all the way back to 1.42. While most of the analysts' predictions were proven incorrect, investors who paid heed to the COT report knew that the time had come to cover short positions.

■ Large Speculators versus Small Speculators

Because the COT report provides an abundance of facts and statistics, the information it provides can be used in a variety of ways. One method involves comparing the positions of the non-commercial traders to those of the non-reportable traders. Some believe that when the two are in opposition, the right move is to take the side of the non-commercials and trade against the non-reportable traders.

What is the philosophy behind this strategy? The non-commercial category, which is sometimes referred to as the "smart money," consists of large speculators and includes institutional traders. It's assumed that the large speculators have more money and better research than their smaller counterparts.

While this type of strategy may have worked in the past, individual traders now have access to information that wasn't previously available to them. While the playing field may not be exactly level, small speculators have been known to occasionally outperform their well-heeled counterparts.

Figure 23.11 provides an example of this, using a COT report that shows positions in the New Zealand dollar as of April 7, 2015. At that time, non-commercial traders were long 16,950 contracts and short 11,172 contracts, meaning they were net long.

Meanwhile non-reportable positions were net short with 2,982 long contracts vs. 4,320 short contracts. Large speculators were anticipating that the New Zealand dollar would rise, while small speculators were expecting it to fall.

What happened next is documented in Figure 23.12. The New Zealand dollar (NZDUSD) took a massive tumble from 77 cents versus the U.S. dollar to 65 cents over the course of three months. An arrow points to April 7, 2015, the date of the COT report referenced before.

```
NEW ZEALAND DOLLAR - CHICAGO MERCANTILE EXCHANGE              Code-112741
FUTURES ONLY POSITIONS AS OF 04/07/15                   |
--------------------------------------------------------| NONREPORTABLE
       NON-COMMERCIAL      |   COMMERCIAL   |    TOTAL   |   POSITIONS
--------------------------|----------------|------------|-----------------
 LONG  | SHORT  |SPREADS  | LONG  | SHORT  | LONG | SHORT | LONG  | SHORT
--------------------------------------------------------------------------
(CONTRACTS OF NZD 100,000)                      OPEN INTEREST:     24,920
COMMITMENTS
 16,950  11,172      499   4,489   8,929  21,938  20,600   2,982   4,320
```

FIGURE 23.11   COT Report for the New Zealand Dollar

Source: Commodity Futures Trading Commission (CFTC.gov)

FIGURE 23.12 NZDUSD Bearish Channel: Small Speculators Were Net Short, While Large Speculators Were Net Long

Not only were the non-commercials on the wrong side of the trade, but they also were on the wrong side of an extremely large move. While institutional traders tend to have better research and more experience than their retail counterparts, they are not infallible.

■ Final Thoughts on Sentiment Indicators

Imagine a boat. Something interesting appears on the horizon, and a crowd of passengers rushes to one side to get a better view. When the boat starts to tip, the passengers feel unsafe and rush to get back to the other side of the boat.

Metaphorically speaking, sentiment indicators are useful because they tell us when the crowd is on one side of the boat. Eventually, something will send them scrambling in the opposite direction. The COT report allows us to anticipate and prepare for this movement in advance.

PART X

POINT AND FIGURE CHARTING

CHAPTER 24

Psychological Aspects of Technical Analysis

Employing technical analysis can help us to avoid many of the pitfalls we all face as investors and traders. By encouraging us to focus on the price, technical analysis helps to prevent us from being drawn in to the noise created by opinion and emotion.

However, even the best technical analyst can still fall prey to the psychological and emotional traps that all investors face. What is the best way to avoid these traps?

We can start by understanding what these traps are and how to identify them. It's much easier to deal with these issues when we know that others have faced and conquered similar problems in the past.

Fortunately, there is an entire field of study, known as "behavioral finance," which focuses on these traps. The issues that traders confront on a daily basis have already been studied, defined, and examined. As a result, there is a wealth of knowledge and information on this subject from which investors can draw.

■ Behavioral Traps

Behavioral traps are a challenge to every market participant, including institutional traders. Some retail traders assume that professional traders are inoculated from these problems, and institutions certainly go to great lengths to keep these issues in check.

Despite these measures, which include on-staff psychologists and dedicated risk management teams, major institutional blowups do occur. Nick Leeson's single-handed destruction of Barings Bank is a matter of public record, as is Long Term Capital Management's estimated $4 billion loss in 1998.

Clearly, if the world's biggest banks and hedge funds have failed to solve these problems, then we are all at risk. Learning to recognize and identify these traps will help investors to avoid them.

The following paragraphs list the behavioral traps that are most likely to lead to trouble.

The Need to Know: As human beings, we can only process a limited amount of information. Therefore, a larger quantity of information doesn't necessarily translate into better decision-making.

However, possessing additional information has been shown to lead to overconfidence. This is true even when the information is irrelevant. In this sense, possessing either too much information or irrelevant information can actually be harmful.

What is the solution? It's not what you know that matters; it's what you can accomplish with what you know. Define your process and keep it streamlined; use only the information you need to perform it. Apply the appropriate risk management measures and filter out the noise.

Making Predictions: Go to any financial news TV channel or website, and you'll be inundated with predictions. Stocks will go higher, oil will go lower, the euro will go sideways, and so on. Since we are surrounded by forecasts, we might begin to believe that markets are predictable and attempt to make our own forecasts.

In truth, nobody can consistently and accurately predict the future. Just look at the number of hedge funds and mutual funds that underperform the markets on a consistent basis. Even the best of the best know that any one prediction could turn out to be wrong.

Why so many predictions? Financial television networks and websites need to create many hours of content every day and must keep their audiences engaged. How boring would it be if that content consisted of one guest after another admitting that they had no idea what was going to happen next? It's much more entertaining to watch someone risk embarrassment by taking a stand.

What is the solution? Take all predictions with a grain of salt—including your own! Instead of predicting where a stock, commodity, or currency is headed, react to what you see happening on the chart.

Special Snowflake Syndrome: The two most common errors in behavioral finance are overconfidence and over-optimism. Average traders and investors typically believe that they are above average.

Let that sink in for a minute. Almost everyone in this business believes they are above average, but there is no possible way that this could be true. In the world of finance, the belief that one is above average is a very average thing to believe.

What is the solution? Understand that believing you are a special snowflake doesn't make you one.

Impatience: Everybody wants to be a winner, and the sooner we can make this happen, the happier we imagine we'll be. We all have a desire for instant gratification.

However, if chasing instant gratification translates to the exclusive use of very short time frames, we could find ourselves trading pure noise. Even if our analysis is correct, we may be out of the trade before that analysis has had a chance to play out due to impatience.

What is the solution? Avoid increasing risk to achieve short-term goals and spend more time focusing on longer time horizons.

Story Time: It is human nature to place greater belief in facts that are woven into a compelling story, as opposed to facts that stand alone. To the logical mind, there should be no difference between a plain fact and one that is wrapped in a tale.

Yet studies have shown that the more compelling the story, the more likely we are to believe it. The quality (or lack thereof) of the facts becomes secondary to the story that surrounds them.

What is the solution? Understand that we are all susceptible to this tendency. Focus on the facts and reduce your exposure to storytelling.

Groupthink: In theory, a group can make better decisions than an individual. We tend to believe that a group of people, working together, will offset each other's biases and cancel out each other's weaknesses.

In reality, the opposite often occurs. Instead of counterbalancing misconceptions and errors, groups sometimes amplify them.

Instead of providing an honest answer, some members of the group may try to provide the answer that they believe the group wishes to hear. Other members may simply adopt an agreeable stance in order to avoid conflict.

When group members behave this way, it is easy for the group to reach a consensus. Even worse, the group's ability to reach a consensus may create an unwarranted optimistic attitude among them.

What is the solution? Make your own decisions and avoid following a herd mentality.

Respect for Authority: Stock analysts frequently meet with company executives to learn more about the company's plans for the future. The goal of the meeting is to determine if the stock is worth buying. In theory, this makes sense and is perfectly reasonable.

However, in actual practice this can do more harm than good. Because executives are the authority figures of the company, we place greater weight on their words and have a tendency to believe what they say. That's fine if they are sharing facts, but it can be harmful if they are sharing opinions.

Analysts' misconceptions about a company are often compounded by the illusions of individuals at the company, who have a tendency to be overly optimistic. As the leaders of the company, it is their job to present the company in a positive light.

What is the solution? Take company pronouncements with a grain of salt. Understand that just like the rest of us, company officials have their own biases.

■ Ten Trading Biases

As traders, all of us fall into the same psychological traps and make the same mental mistakes. The first step to breaking the cycle and avoiding counterproductive behavior is to gain an understanding of the biases we face. This helps us to identify these biases when they arise in our own trading.

The following is basically a catalogue of the psychological errors to which traders fall victim. Because we are all human, and because we are all influenced to various degrees by fear and greed, our biases can be somewhat predictable. Here are some common biases we should all seek to avoid.

1. *THE ILLUSION OF KNOWLEDGE:* At one time or another, we all fall victim to the illusion that having more information will result in a better outcome.

    In reality, too much information can be a negative, as it can result in "paralysis by over-analysis." It is much more important to have meaningful information than it is to have a large quantity of information. Meaningful information is what moves the market.

2. *THE ILLUSION OF CONTROL:* This is the belief that we can influence the outcome of an uncontrollable event. This false belief causes traders to veer away from their trading plans or to make constant adjustments to their trades. All of this tinkering nourishes the illusion that the trader is in control of the situation, when in fact, there is always a degree of random activity present in any market.

    Meanwhile, the result of the original strategy or tactic remains unknown. The illusion of control causes the trader to veer off course. He or she is no longer following a plan, which makes it impossible to judge the plan's effectiveness.

3. *CONFIRMATION BIAS:* We tend to believe that which supports our current beliefs, and we tend to ignore that which challenges those beliefs. If someone agrees with our beliefs, we tend to think that person is intelligent and perceptive. If someone disagrees with our beliefs, we tend to disregard their opinions because we believe them to be uninformed.

    For an everyday example of confirmation bias, look no further than media outlets that pander to a particular ideology or philosophy. Consumers of such information tend to prefer a source that confirms, rather than challenges, their current beliefs. Because of this narrow-minded approach, potentially important information is often disregarded.

4. *SELF-ATTRIBUTION:* Have you ever noticed that traders blame external forces when their stops are hit, but never give credit to those same forces when their targets are hit? This is absurd when you consider that one trader's protective stop may be in the exact same location as another trader's target.

Yet the trader whose target is achieved assumes all of the credit, while the trader whose stop is hit seeks to avoid any blame. In the latter case, the blame is usually deflected to an exterior source.

When we are victorious, we want to believe that it is due to our brilliant decision-making skills, rather than luck. When we lose, we want to believe that it is due to bad luck. Otherwise, we'd have to admit that our losses could be due to poor decision-making skills. That's something that all human beings, including traders, aren't keen to admit.

Taking responsibility for both wins and losses is necessary to succeed in trading. If we attribute all of our negative outcomes to bad luck, then we are ignoring the possibility that there might be something wrong with our approach. It's impossible to correct our mistakes if we fail to acknowledge their existence.

5. *HINDSIGHT:* Have you ever looked at a chart and automatically assumed that you would have known exactly when to enter and exit a trade that occurred in the past? This use of hindsight is very common, and it gives traders a false sense of confidence in their trading abilities.

It's easy to look at a historic chart and believe that we would have known exactly what to do at just the right moment. In hindsight, anyone can see that tech stocks were in a bubble in 1999, or that the broad market was a screaming buy in March of 2009.

However, things that seem obvious in hindsight were much less obvious at the moment they occurred. As the saying goes, "hindsight is 20–20."

6. *ANCHORING:* This is the name given to the common process of latching on to irrelevant numbers. In trading terms, the number most likely to fill this role is the entry price of a trade. Many traders care a great deal about an investment's current price vs. its entry price, but the latter is irrelevant to the future movement of the price.

Mentally anchoring the trade to the entry price can lead to poor trading decisions. For example, imagine that you purchased a stock near support at $25. The stock then breaks support and falls to a new 52-week low at $22.

Technically speaking, the stock is now a sell. However, the trader may be reluctant to exit the position because he or she wishes to break even. The trader only cares about getting out at $25, and thus ignores important information. It's easy to see how the trader could make the wrong decision and hang on to the position due to being mentally anchored to the entry price of $25.

In reality, the entry price has no bearing on what will happen next, or on how we should react to what happens next. The important information in the previous paragraph is that the stock has broken support and reached a major new low. The entry price of $25 is now irrelevant. You may care about your entry price, but the market does not.

7. *CHASING PERFORMANCE:* People have a tendency to base future projections on past performance. This leads to a behavior known as "chasing performance." This tendency is the reason why the disclaimer "past performance may not be indicative of future results" appears so frequently in investment literature and advertisements.

For example, it is usually a poor investment decision to buy last year's top performing mutual funds. However, investors have a tendency to do exactly that. We do this because we assume the same level of outperformance will continue, but it rarely does.

This bias leads to the meaningless extrapolation of figures. Suppose a trader achieves a 10% profit in his or her first month of trading; due to a lack of experience, the trader may believe that such results can be duplicated on a monthly basis. The trader then begins the mental process of extrapolating that figure forward, creating a false expectation and a sense of overconfidence.

In reality, such extrapolations are worthless; the random return generated during any given month likely has no bearing on what will occur in subsequent months.

8. *PERSONAL EXPERIENCE:* We tend to place greater emphasis on our own personal experiences, while giving less consideration to the experiences of others. We tend to place an even greater emphasis on experiences that happened in the recent past.

For example, have you ever found yourself in a profitable trade, yet you were unhappy with the result? Have you ever believed that you should have made more money on a winning trade?

Imagine the following scenario: Trader 1 buys a stock at $30 and exits at $35 for a $5 per share profit. Trader 2 buys the same stock at $30 but doesn't exit at $35. He continues to hold the stock as it rises to $40. As he continues to hold, the stock then falls back to $35. At that price, Trader 2 exits.

Both Trader 1 and Trader 2 achieved the same result by buying at $30 and selling at $35. However, their experiences were not the same. Trader 1 is probably pleased with the result and may not even be aware that the stock subsequently climbed to $40.

Meanwhile, Trader 2 had the opportunity to sell at $40 but failed to do so, and because of this is less enamored with the result. Trader 2's emotional reaction comes as a result of placing too much emphasis on what he personally experienced.

What Trader 2 needs to realize is that he's not psychic. There is no way he could have known for certain that the stock would continue to rise after he sold it.

There is no point in kicking yourself because you didn't buy at the bottom or sell at the top. Picking tops and bottoms may seem easy in hindsight, but attempting to do so in real time can be difficult. There is no way to know for certain that the price has reached a major high or low, except in hindsight.

9. *FRAMING:* Traders and investors are constantly faced with questions. Should we buy the stock at this price? Is this currency undervalued? Should we hold on to this trade or should we get out?

Studies have shown that the answer we give to a question depends on the way the question is posed or "framed." The conclusions that we draw can be affected, and sometimes manipulated, based on the manner in which the question is posed.

A trader who understands the concept of framing can affect his or her own behavior by consciously determining the meaning and the context of a win or loss. The ways in which traders frame their losses can help determine their future success or failure in trading.

For example, Trader 1 may believe that taking a loss makes him or her a loser. By taking this stance, Trader 1 is mentally framing the loss in a harsh context. There is a good chance that Trader 1 will feel tempted to hold on to a losing positon, because he or she wishes to avoid being labeled a loser.

Meanwhile, Trader 2 frames losses differently from Trader 1. Trader 2 views taking a loss as just another part of the trading game; therefore, his or her self-worth is unaffected by the outcome of the trade. Because of this, Trader 2 finds it easy to take a loss and move on. The way that Trader 2 frames the situation makes it less likely that he or she will fall into the trap of holding on to losses.

10. *THE ENDOWMENT EFFECT:* Most people have a tendency to place greater value on an item that they already own than outsiders do. For example, a homeowner who is enamored with their residence might be unwilling to part with it, even if offered a price significantly above market value.

Meanwhile, the market values the house in a very different way. To the rest of the world, it's just another house. Like any other property, its value is determined by its location, size, and condition.

Investors are also subject to the endowment effect. We may be reluctant to exit a trade at its current price, even if it is the right thing to do, because we attach a greater value to the investment than the market does. This can lead to "arguing with the market," which is highly inadvisable.

To avoid the negative impact of the endowment effect, consider that you may be attaching an arbitrary value to an investment based on your own biases. Assume that the market price of an investment is the correct price, and you'll usually be right.

■ Fallacies, Herding, and More

When dealing with the psychological aspects of trading, there are numerous terms that appear repeatedly. Here are a handful of frequently encountered psychological terms, along with an explanation of how each of them applies to trading.

1. *The Gambler's Fallacy:* This is the false belief that the odds favor a certain outcome, based on a series of random or meaningless events.

    A good example of this is a coin toss. If we flip a coin three times, and the coin lands with the head facing up all three times, what are the odds that the next flip will produce a different result?

    It's common to believe that the odds are now in favor of the coin's landing with its tail facing up. However, this is a fallacy. Every toss of a fairly balanced coin has 50–50 odds of coming up heads or tails, regardless of the results of the previous flips. This is because the prior outcomes have no bearing on the outcome of the current coin toss.

2. *Herding:* Many types of animals form herds to protect themselves from predators or to obtain food. Because there is safety in numbers, we humans also display this herding tendency.

    By conforming to the standards of a larger group, an individual lessens the risk of the pain due to rejection. This explains popular fashion, in which large groups of individuals arrive at similar decisions regarding their clothing choices. These decisions are often mocked in retrospect, but at the time they are encouraged.

    Herding also occurs in finance; many mutual funds and hedge funds make similar investments at the same time. The danger of herding in finance is that such groupthink sometimes leads to the formation of bubbles. Herding also makes it more difficult to outperform the group, since the individual has chosen to be a part of that group.

3. *Information Cascade:* This describes the actions of individuals who abandon their own view in favor of the view of the herd. This concept helps explain why markets do not always behave rationally or efficiently.

    This brings up an interesting point: There are times when running with the herd is advisable. For example, suppose you are bullish on a stock, but the overall market takes an overwhelmingly bearish stance against it.

Are you better off standing your ground and holding on to the stock, or abandoning your opinion and joining the herd in selling it? If the vast majority of market participants are selling, the latter of the two choices is usually the correct one.

4. *Impact Bias:* This occurs when we overestimate the impact of an event. For example, when a romance ends, it may seem as if the world is coming to an end. However, over time, such feelings fade, and the participants get over it.

   The same type of feelings can be attached to trading wins and losses. Traders tend to overestimate the impact of a win or loss. Chances are, the lasting impact of a win or a loss won't be as great as we believe.

5. *Empathy Gaps:* Individuals can't always accurately predict how they will react in a stressful situation. For example, a wealthy person may firmly believe that he would never commit a robbery. Years later, homeless and starving, he robs a store. The same person who couldn't empathize with criminal behavior under one set of circumstances became a criminal himself under a different set of circumstances.

   Empathy gaps can also be applied to trading. For example, a person who is not currently involved in a trade may believe that he will always adhere to his plans and execute them flawlessly. However, when that same person is engaged in trades and dealing with the pressures that accompany them, there is a heightened danger that he may break his rules and abandon his plan.

   If we can understand that we don't know in advance how we'll react under a particular set of circumstances, we can also understand the importance of strict adherence to a set of rules. This is why, for many traders, risk management rules override all other considerations when involved in a trade.

6. *Loss Aversion:* Individuals, including traders, have an intense dislike for losses. If we were logical beings, we'd probably give equal weight to equivalent losses and gains. The fact is, we dislike losses far more than we like equivalent gains—about twice as much, according to studies.

   Loss aversion helps to explain why trading is hard. Nobody likes to lose money; in fact, we dislike it intensely, but losing is a necessary ingredient in successful trading. To put it into military terms, you have to be willing to lose some battles if you want to win the war. Understanding and overcoming loss aversion aids traders in taking small but necessary losses as part of an overall trading plan.

7. *Dispositional Affect:* Most people can be defined as having a positive, neutral, or negative disposition. This is evident in everyday life; some people focus on the dark clouds, while for others there is always a silver lining.

   However, while many good things can stem from a positive attitude, it doesn't necessarily help in the field of trading. In fact, portfolio management studies have shown that highly positive affectivity can lead to a lack of diversification. This may be due to overconfidence.

Meanwhile, portfolio managers who demonstrated low positive affectivity showed a greater tendency to protect their investments via diversification. There is nothing wrong with hoping for the best, as long as one is prepared for the worst.

8. *Cognitive Reflection:* This describes the ability to switch from one type of mental process to another. Specifically, it describes the ability to shift from emotional thinking to logical reasoning.

Think of a person as having two minds. One works quickly and effortlessly, as if by default. This could be considered the emotional brain. The other can only move one step at a time, as each step in the process must be justified by logic before moving on to the next step. This is the analytical brain.

The emotional side is quick and effortless, but also primitive. This side of the brain is hard-wired and causes traders to herd and to seek short-term gains.

The analytical side of the brain allows traders to override their emotions. It enables them to create plans and execute them, regardless of the circumstances.

While emotion may be a necessary ingredient in the ability to make trading decisions, highly emotional trading can be disastrous. A trader needs to be able to shift from emotional thinking to logical thinking in order to succeed.

9. *Cognitive Reflection Task:* This is a test designed to determine a subject's ability to shift from emotional thinking to logical thinking.

In this exam, the "obvious" answer, which is usually generated by the emotional brain, is often incorrect. The test is designed to encourage the subject to engage in logical thinking in order to answer the questions correctly.

■ Final Thoughts on Traps, Biases, and Fallacies

Even the best technical analyst can fall prey to the psychological and emotional traps that all investors face. We can neutralize some of these issues by understanding that they are a normal part of trading, and that nearly all traders face similar issues.

CHAPTER 25

Understanding Bubbles

What is a bubble? Is it a fundamental event that occurs when valuations reach astronomical proportions? Or is it a technical event that can be measured by large movements in price over a short span of time?

Actually, a bubble is neither a fundamental nor a technical event. A bubble is a behavioral event.

■ The Five Stages of a Credit Cycle

According to Hyman Minsky, the late economics professor and perhaps the most widely referenced authority on the subject, there are five stages to a credit cycle: displacement, boom, euphoria, crisis, and revulsion. Here is a closer look at each of these stages:

1. *Displacement:* This phase is a shock to the status quo that creates opportunity, and often involves the introduction of a revolutionary or disruptive technology. A good example of this would be the early stages of the widespread use of the Internet in the mid-to-late 1990s.

    The introduction of the Internet created a major disruptive change, both for businesses and for individuals. The excitement generated by this change led to a bubble in Internet-related stocks that finally collapsed in 2000/2001.

2. *Boom:* This phase is marked by the widespread availability of cheap money. For example, a combination of low interest rates and easy lending terms led to an explosion in real estate values in the U.S. in the early 2000s. That real estate bubble collapsed in 2007/2008, after the low quality of many of the real estate loans made at that time became apparent. This event helped to spark a global financial crisis.

3. *Euphoria:* In this phase, over-optimism leads to rampant speculation. The public becomes enamored with a market as prices begin to rise at an accelerated rate. Market news begins to dominate headlines, pulling in unsophisticated investors. There is widespread trading and investing with borrowed funds.

   In this phase, the market becomes inescapable and is featured on television and on magazine covers. Talk of stocks or real estate begins to dominate discussions at parties. By this point, everyone either knows of or has heard of someone who has made big money in the market.

   Jealousy and the fear of missing out now join greed as emotional factors driving the bubble. Everyone wants a piece of the action, and nobody wants to be left behind.

4. *Crisis:* This phase of a bubble is marked by financial distress. Selling by company officials and other insiders increases sharply. Companies rush to offer stock to the public in the form of IPOs (initial public offerings). From the company's perspective, an IPO is a way to get the stock off of their books and into the public's hands before it loses its perceived value.

   In this phase, knowledgeable insiders are exiting the market and selling to retail investors who are still hopeful that the market will spiral ever higher. Eventually, a point is reached where retail investors have "loaded the boat," meaning that they are fully long and can afford to buy no more. Meanwhile, institutional investors have already exited the market and have no interest in buying. The absence of new buyers means that the path of least resistance is now lower.

5. *Revulsion:* Prices begin to fall sharply. This phase is marked by panic selling and capitulation. Fear grips the market as participants see their gains quickly evaporate, and this fear causes the selling to accelerate.

   By this point, many investors have lost money and no longer wish to participate in the market. Prices continue to fall until they are well below fair value. Eventually, institutions start to buy again.

Note that none of the five stages includes a fundamental or a technical requirement. Although bubbles are neither technical nor fundamental in nature, they are marked by certain behavioral patterns.

■ China Stock Bubble 2007

For example, when I visited China in 2007, I was told that no maid service was currently available in my hotel. The reason? There was no maid service because many of the hotel's employees had quit to trade in the stock market. That behavior was indicative of a bubble.

The result of the behavioral patterns that created China's 2007 bubble can be seen in Figure 25.1. The Dow Jones Shanghai Exchange ($DJSH) nearly tripled in value that year and reached a major peak in October of 2007. After a pullback, the index rallied again, only to be rejected at a similar level in early 2008.

This resulted in a double top, which also served as the head of a massive head and shoulders pattern. The index spent much of 2008 surrendering the gains it had acquired during the previous year.

■ NASDAQ Stock Bubble 1999

In 1999, the NASDAQ Composite Index gained 85.59%, after climbing 39.63% the year before. Many participants declared this market to be in a bubble well before it reached its peak. In hindsight, this was clear not only by the market's gains, but by the behavior exhibited by many of its participants.

FIGURE 25.1   A Bubble in the Dow Jones Shanghai Exchange ($DJSH), 2007/2008

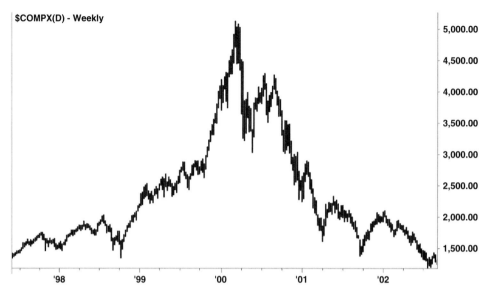

FIGURE 25.2 A Bubble in the Nasdaq ($COMPX), 1998/2002

At that time, it seemed that nearly everyone wanted a piece of the action. Suddenly, people who had never owned stocks—and who had no business being in the market—wanted to buy. Instead of buying familiar names like AT&T (T) or General Electric (GE), they gravitated toward the wildly volatile shares of companies they barely knew existed just months earlier. These companies included names like JDS Uniphase (JDSU), Applied Micro Circuits (AMCC), and America Online (AOL).

Television dramas that focused on the stock market began to appear on prime-time network TV. The stock market became a constant topic of discussion, both in the workplace and at social events. All of these behaviors were indicative of a bubble.

The NASDAQ Composite Index peaked in March of 2000. Over the following two years, it surrendered more than two-thirds of its value, as shown in Figure 25.2.

■ China Stock Bubble 2015

In 2015, BNP Paribas reported that 170,000 people—the equivalent of the population of Cape Coral, Florida—were opening new stock trading accounts in China *every business day*. Naturally, this behavior was indicative of a bubble. When the Dow Jones Shanghai Index climbed by over 100% in less than one year's time, it merely confirmed that suspicion.

Once again, the familiar behavior that accompanies a bubble began to spread. The results of this behavior are visible on the chart of the Dow Jones Shanghai Index ($DJSH), as seen in Figure 25.3.

FIGURE 25.3 A Bubble in the Dow Jones Shanghai Exchange ($DJSH) in 2015

From October of 2014 through June of 2015, the index gained over 100%. At the time, China's citizens were encouraged to invest in stocks by their government, which also provided the leverage to do so via an official government agency. The index then formed a head and shoulders pattern, and the gains were quickly reversed.

In July of 2015, as the stock market plunge accelerated, China's government stepped in and started buying stocks (circled). Brokers were strongly encouraged to join in the buying. Hedge funds and mutual funds that held more than 5% of a company's stock in its portfolio were warned not to sell those shares. Some institutions that engaged in short selling found themselves under the threat of investigation for "trading irregularities."

Clearly, China was doing everything in its power to stabilize its markets. New rule changes were announced on an almost daily basis. However, these official actions had unintended consequences. Any institution buying shares under these circumstances was now taking the risk that China might outlaw institutional selling entirely. These concerns may have delayed the market's eventual recovery.

■ Final Thoughts on Bubbles

In each of these cases, the chart is not the culprit. The charts are merely a reflection of a behavioral pattern that has existed for centuries. People come and go, but human behavior essentially remains the same. As long as this remains the case, we should expect to see similar bubbles in the future.

CHAPTER 26

Trading versus Reality

O ne of the more popular aspects of technical analysis is trend trading, and volumes have been written on this subject. Trend trading is a catchphrase for the numerous techniques that have been designed to capitalize on the directional momentum of a stock, currency, or commodity.

Long-term trends can create numerous opportunities. They can also simplify the trading process; when a trend trader identifies a trend, he or she already knows that the next trade will be in the same direction as that trend. All that remains is to identify the correct entry, stop, and targets. On the other hand, if there are no signs of a clear trend or of a trend reversal, the trader has no directional edge.

Despite the advantages of trend trading, traders fight against trends every day. Every trend is littered with the losses of traders who tried to fight against that trend.

Why is trading against the trend such a prevalent behavior? One reason is because it is a learned behavior. Traders who fight against trends are only doing what the world has taught them to do.

To a degree, we are all influenced by events that occurred earlier in our lives. For example, imagine that you were a novice stock trader in the mid-1990s, during what was then described as the biggest bull market of all time. The market was trending strongly, and traders were rewarded for trading in the same direction as that trend.

Those who traded with the trend at that time were richly and repeatedly rewarded. Because of this, there is a good chance that a trading career that started around that time continued well into the future.

On the other hand, those who fought against that same trend probably had a negative experience. They lost money, and for many of them, their trading careers ended at that point.

This leads us to the effect of survivorship bias. Some of the traders who were successful in the 1990s shared their experiences and became known as successful trend traders. Meanwhile, little was written about counter-trend techniques, because those who employed them may have found it difficult to survive.

Figure 26.1 presents an example of an extremely strong trend in the S&P 500 Index ($INX). Consider how you may have reacted to this chart at that time. Assume that you had no knowledge of what was to come. Would you go long, sell short, or remain on the sidelines?

By 1997, which is the right edge of the S&P 500 chart, the financial press and many market participants were already shouting the word "bubble." Eventually they were right, but stocks continued to rally for several more years, culminating in an incredible 85 percent gain for the NASDAQ composite in 1999.

It would be easy to look at the chart in Figure 26.1 and say, "You should have gone long," but at the time, many traders couldn't bring themselves to do it. In fact, most of us have a tendency to go against a strong trend.

To understand why, imagine that a stock is trading at $78. You consider buying it, but for whatever reason, you don't. One week later, the stock is trading at $86. Now it is even harder to buy the stock, because it has already moved up. That's a natural reaction, based on the way most of us were raised.

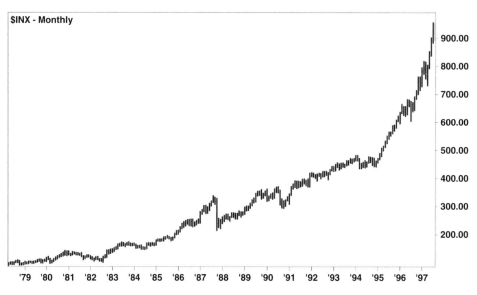

FIGURE 26.1   An Extremely Strong Trend in the S&P 500 ($INX)

From the time you were a small child, you've paid various prices for various things. Maybe you heard that your favorite candy was on sale for half-price at the store. You went to the store, but the sale had ended. What did you feel? Regret and disappointment. The feeling of missing out.

When you were a little bit older, the same thing happened again, only this time it was a pair of shoes or a new car. You could've gotten it at a great price, but you missed the opportunity. It's disappointing.

Then again, there were times when you did get the item that you wanted at the price you wanted to pay. How did that feel? It felt great.

■ Real World versus Trading World

Try to imagine that the real world and the trading world are two separate places.

Since early in our lives, the real world has been teaching us to hunt for bargains. We've been trained to avoid buying after the price has risen. In the real world, we prefer to buy things that are on sale. Another way to express this is to say that we want to buy after the price has fallen.

Unfortunately, the real world has trained us to do the exact opposite of what will work in the trading world. In the real world, we love to buy the things we desire when they're on sale.

However, when a stock, currency, or commodity drops in price, often it is just the beginning of a downward spiral. In the trend trading world, that which is cheap has a tendency to get cheaper. Conversely, that which goes up in price tends to keep going higher.

We have to unlearn what the real world has taught us, or at least learn to avoid applying it to the trading world. The problem is that most of us don't even realize that we've been trained.

■ Anchoring and Trends

It isn't hard to determine what occurs during a trend. If the trend is bullish, some participants sell short because the price is, in their estimation, too high. They assume that the price will fall back to a price they have seen earlier.

Why make this assumption? Think again about stock XYZ, which is trading at $86. You recall that you recently saw stock XYZ trading at $78. For most of us, it's not hard to imagine XYZ returning to $78 at some point in the future.

On the other hand, XYZ has never traded at $94. We've never seen it trade at that price, so it's a little harder to imagine the price moving to that level. It would be easy to make the assumption that the price has a better chance of returning to a familiar price, $78, than it does to continue moving higher to $94, a price we have never associated with that stock. This is what the real world teaches us.

In the trading world, the opposite may be true. We know that the price has already moved from $78 to $86. Since the stock is moving higher, there's a good chance that it's in an uptrend. If that's the case, then the stock may have a better chance of reaching $94 than it does of falling back to $78.

When Profits Hurt

There are other ways in which experiences in the real world can undermine success in the trading world. For example, many traders take profits too quickly. Perhaps you've heard the saying, "You can't go broke taking a profit."

This is a fallacy. If we habitually take profits prematurely, our gains will be small and could easily be outweighed by our losses.

Imagine that you've made a good entry, but then took your profit quickly because it seemed like the right thing to do. You're not going to lose money on that particular trade. Besides, it feels good to win. Everyone wants to feel like a winner. This positive feeling reinforces the behavior.

The trouble is that we need to make large gains, at least occasionally, to counterbalance the inevitable small losses that all traders face. Nobody wins all the time, and hot streaks eventually end. There are no perfect traders, and there are no perfect trading systems or strategies. In order to make money, your gains have to outweigh your losses.

Instant Gratification

The real world has trained us to take profits too soon. It feels good to win, and taking a profit alleviates the discomfort that we feel while we're in a trade. We feel discomfort because we're afraid that the price will turn against us. We're afraid that we'll lose what we've gained.

In order to hold onto those gains, we have to be willing to delay gratification. Isn't that the opposite of what the real world teaches us? Entire industries have been built upon the concept of instant gratification. The most successful companies are the ones that provide what we want, when we want it. Not surprisingly, the desire for instant gratification works against us in the world of trading.

We have to be willing to look at trading in a different context and accept the fact that losses come with the territory. In order to win the war, we have to be willing to lose some battles along the way. By taking the route of instant gratification, we may eliminate the chance of a loss, but we also eliminate the chance for an outsized gain.

Occasionally, situations arise where a trader can make money via the instant gratification route. For example, there was a brief period during the 1990s when individual retail stock traders flourished. At that time, the introduction of new technologies like the Small Order Execution System (SOES) created an imbalance where individual traders had a significant edge, and a small fortune could be made via quick trades.

Then the markets changed, as they always do. The rules were changed as market makers sought to regain the edge that they'd unwittingly surrendered. Individual traders who failed to adapt were now at a disadvantage. The window of opportunity was open only for a few short years, but people still speak wistfully of those days because it plays to their fantasies of easy money and instant gratification.

■ The Humble Trader

These traps are difficult to overcome if you understand that they exist. They are nearly impossible to surmount if you do not. It's fortunate for us that others have blazed this path.

It's been said that trading is simple but not easy. Investors and traders don't require special intelligence to succeed, but they do need to understand that they've been programmed to fail. If you understand that certain learned behaviors make trading more difficult, then it's easier to disregard the desire to engage in those behaviors.

A career as a trader can alter an individual's programming in numerous ways. For example, one learns, sooner or later, that when it comes to trading, arguing with the market can be expensive. If you approach the market with arrogance, you quickly learn a lesson in humility.

Every day, at any given moment, traders are forced to accept the fact that they could be wrong. It is difficult to be arrogant or argumentative when you are constantly on the verge of admitting a mistake.

Why do people argue? We argue because we think that we're right. We want to defend an idea. Traders can't afford to be tied to an idea, and can't allow their self-worth to be dependent upon being right.

If you strongly believe that you're right, and the market disagrees, you may start arguing with the market. Do this, and the market will crush you.

Once a trader learns humility, it can transfer it over to their personal lives. The description "humble trader" is as far as can be from Hollywood's typical Wall Street stereotype, yet in reality there are many humble traders.

There is even a saying you might occasionally hear on a trading floor that references this humility. Occasionally, you might witness a trader spouting off about his talents, but that kind of boastfulness doesn't go over well on a trading floor.

At such times, you may hear one experienced trader turn to another and mutter, "The Market gods will not approve of this." It's a reminder that a loss of humility is often followed by losses in the market.

The Adversary

Many of us view the market as an adversary. Not coincidentally, behavior in a trading environment can sometimes mirror patterns that were formed early in life when dealing with adversaries.

Most of us had childhood adversaries. Perhaps when you were a child, Little Billy was your adversary. Maybe he made a habit of insulting you or a member of your family.

One day, you got into a heated argument with Little Billy, and the argument escalated into a fight. Even though you were punished for doing so, perhaps the act of striking Little Billy provided a catharsis.

As we grow, Little Billy appears in various forms throughout our lives. Although the acceptable method of dealing with these adversaries begins to change, we still seek a form of catharsis. We still have a desire to demonstrate to our adversaries that we are superior to them.

Eventually the market becomes our chief adversary, and it may be the most difficult adversary we will ever face. You say stock XYZ is going up; the market says it's going down. You are tempted to argue "I'm a successful trader, I'm not wrong, I'm right." There's a danger that we might take our adversarial relationship with the market personally and respond in a method better suited to a child.

The problem is, Little Billy is now personified by the market. Little Billy is now a monster that can crush us in a second. But somewhere deep in our minds, we're still arguing with that kid in the schoolyard.

What is the solution? We have to be willing to say, "You know what? Maybe you're right, Little Billy. Maybe my eyes are too far apart. So what?"

I guess that's what we call maturity: when we stop caring so much about the opinions of others. We need to stop caring so much about being right. As my friend Dollar Bill once asked of me, "Ed, do you want to be right, or do you want to make money?"

Hard Work

In the real world, there is a clear connection between hard work and success. John studied hard at school and he was rewarded with good grades. When he graduated, he worked as hard as he could at his new job, and was rewarded with a raise and a promotion.

After John built up some wealth, he attempted to trade the markets. At first he was unsuccessful, so he tried harder, because extra effort is what has always worked for John in the past.

John responded by doing what he has always done: try harder. Unfortunately, the harder he tries, the harder trading becomes.

John's problem is that he is applying lessons learned from the real world to the trading world.

Whenever John was faced with a problem at school or at work, he would study or work through the night if necessary to complete the task at hand. He would do whatever it takes to succeed.

What is the one thing he would never allow himself to do? When faced with a problem, the last thing John would consider doing is this: push away from the desk, stand up, and walk out the door.

Here is the conundrum: John won't allow himself to walk away, but he will have trouble succeeding as a trader until he learns to do so. It's the exact opposite of everything the real world has taught him.

In trading, we always have to be willing to close our positons and walk away. There are going to be times when we are out of sync with the market, or when the market is just uncooperative. During these times, the risk of loss is greater than normal.

Learning how to trade can be hard work, but trading itself shouldn't be. Markets are dynamic, and they are not always cooperative. If you are working too hard and trying to force the issue, you may be internalizing an external issue.

■ Final Thoughts on Trading versus Reality

Trading can be difficult because it is often counterintuitive. This means that the types of actions that normally create positive results in day-to-day life often do not apply to trading. Understanding this problem is the first step in overcoming it. If we understand that trading is counterintuitive, we are less likely to draw on our day-to-day experiences in order to solve problems that occur in the realm of trading.

PART XI

ODDS AND ENDS

CHAPTER 27

Unconventional Patterns

While most of the technical patterns covered in this book fit neatly into well-defined categories, there are other formations that are not so easily classified.

Some of these unconventional formations include unique sets of conditions, and not all of these conditions fall under the auspices of traditional technical analysis. Two such patterns that have gained notoriety in recent years are the Hindenburg Omen and the Three Peaks and a Domed House pattern.

■ The Hindenburg Omen

On May 6, 1937, the German passenger airship *Hindenburg* caught fire and crashed while attempting to dock in Lakewood, New Jersey. The crash resulted in 36 fatalities and numerous injuries.

The tragedy became infamous because it was one of the first disasters of its kind to be captured on a video recorder. It was also described vividly by reporter Herbert Morrison on a radio broadcast.

The Hindenburg Omen is a technical analysis indicator that predicts a crash of a different kind. There is a list of criteria that must be met for the Hindenburg Omen to occur. All of the following must occur within a short time span:

1. At least 2.8% of the stocks that advanced on the New York Stock Exchange on a particular day must reach new 52-week highs. On the same day, at least 2.8%

of the stocks that declined on the NYSE must reach new 52-week lows. This indicates that a large number of stocks are reaching new highs and new lows simultaneously, which is an unusual condition.

2. The NYSE index is higher than it was 50 trading days ago. This condition was substituted for a rising 10-week moving average, which was part of the criteria in an earlier version of the indicator.

3. The McClellan Oscillator gives a negative reading. This would mean any reading below zero.

4. The number of new 52-week highs is less than double the number of new 52-week lows.

First we'll deal with conditions #2 and #3. There is nothing unusual about a stock index trading higher than it was 50 trading days previous to today. This only tells us that the market is higher than it was a few months earlier.

Nor is there anything strange or special about a day when the McClellan Oscillator gives a negative reading. These two conditions can be easily met.

The first rule, however, presents an odd condition. There are plenty of days where more than 2.8% of the stocks traded on the NYSE reach a new 52-week high; there are also numerous occasions when more than 2.8% of NYSE stocks reach a new 52-week low. However, having both occur on the same day would be considered strange and suggests a deep fracture within the market.

In some ways, the fourth rule echoes the sentiment of the first rule. In rules #1 and #4, neither the bulls nor the bears are dominating the new 52-week high/new 52-week low lists. Again, this suggests a split beneath the surface of the market.

Perhaps that split is an early warning sign that something is amiss. It could be that certain market sectors are being sold with abandon, while others are still rising.

When all of these criteria are met, the stock market is considered to be in danger of collapse.

Once the Hindenburg Omen signal occurs, it is considered valid for the following 30 days. During that time, traders look for subsequent occurrences of the Omen to confirm the initial signal.

While signals tend to be rare, when they do occur they sometimes appear in clusters. It's not unusual to receive two or three Hindenburg Omen signals within a period of a few weeks.

In recent years, false Hindenburg Omen signals have been the rule rather than the exception. Some traders suggest that the figures are now skewed because of the widespread use of exchange-traded funds, which came into existence in the late twentieth century. This has caused some analysts to adjust or create additional criteria, such as raising the percentage of NYSE stocks required to reach new 52-weeks highs and lows.

■ Three Peaks and a Domed House Formation

George Lindsay is credited with the discovery of the Three Peaks and a Domed House pattern. This is a complex topping pattern that has a very specific set of guidelines and requires the unfolding of a long sequence of events. The pattern is only believed to have formed on a handful of occasions, including several times during the early part of the twentieth century.

Figure 27.1 displays a Three Peaks and a Domed House formation that occurred from late 1964 through mid-1966 on the weekly chart of the Dow Jones Industrial Average ($DJIA). What follows is an abbreviated description of the formation, along with a partial listing of the events that must occur in order for the pattern to form.

The pattern begins with an uptrend. Eventually, three peaks are formed (points 1, 2, and 3). The three peaks should be created over a period of approximately eight months.

This is followed by a deep retracement (point A) that is referred to as a "separating decline." The term separating decline is used because the retracement separates the three peaks from the domed house. The separating decline retracement must break beneath the lows that followed the formation of each of the three peaks.

Next, a short-term consolidation should appear (point B). This is followed by a rapid move higher, which creates the "wall of the first story" (point C). A period of sideways, choppy action forms the roof of the first story (point D), which in this case could also be considered the left shoulder of a head and shoulders pattern.

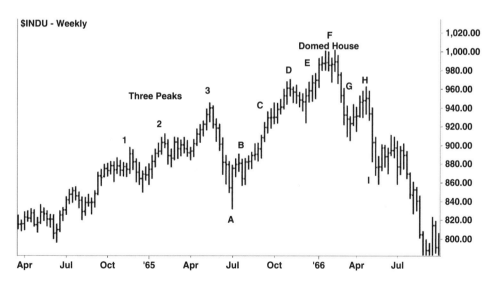

FIGURE 27.1   Three Peaks and a Domed House Pattern on the Dow Jones Industrial Average ($DJIA)

The price then resumes its ascent, forming the "wall of the second story" (point E). This is followed by another period of choppy, range-bound action, which forms the "roof of the second story" (point F). In this case, the second roof could also be considered the head of a head and shoulders pattern.

From here, the price should fall rapidly (point G). Then, a lower high forms (point H) before the price drops sharply to a lower low (point I). This completes the pattern; the price is expected to find support in the vicinity of point A. In the case of Figure 27.1, the price traveled beyond that point before finding a bottom.

As indicated earlier, this chart could also be interpreted as a rally leading to a head and shoulders reversal pattern. That particular formation should be evident and involves a less tedious identification process. Perhaps that is one of the reasons why this pattern gets less attention than some of the better-known formations.

■ Final Thoughts on Unconventional Patterns

The Hindenburg Omen's ominous moniker has made it a favorite on financial television in recent years. Because of this, it has crept into the consciousness of the retail trading community.

Although the Three Peaks pattern is somewhat obscure, it is frequently referenced by Wall Street professionals. These pros include hedge fund manager Doug Kass, who is well known for his fundamental trading style.

CHAPTER 28

Combining Technical and Fundamental Analysis

Technical analysis is focused on price rather than on fundamentals. This is not to say that fundamentals are insignificant; rather, it is an acknowledgement that the fundamental aspects of a stock, currency, or commodity are to some degree already reflected in its price.

Still, there are investors who take both technical analysis and fundamental analysis into consideration, and use the two disciplines in conjunction. One method for doing this involves using a fundamental screen to uncover a pool of potential investments, which can then be charted.

For example, in a bull market, an investor can scan for stocks that feature positive fundamentals, such as a high growth rate combined with an inexpensive valuation. Conversely, in a bear market, investors might seek to identify shorting candidates that have poor fundamentals—for example, stocks that are overvalued and have declining or negative growth rates.

A few examples of metrics that could be used as part of a fundamental screen include price–earnings (PE) ratio, price–earnings to growth (PEG) ratio, enterprise-to-EBITDA (earnings before interest, taxes, depreciation, and amortization) ratio, price to sales (PS) ratio, and free cash flow.

Since the topic of this book is technical analysis, I'm not going to give a detailed explanation of each of these terms here. Definitions and explanations for all of the above are readily available in numerous publications and on a variety of websites.

The fundamental characteristics of a stock can be analyzed via one of the many stock screeners that can be found online. Free stock screeners can be found at websites such as Finviz, Google Finance, Yahoo Finance, MarketWatch, and Morningstar.

■ Bull Market Fundamental Screen

Here's an example of a screen that can be used to identify stocks that have positive fundamental characteristics. This is just one example of many potential screens that an investor might use to locate buying opportunities in a bullish environment:

The stock must have a market capitalization of $2 billion or higher. We use this condition to eliminate illiquid stocks and small cap stocks.

The stock must have a price above $5. We use this condition to weed out penny stocks. Contrary to what stock promoters might say, penny stocks are not good vehicles for trading and investing.

The company must have an average annual sales growth rate of 20% or greater over the past five years. Notice that I used sales growth instead of earnings growth. I chose sales growth (also known as revenue growth) because earnings are easy to manipulate and therefore can be deceptive. Compared to earnings growth, sales growth tends to be a "cleaner" figure.

The stock must trade with a forward price-to-earnings ratio (forward PE ratio) of 20 or less. The question of whether a stock is expensive involves more than just the stock's price. In this case, it's determined by how much investors are willing to pay for a company's earnings.

I call this a "20/20" screen, because it seeks to identify stocks that are growing sales at an annual rate of greater than 20%, yet are valued at less than 20✕ their anticipated future earnings.

Of the thousands of potential choices, this scan produced 134 stocks that fit the previous criteria at the time it was run. Figure 28.1 shows the four criteria mentioned above on the Finviz.com stock screener.

Two of the criteria are described as "fundamental" (forward P/E ratio and sales growth) while the other two are termed as "descriptive" (market cap and price). Descriptive criteria can be added to both fundamental and technical screens to weed out companies with undesirable properties.

Now that the fundamental screen is complete, and a pool of candidates has been identified, the analyst can apply technical analysis to the results. The stocks that met

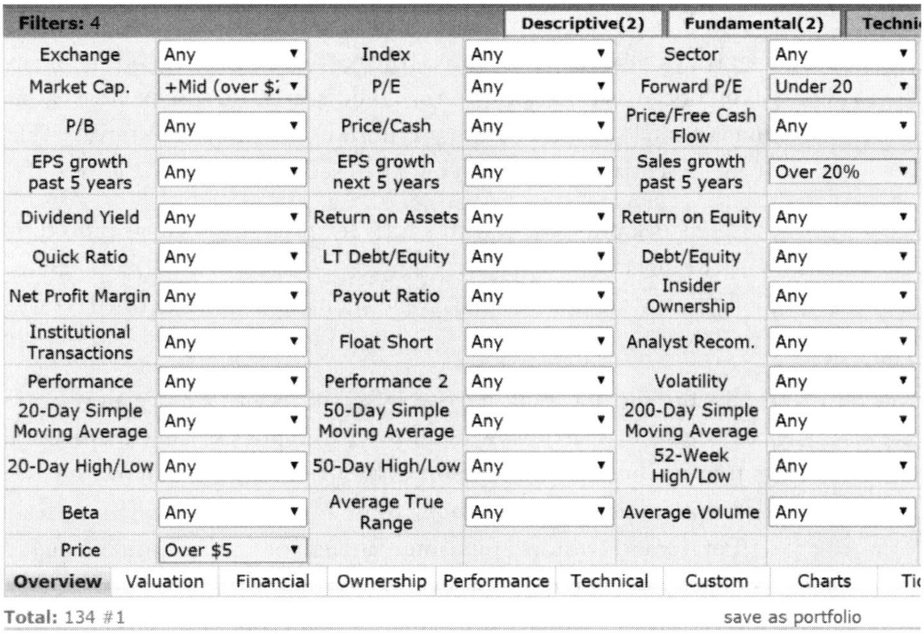

Filters: 4					Descriptive(2)	Fundamental(2)		Techni
Exchange	Any ▼	Index	Any ▼	Sector	Any ▼			
Market Cap.	+Mid (over $2 ▼	P/E	Any ▼	Forward P/E	Under 20 ▼			
P/B	Any ▼	Price/Cash	Any ▼	Price/Free Cash Flow	Any ▼			
EPS growth past 5 years	Any ▼	EPS growth next 5 years	Any ▼	Sales growth past 5 years	Over 20% ▼			
Dividend Yield	Any ▼	Return on Assets	Any ▼	Return on Equity	Any ▼			
Quick Ratio	Any ▼	LT Debt/Equity	Any ▼	Debt/Equity	Any ▼			
Net Profit Margin	Any ▼	Payout Ratio	Any ▼	Insider Ownership	Any ▼			
Institutional Transactions	Any ▼	Float Short	Any ▼	Analyst Recom.	Any ▼			
Performance	Any ▼	Performance 2	Any ▼	Volatility	Any ▼			
20-Day Simple Moving Average	Any ▼	50-Day Simple Moving Average	Any ▼	200-Day Simple Moving Average	Any ▼			
20-Day High/Low	Any ▼	50-Day High/Low	Any ▼	52-Week High/Low	Any ▼			
Beta	Any ▼	Average True Range	Any ▼	Average Volume	Any ▼			
Price	Over $5 ▼							

Overview Valuation Financial Ownership Performance Technical Custom Charts Ti

Total: 134 #1   save as portfolio

FIGURE 28.1 A Screen for High-Growth Stocks, Reasonably Valued Stocks

Source: Finviz.com

the fundamental criteria would now be charted to determine if they possess bullish technical properties. Ideally, this will yield a smaller list of candidates that are strong both technically and fundamentally.

■ Bear Market Fundamental Screen

In a bear market, the analyst would screen for stocks that have poor fundamental characteristics, such as a high valuation and/or a low growth rate. Once the results are available, the analyst would scan the charts of these stocks in search of weak technicals—stocks that are in downtrends, or have formed a head and shoulders, descending triangle, or other bearish pattern. This way, the analyst can create a pool of shorting opportunities by finding stocks that are both technically and fundamentally weak.

The bear market fundamental screen would contain similar descriptive properties to those listed in the bull market version. Whether searching for long or short trades, investors should avoid stocks that have very low prices and/or very small market capitalizations.

Low-priced stocks and small cap stocks are often thinly traded, and it can be difficult at times to find a participant who is willing to take the other side of your trade. Every prospective buyer needs to find a seller, and every prospective seller needs an available buyer. This is true regardless of which side of the market one is on.

In a bear market, an investor could search for companies that have undesirable fundamental qualities by using criteria similar to the following. This is just one of many potential screens that could be used to find candidates to sell short:

The stock must trade with a forward price-to-earnings ratio (forward PE) of 30 or higher.

The company must have average annual sales growth of 10% or less over the past five years.

By turning the bullish criteria on its head, we are now seeking to identify companies that are growing slowly, yet possess an excessive valuation. While extreme valuations are sometimes forgiven during a bull market, stocks that fit this description are often first among those to be punished when a market turns bearish.

For some investors, fundamental analysis can be intimidating. It is somewhat complex, and it requires a level of comfort with mathematics. Also, fundamental analysis doesn't lend itself to simple visual representations in the way that technical analysis does.

■ Technical Screens

Just as investors can use fundamental analysis as a filter, it is possible to create a screen to identify stocks that possess positive technical properties. In addition to screening for market capitalization and stock price, there are other applicable conditions. For example:

The stock must have a beta of greater than one. Beta refers to the volatility of the S&P 500, which has a beta of one. Therefore, any stock with a beta of greater than one is more volatile than the S&P 500—a trait that some traders find attractive.

Market participants who enjoy volatile trading might further narrow their search by identifying stocks that have a beta of greater than two. This is a descriptive term that could be applied to both bullish and bearish trading opportunities.

The stock must have a bullish candlestick pattern. Many stock screeners are capable of locating bullish candlestick patterns such as the hammer or bullish engulfing patterns. A bearish version of this screen might seek to identify shooting star or bearish engulfing patterns.

The stock is trading above its 20-day, 50-day, and 200-day moving averages. A stock that can maintain its position above these moving averages is considered strong. This condition could be used to locate strong stocks that have yet to reach new highs. A bearish version of this screen might search for stocks that trade below their key moving averages, which is considered a sign of weakness.

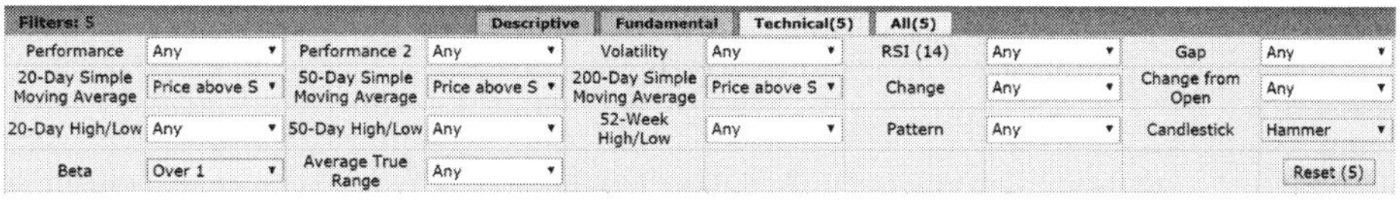

Filters: 5					Descriptive	Fundamental	Technical(5)	All(5)					
Performance	Any	▼	Performance 2	Any	▼	Volatility	Any	▼	RSI (14)	Any	▼	Gap	Any	▼
20-Day Simple Moving Average	Price above S	▼	50-Day Simple Moving Average	Price above S	▼	200-Day Simple Moving Average	Price above S	▼	Change	Any	▼	Change from Open	Any	▼
20-Day High/Low	Any	▼	50-Day High/Low	Any	▼	52-Week High/Low	Any	▼	Pattern	Any	▼	Candlestick	Hammer	▼
Beta	Over 1	▼	Average True Range	Any	▼								Reset (5)

FIGURE 28.2 A Screen for Bullish Technical Properties

Source: Finviz.com

Figure 28.2 depicts this technical screen as it would appear on Finviz.com.

Next is another variation of the technical screen. This version would be used to locate strong stocks.

The stock is hitting a three-month, six-month, or year-to-date high on heavy volume. Stocks that are breaking out to new three-month or six-month highs often have already broken through resistance. Stocks that trade at all-time highs have no true resistance. Support and resistance are created by prior price action—in some cases, by market participants who are attempting to break even due to their involvement in that prior price action.

If the price ventures into a previously untouched area and reaches a new all-time high, the only potential selling would be by longs seeking to take a profit, or by shorts seeking to establish a position. There can be no potential sellers attempting to break even to avoid a loss, since there were no previous opportunities to buy in this price area.

The bearish version of this screen would search for stocks that are breaking to new three-month, six-month, or year-to-date lows on heavy volume, as stocks that fit this description are often breaking support. A stock that is hitting an all-time low has no true support. This is because there can be no traders seeking to break even due to prior short trades taken at those prices.

Both the bullish and bearish versions of this screen include heavy volume as a condition. Not only is the price breaking to new levels, but the buying or selling is intense and enthusiastic. High volume indicates that the price movement is likely driven by institutions, which tend to have more capital and better information than the average investor.

The term "heavy volume" commonly refers to a multiple of average daily volume. Many traders use double or triple the average daily volume as a condition when scanning for stocks reaching new highs or lows.

Another way to incorporate this concept would be to compare the stock's intraday volume to its average volume at a particular time of day. For example, if stock XYZ normally trades three million shares by 11 a.m., but has traded nine million shares by 11 a.m. today, we could say that XYZ is on a pace to trade triple its average daily volume by day's end. This could also be used as a condition of a screen.

Once the scan is complete, the results can be further scrutinized for additional positive technical qualities. Examples include stocks that are in an uptrend, or have formed an inverted head and shoulders, or that repeatedly bounce higher when coming into contact with a moving average.

This would result in a shorter list of stocks that possess multiple positive technical qualities. Conversely, in a bear market an investor would search for stocks that have multiple negative technical qualities.

■ Screens for Other Asset Classes

Most of the technical criteria that is used in scanning for stocks also applies to other asset classes.

Technical analysis can also be applied to bonds, currencies, and commodities. Therefore, technical screens can be run for these asset classes by employing many of the same criteria that are used for stocks.

However, the application of fundamental analysis to these instruments can present a problem. For example, because gold has no earnings, there can be no such thing as a forward price/earnings ratio for gold. Currencies have no enterprise value, so there can be no such thing as an enterprise value-to-EBITDA ratio for the British pound. The fundamentals used by stock traders cannot be applied to every asset class.

This issue is further complicated in the world of currency trading, where the fundamentals of two separate entities are pitted against one another. Currency fundamentals revolve around interest rates, which can attract or repel capital, and fundamental measures such as purchasing power parity.

■ Final Thoughts on Combining Technical and Fundamental Analysis

Although technical and fundamental analysts are frequently at odds, the two disciplines are not mutually exclusive. Most major trading institutions employ both technical and fundamental analysts. In addition, there are many traders who study both disciplines and seek out situations where the two schools of analysis are in harmony.

PART XII

BEHAVIORAL ASPECTS OF TECHNICAL ANALYSIS

CHAPTER 29

Final Thoughts on Technical Analysis

Experienced traders know how it feels to be involved in a winning trade or a losing trade. When other traders win or lose, they experience similar emotions. If you can understand and empathize with the other participants in the trade, then you'll recognize and understand exactly what those participants are experiencing when you see it on a chart.

This ability to empathize with other traders has value. If we think of other traders as our opponents, and we are aware of the pressures that they face and the emotions that they experience, then this information can be used to anticipate their next move.

There are investors and traders who use technical analysis not to determine their own entries and exits, but to understand how their opponents view the markets. They use it to determine where other traders might buy or sell, and then use that information to their advantage.

Long-term investors who have no intention of ever placing a short-term trade, who hold only mutual funds or bonds in their portfolios, can still reap tremendous benefits by understanding technical analysis. If a long-term bull market appears ready to transition to a bear market, such an investor can simply move funds to cash. There is no reason to be fully invested during a bear market, and markets rarely crash (or skyrocket) without first giving sufficient technical warning.

There are always going to be naysayers, those who will believe that technical analysis doesn't work. Everyone is entitled to their opinion, but perhaps the reason behind this belief is because they don't really understand technical analysis. As is so common in society these days, those who understand the least often have the loudest voices.

I imagine that to the uninformed, technical analysis appears to be a kind of crystal ball that can supposedly foretell the future. This is far from the truth. Technical analysis doesn't provide any guarantees, and it doesn't always provide the correct answer. Imagine how easy the game of trading would be if it did.

Instead, think of technical analysis as something that can put the odds in your favor, similar to counting cards while playing blackjack. The card counter waits until the count is out of balance. When the card counter knows that there are more high-value cards left in the deck than low-value cards, he or she places a bet that anticipates the appearance of a high card.

This gambit is not successful on every hand of blackjack; nor is it supposed to be. The card counter is simply playing the percentages. When the odds of a high-value card are greater than 50%, this is the only sensible bet, but it is not a guarantee of success. A sensible bet isn't always a winning bet.

Sometimes the card counter is right, and sometimes not, but if he or she continues to play the percentages over time, the gambler will be right more often than wrong. He or she will know when to bet gingerly, and when to press the advantage and push the chips to the center of the table.

This is why casinos go to great lengths to prevent gamblers from counting cards. Technical analysis is similar in that it guarantees nothing, but it allows traders and investors to place intelligent bets.

Sometimes, the tale that is told by a chart is exciting, but not always. You shouldn't expect to view twenty charts and come away with twenty great trading ideas or twenty high-quality trades. Realistically, you should come away from any chart viewing session with one or two good ideas. If you see that no high-quality opportunities are available, simply refrain from placing a trade. As you progress in your understanding of this subject, quality opportunities will become easier to identify.

There are always more charts to see. Some traders search through charts for specific types of setups. I believe there is a danger in doing this, since people have a tendency to see what they wish to see. Instead of searching for specific technical setups, I'll flip through charts until something useful appears. You can always find a high-quality trade, if you're willing to look at enough charts.

Technical analysis continues to evolve. New indicators are created every day. However, at its core, technical analysis is simply a visual study of human behavior. Some day, human behavior will be fundamentally different than it is today. Until that day comes, technical analysis will continue to remain an effective tool for trading the markets.